The History of Roman Legion VI Victrix

The History of Roman Legion VI Victrix

The Original Watchers on the Wall

Tony Sullivan

PEN & SWORD **HISTORY**

First published in Great Britain in 2023 by
Pen & Sword History
An imprint of Pen & Sword Books Limited
Yorkshire – Philadelphia

ISBN 978 1 39908 857 2

A CIP catalogue record for this book is
available from the British Library

Typeset by Mac Style
Printed in the UK by CPI Group (UK) Ltd, Croydon, CR0 4YY.

Pen & Sword Books Limited incorporates the imprints of After
the Battle, Atlas, Archaeology, Aviation, Discovery, Family History,
Fiction, History, Maritime, Military, Military Classics, Politics,
Select, Transport, True Crime, Air World, Frontline Publishing, Leo
Cooper, Remember When, Seaforth Publishing, The Praetorian Press,
Wharncliffe Local History, Wharncliffe Transport, Wharncliffe True
Crime and White Owl.

For a complete list of Pen & Sword titles please contact

PEN & SWORD BOOKS LIMITED
47 Church Street, Barnsley, South Yorkshire, S70 2AS, England
E-mail: enquiries@pen-and-sword.co.uk
Website: www.pen-and-sword.co.uk
or
PEN AND SWORD BOOKS
1950 Lawrence Rd, Havertown, PA 19083, USA
E-mail: Uspen-and-sword@casematepublishers.com
Website: www.penandswordbooks.com

Contents

Acknowledgements

A special thanks to the various re-enactment groups for the expert advice, pictures and general enthusiasm and encouragement.

Firstly, Matthew Parkes from Petuaria Revisited. Petuaria is the Roman name given to Brough in East Yorkshire. The group was set up for those who live within the community and have a strong passion for the historic past of Petuaria and all things Roman locally. The town council and the community of Elloughton cum Brough have aspirations of bringing back to life the ancient Roman settlement of Petuaria, firstly in a physical sense and then in an 'Augmented Reality' sense with the help of Dr Peter Halkon and his team at Hull University (subject to a successful application to the Heritage Lottery Fund).

www.petuariarevisited.co.uk
https://www.facebook.com/petuaria

Secondly, Ross Cronshaw of Magister Militum. This is a re-enactment group focusing on recreating soldiery from the ancient period, predominantly Romans in the fourth century AD. Based in the north of England, it focuses on the *legio palatina* (elite imperial legions) of the late fourth and early fifth centuries AD. They demonstrate impressions of senior officers, junior officers and legionaries in battle dress and a variety of living history camping skills from writing, games and religion to blacksmithing and engineering. They also produce impressions of other soldiers of antiquity, from classical-era Greeks through to the Viking period.

info@magister-militum.co.uk
admin@magister-militum.co.uk
https://www.facebook.com/magistermilitumreenactment
https://magister-militum.co.uk

Thirdly to Dave (Optio Marcus) of Legio VI Victrix Eboracum, a re-enactment group based at York, the home of Legion VI Victrix where

Artorius Castus was *praefectus castrorum*. Supporting the Roman Bath museum, York. A re-enactment group of VI Victrix, Eboracum Legionary soldiers.

http://www.legiovieboracum.org.uk
https://www.facebook.com/groups/legiovi

Also many thanks to John Richardson of the Antonine Guard for his advice and photographs. The Antonine Guard is a registered Scottish charity, founded in 1996 to promote awareness of Scotland's Roman heritage. At events across the UK and overseas they bring to life Roman history of the late first and early second century AD. From military drill displays to school visits and talks, they portray the people who campaigned, built, and patrolled on the northern edge of the Imperium Romanum. It recreates a detachment of Legio VI as it would have appeared during the mid-second century AD.

https://www.facebook.com/The-Antonine-Guard
http://www.theantonineguard.org.uk

I'd also like to thank the following for their kind advice: Frederick Hopkins and Richard Hughes from the Practical HEMA Facebook Group (Historical European Martial Arts); and Alexander Iles, a tour guide and part of the Autonomous Re-enactment Collective Group, who walked the Wall in February 2022 to highlight the Hadrian's Wall 1900 event.

Tables

Figures

Introduction

This book concerns the history of the Sixth Legion in Northern Britain. It owes a great debt to the many re-enactment groups and enthusiasts who help to bring history to life. Their advice and guidance has been invaluable. It is hoped the inclusion of practical experience makes this book more readable and relatable. The focus is on northern Britain and as such will also touch on the many auxiliary units stationed on the frontier as well as the two famous walls built during the reigns of Hadrian and Antoninus. I have chosen the Sixth Legion as it was the main military force in the north for nearly three centuries. We also have a reasonable amount of epigraphical and literary evidence supported by archaeology to provide an interesting case study for the evolution of Roman power across the centuries. First, though, we must turn to the Legion's origin.

The Sixth Legion was founded by Octavian in around 41 BC during a tumultuous time in Roman history. A decade and a half before, Julius Caesar had twice invaded Britain, first in 55 BC, then a year later. His crossing of the Rubicon and march on Rome in 49 BC set up the political situation that resulted in Octavian becoming the first Emperor and the formation of the Sixth. Caesar's death in 44 BC led to a vicious civil war that effectively ended at Philippi, after which Brutus and Cassius, two of the chief architects of the assassination, committed suicide. These events led to the Second Triumvirate and an uneasy truce between Octavian and Mark Antony. Mark Antony took control of Egypt and the eastern provinces, Lepidus, North Africa, leaving Octavian in Rome and the West.

It was during this period that the Sixth was formed and we have evidence of sling shots with the inscription 'VI' supporting their presence at the siege of Perugia in Italy c. 41 BC. The resettlement of soldiers in Italy had caused some disquiet. Mark Antony's brother, Lucius Antonius, raised an army in Italy but was forced to surrender at Perugia in c. 40 BC. The Sixth was also involved in action against Sextus Pompeius, son of Pompey the Great, who had occupied Sicily and threatened the grain supply to Rome. In this conflict Antony aided Octavia but their alliance could not last and events came to a head at the climactic battle of Actium in 31 BC. The Sixth played little part in the naval victory and the following year they were sent to the province of Hispania Tarraconensis in north-eastern Spain.

The death of Antony enabled Octavian to take full control of the Empire and by 27 BC he was named Augustus and given unprecedented powers by the senate. This effectively ended any semblance of the former Republic and marks the start of the imperial age. Between the years 29–19 BC the Sixth fought in the *Bellum Cantabricum et Asturicum*, Cantabrian and Asturian Wars. The legion was initially called *Hispaniensis*, meaning simply 'stationed in Spain'. The name *Victrix*, or 'Victorious' is first attested during the reign of Nero, AD 54–68. Towards the end of Nero's reign the legion supported its legate and provincial governor, Galba, in the civil war of AD 68. This resulted in Nero's death and the 'Year of the Four Emperors'. Galba was followed quickly by Otho and Vitellius before Vespasian stabilised the political situation. It was Vespasian who sent the Sixth to the Rhine border in AD 70 to quell a revolt by the Batavians. This resulted in a victory at Xanten, near the legionary base Vetera, on the Lower Rhine in the same year.

Shortly after a monument, found near Vynen north of Xanten, was erected, dedicated to Vespasian and his son Titus:[1]

> To Vespasian and Titus, son of the Imperator Vespasian Augustus, holder of the tribunician power, acclaimed Imperator for the fourth time, Consul twice and appointed as Consul for the third time, appointed as Censor, Legio VI Victrix dedicated this, when Aulus Marius Celsus was pro-praetorian legate of the emperor and Sextus Caelius Tuscus was legate of the emperor.

The Legion stayed in Lower Germany at Novaesium, Neuss. In 89 they were sent to quell a rebellion by the governor of Upper Germany against the Emperor Domitian. For this they were awarded the title *Pia Fidelis Domitiana*, Dutiful and Loyal of Domitian. This was dropped after Domitian was assassinated and his name suffered *Damnatio* in the year 96. Subsequently Novaesium was abandoned and the legion moved to Xanten in Germany. The next campaign the legion is thought to have taken part in is the Dacian Wars of 101–106 under Emperor Trajan.

However this book is concerned with the legion's time in northern Britain and so we must go back a little to the year AD 43 when the Sixth were still in northern Spain. All dates from now on will be AD unless stated otherwise. Around eighty years after Caesar's first forays Claudius gained a large part of the island. Over the next fifteen years the Romans expanded their control, reaching the Humber in the north and as far west as Anglesey in North Wales.

The Boudican revolt in 60–1 demonstrated just how precarious Rome's grip on the island was.

At this point there were four legions in Roman Britain: II Augusta; IX Hispana; XIV Gemina; and XX Valeria. In the 60s II Adiutrix replaced XIV Gemina which was removed itself a generation later. This left three legions. There is a mystery surrounding the fate of the ninth legion which will be discussed later. The arrival of VI Victrix in c. 122 may have raised the garrison strength to four legions. However, by the early 130s IX Hispana was no longer present, reducing the legions strength back to the usual three which is how it remained for most of Roman Britain.[2] The Sixth took over the Ninth's base at York.

In 121, the Emperor Hadrian was in Germania Inferior where he ordered the construction of the Lower Rhine limes. The governor, Platorius Nepos, was a personal friend of Hadrian and he likely used the Sixth for this task. It is possible this experience convinced Hadrian to transfer Nepos and the Sixth to Britain in 122. It was in that year Hadrian visited Britain and ordered the famous wall bearing his name to be built. An inscribed building stone near Haltonchesters places and dates the legion to the north of Britain for the first time between c. 122–6 where it helped to build the wall between Newcastle and Carlisle.

Further inscriptions show it took part in the construction of the Antonine Wall, which was started c. 142. A few years before, similar evidence demonstrates it was also involved in repairs of Hadrian's Wall near Heddon near Newcastle. Around 160 the Antonine Wall was abandoned and we see part of the legion was stationed at Corbridge, although by this time the legion's main base had become York.[3] We will see this was not the last time Rome extended its reach into modern Scotland only to pull back later to the Tyne-Solway isthmus.

Another period of significant upheaval in Britain was during the reigns of Marcus Aurelius and his son Commodus. As well as barbarian raids there was much internal unrest and mutinies by the army and the Sixth played an important part. The legion also no doubt played a significant role in the subsequent civil war between Septimius Severus and Clodius Albinus. It was the infantry of the British legions that nearly won the climactic battle at Lugdunum in 197. By 208–11 they formed an integral part of the invasion force of Septimius Severus into Scotland. We see evidence of the Sixth alongside II Augusta at Carpow on the River Tay, south-east of Perth. To the legion's name was now added *Victrix Britannica pia Fidelis* suggesting it had at some point displayed a level of loyalty.

We hear very little during the third century. Detachments from legions, vexillations, may have been sent to the Rhine whilst the legion remained in

Britain during the Gallic Empire (260–74) and the short-lived reigns of the usurpers Carausius and Allectus (286–97). Back under control of the Empire, it was the Sixth that declared Constantine I as emperor when his father died at York in 306. The fourth century is mostly silent despite the many raids and political upheavals but the early fifth century *Notitia Dignitatum* possibly includes the legion's name under the command of the northern military command led by the Dux Britanniarum. This will be covered in greater detail in the final chapter.

Towards the end of Roman Britain only one legion remained, Legio VI Victrix.[4] It may have been removed by the general Stilicho in 402 or accompanied Constantine III to Gaul in 407. One theory is it was destroyed in the wars leading up to the sack of Rome in 410.[5] It is also likely a remnant of the Sixth remained in Britain to protect the northern border from increasing incursions of Picts and Irish raiders. Whatever the case it was the last legion left to defend the northern frontier.

This book is not just about legions and battles though. It will also cover day-to-day life of civilians as well as soldiers, many from faraway lands and sent to a remote corner of the empire, posted to guard a border against the fierce northern tribes. HBO's enormously successful *Game of Thrones* television series is based on George Martin's books, *A Song of Fire and Ice*. The great northern ice wall in the book, 700-feet high, is said to have been inspired by a visit to Hadrian's Wall. In the books, the Night's Watch guard the seven kingdoms against the wildings, giants and the White Walkers. Great fantasy fiction often has an element of reality at its core but twists and exaggerates to produce something entertaining.

A soldier of the Sixth looking northwards from a mile-castle along Hadrian's Wall might be forgiven for wondering just what lay beyond the horizon. Tales of fierce tribes and bloody battles would have been handed down generation after generation. What would he have felt after growing up in Egypt or Syria, perhaps never having seen snow in his life? Now looking out through a blizzard, his cloak the only protection against the cold of a fierce northern winter, far away from family and friends. For 300 years such men guarded the empire's border. Not against the fantasy of dragons and dire-wolves but very real terrors armed with spear and sword. These were the original 'Watchers on the Wall'.

Sources

The main epigraphical and contemporary sources used are as follows:

CIL The *Corpus Inscriptionum Latinarum* collection of ancient Latin inscriptions.
RIB Roman inscriptions of Britain number
Bellum Gallicum by Julius Caesar, 100–44 BC
The Histories, The Annals, Germanaia and *Agricola* by Tacitus 56–120
Historia Romana by Cassius Dio c. 155–235
History of the Roman Empire since the Death of Marcus Aurelius by Herodian c. 170–240
Historia Augusta anonymous author, 4th century
Epitoma rei militaris by Vegetius, 4th century
Res Gestae by Ammianus Marcellinus c. 330–400

Chapter 1

Rome and Britannia Before the Wall

Before we come to the arrival of the Sixth Legion in Britain we will briefly look at the nature of the Roman Empire in the second century. It will be necessary first to describe how the Roman Republic evolved into an imperial system and how Britain in particular was governed. It is also important to note the social and cultural structures and have an understanding as to how people fitted into the social hierarchy. The differences between senators, equestrians and plebeians are crucial in understanding Roman society. Despite the relative rigidity, advancement was possible and we shall see how at least one man, a tribune of the Sixth in the second century, rose from being the son of a freedman to the highest office of all. That man was Pertinax, emperor in 193 after Commodus met his untimely end in the bath, at the hands of his wrestling partner. We will also need to look at the structure of the army along with their weapons, armour and tactics. Contemporary accounts of battles, evidence from modern re-enactors and weapons testing will also aid our understanding of the lives of some of the individuals we will meet on our journey across three centuries.

Rome

Rome's founding is traditionally dated to 753 BC on seven hills above the River Tiber. The foundation myth told by Livy in the first century BC is worthy of note. Aeneas, a prince of Troy, escaped the destruction of that city and settled on the west coast of Italy. His descendant Numitor, grandfather to our two heroes of the tale, was overthrown by his brother Amulius who forced Numitor's daughter, his niece Rhea Silvia, into the temple, hopefully ensuring no future male rivals. Unfortunately for the usurper, not to mention Rhea herself, she was raped by Mars, the God of War. The resultant twin boys were thrown into the Tiber to drown. But Romulus and Remus were rescued and suckled by a she-wolf. Livy, perhaps sceptical of the tale, states the Latin word for wolf, Lupa, was also a colloquial term for prostitute.[1] The boys were found and raised by a shepherd, Faustulus, and his wife, Acca Larentia. They grew to manhood, killed their uncle, restored their grandfather to the throne and set out to found a new city. An entertaining tale of usurpation, rape, attempted infanticide and revenge. Finding the seven hills by the famous river, they each choose one, Romulus the Palatine Hill and Remus the Aventine Hill.

In a biblical twist Romulus kills his brother and declares Rome an asylum, attracting exiles, refugees, runaway slaves, convicts and the 'rabble and dispossessed of the rest of Italy'.[2] Lacking women he planned a ruse to abduct those of the Sabines and Latins which unsurprisingly caused a war. The result of this conflict left Romulus as the first of seven kings, a concept that later plays a crucial role in the Roman mindset. It was the fear of kingship that drove Caesar's assassins hundreds of years later. The last king of Rome, Lucius Tarquinius Superbus, is dated to c.509 BC. Coincidently the man who killed him was another Brutus. The oath he asked the Romans to swear gives us an insight into Roman attitudes: 'First of all, by swearing an oath that they would suffer no man to rule Rome, it forced the people, desirous of a new liberty, not to be thereafter swayed by the entreaties or bribes of kings.' This may be legend, but the Romans took such things seriously and it played an important part in the development of the republic. The letters SPQR stand for '*Senatus*

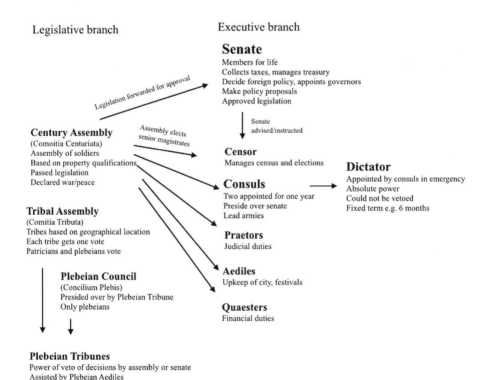

Figure 1: Governmental structure under the Roman Republic.

Populusque Romanus', 'the Senate and People of Rome'. This phrase embodies the ideal, if not the reality, of Roman government.

In the early republic power resided among a few aristocratic families. Subsequent political and social upheavals changed the balance of power, one example being the 'conflict of orders' (c. 500–287 BC) which resulted in formation of The Plebian Council and the 'Laws of the Twelve Tables' displayed in the forum. This laid out rights and duties of all citizens, creating a balance and separation of powers. This worked reasonably well in a city state; however, as the empire expanded tensions between competing powers increased. The coalescence of power, around, first, Caesar then Octavian, could be viewed as the inevitable consequence of the need for a central authority to control the vast empire. Octavian became Augustus and ruled 27 BC to AD 14, making a number of reforms.[3] Senatorial decrees were given the force of law along with Imperial pronouncements and formed the basis of Roman legislation.

Meanwhile the social hierarchy had also changed. From the earliest days of the republic there had been a distinction between patricians and plebeians in Roman society. The definition of patrician evolved and divided into a stratified upper-class of wealthy aristocrats, senators and equestrians. The development of a relatively large equestrian class, of up to 30,000 at any one time, provided a crucial source of military and civilian officials to help run the empire. The plebeians formed the bulk of the population and beneath them came freedmen and, lastly, slaves. As the empire expanded, social mobility increased. Plebeians were able to rise to equestrian status and from there even to the senate.

The career ladder of the senatorial class, the *cursus honorum*, gave aspiring nobles a route to high office. Equestrians could progress through military posts, the *tres militiae*, and from there one of the procuratorial posts, or one of the four great prefectures of Rome. As the empire expanded more men from

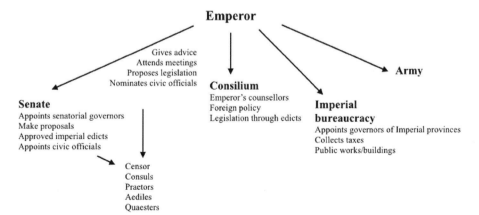

Figure 2: Governmental structure under the Roman Empire.

the provinces were awarded equestrian status and some began to enter the senate. Figure three shows the cursus honorum in the republican era and when the role of 'dictator' was originally restricted to a set time to address a specific emergency. A month before his murder, Julius Caesar had been appointed dictator, for life and this role ultimately evolved into that of emperor. The official title was *princeps*, which owed its origins in the *princeps senatus* of the republican era, a position held by an ex-consul for five years and which gave precedence to for speaking in debates. The officer class of the Sixth were drawn largely from the equestrian class. But up until the mid-third century the legions were led by senatorial legates. The bulk of the soldiers though would have been plebeians. Importantly they had to be classed as citizens. By the time of Hadrian the bulk of these citizen recruits came from outside the Italian peninsula.

A Roman citizen of the plebeian class might see the army as providing one of the few opportunities for regular reasonably well-paid employment as well as one providing a rare path for social advancement. A soldier of the Sixth could rise to centurion and if he became the *primus pilus*, the leading centurion of the first cohort, or even *praefectus castorum*, he would be eligible for equestrian status. One *praefectus* of the Sixth who we will meet later, Lucius Artorius Castus, did just that and retired to become a procurator of Liburnia in modern Croatia. He would, of course, have stiff competition from one of the 20,000 to 30,000 equestrians across the empire, all of whom would

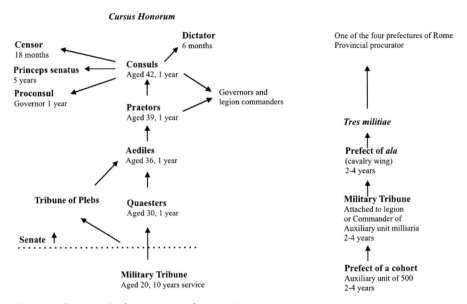

Figure 3: Career paths for senators and equestrians.

be eager for their children to follow their footsteps. For these the centurion route was one option. Perhaps the better known was the *tres militiae*. A young equestrian might obtain a post as a praefectus of an infantry cohort of auxiliaries, usually numbering 500. If he proved his worth he could serve as one of the five tribunes of a legion, advising the senatorial legate who commanded. Next would be a *praefectus alae*, commander of a cavalry wing. From here he could advance to become a procurator of a province which normally entailed financial responsibilities and was subordinate to the governor, although he reported direct to the emperor. Finally came one of the four great praefectures:

- Praetorian prefect, *praefectus praetorius*, based in Rome and consisting of usually nine cohorts.
- Prefect of the grain supply, *praefectus annonae*, again based in Rome.
- Prefect of the Vigiles, *praefectus vigilum*, commanding seven cohorts, also in Rome.
- Prefect of Egypt, *praefectus Aegypti*, controlling the strategically important province of Egypt with its number of legions and importance of its grain supply.

Pertinax held a number of these posts and was eventually promoted to the senate. The senatorial career path often began with a posting as military tribune to a legion in the early twenties. He could then progress to *quaestor* and *aedile* both of which placed him in the senate. If competent he could serve as *praetor* and even consul (of which there were generally only two each year). He was then eligible to serve as a legion commander and governor. Thus governors were called proconsuls or propraetorian legates. Pertinax, having previously served as an equestrian tribune of the Sixth, returned as a senatorial propraetorian legate and governor of Britain in 185–7.

Despite an increase in social mobility there remained high levels of inequality within a rigidly stratified social hierarchy based on property ownership and wealth.[4] The property qualification for a senator was 1 million sesterces and for an equestrian 400,000.[5] To serve as a juror required 200,000 and municipal councillors 100,000. Beneath these, salaried workers such as doctors, teachers and shop owners were luckier than the bulk of the population who lived a hand-to-mouth existence. Slaves made up one-in-six of the empire's 70–80 million population, and up to half of Rome's estimated one million. With regard to wages we can see the disparity: at the time of Cicero in the first century BC average wages were less than 1,500 a year whilst the famous statesman and orator earned 555,555 sesterces from his legal work alone.[6] A peasant family could live on an estimated 500 sesterces a year whilst senatorial governors earned 400,000; equestrian procurators 60,000–300,000 whereas a legionary soldier could expect 1,200 sesterces. However, a centurion earned 18,000. For a poor citizen the military not only guaranteed a reasonable income and food but was one of the few avenues open for economic and social advancement.

During the early principate, provinces were divided between those directly ruled by the emperor and those by the senate. With some exceptions, such as the important province of Egypt, provinces were governed by those of senatorial rank and legions commanded by senatorial legates. The number of proconsular provinces reporting directly to the senate had dwindled in number by the time of the Sixth's arrival in Britain. The majority of provinces were imperial provinces reporting direct to the emperor and administered by a proprietorial of senatorial rank. Legions tended only to be posted to imperial provinces. Where only one legion was present the legate often also served as the governor.

Assisting the governors were procurators responsible for financial matters who were generally of equestrian rank although increasingly emperors, such as Commodus, used trusted freedmen in important positions. However, some minor provinces were administered by equestrian procurators from the time of Augustus. The one exception was Egypt, governed by a *praefectus Aegypti*, which made up one of the four great prefectures, three of which were based in Rome: The Prefect of the grain supply, *praefectus annonae*; Praetorian

Figure 4: Map of Imperial and Senatorial provinces AD 117. (*Wikimedia Commons*)

prefect, *praefectus praetorius* commanding nine cohorts; and Prefect of the Vigiles, *praefectus vigilum*, with seven cohorts. These were the pinnacle of the equestrian career. The urban cohort, consisting of four cohorts, was led by someone of senatorial rank.

Such was the political and social structure of the Roman Empire when the Sixth arrived in Britain in the early second century. Augustus had reduced the number of senators from 900 to 600 and from such men were appointed the governors and legion commanders that controlled the empire. Beneath them were several thousand equestrians in various military and civilian roles. The common soldiers and plebeians could only dream of reaching such heights, although there were rare exceptions. Most lived, fought and died as legionaries but if they were lucky survived to enjoy retirement. It is to the army we will now turn.

The legions

By the end of the first century AD a legion numbered approximately 5,500 and was made up of generally professional volunteers drawn from citizens. Conscription was also used in times of emergency. Auxiliary troops were raised from the provinces and organised into units of infantry, cavalry or mixed, numbering either 500 or up to 1,000. By the beginning of the second century this was also a largely volunteer force. The number of legions under Augustus rose from twenty-five to thirty-three under Caracalla whilst auxiliary units rose from 250 to 400. Whilst the total number of troops across the empire increased the percentage of legionaries dropped below 50 per cent. Auxiliary units were led by equestrian prefects as part of the *tres militiae*. The empire also hired mercenary barbarian units called *numeri*, led by their own native leaders.

The Sixth Legion in the early second century had a clearly defined hierarchy that would be familiar to any disciplined and well-trained armed force from ancient to modern times. In second century Britannia the legion commander of the Sixth based at York reported to the provincial governor, the *legatus Augusti pro praetore*, in London. This legion commander was titled *legatus legionis*, and as we have noted would have been of senatorial rank. The average length of his posting was three to four years.

His second in command was the senatorial tribune, *tribunus laticlavius* ('military tribune of the broad stripe', referring to the toga worn by senators), usually an inexperienced young man. As the Sixth was in Britain, he was also appointed by the Emperor rather than the senate. The legate and his second in command were advised by five military tribunes, *tribuni angusticlavii* ('military tribune of the narrow stripe'), who were normally experienced, battle-hardened men of equestrian class. This formed the second rung on the ladder of promotion for equestrians, the tres militiae.

Equestrians could also be appointed as centurions and come up through the ranks to *primus pilus* and eventually *praefectus castrorum*, the third in command under the legate and tribunes. This route was also open to plebeians who would have been eligible for equestrian status once they reached *primus pilus*. One example we shall meet, Lucius Artoris Castus, had been a primus pilus of Legio V Macedonia on the Danube before his posting to York as praefectus castrorum of the Sixth. He would likely have been 50 to 60 years of age at this point and usually this post would have been his last.[7]

The legion itself was made up of ten cohorts with cohorts two to ten divided into six centuries of eighty men, giving 480 per cohort. The lead centurion of each was called the *pilus prior*. The first cohort, however, consisted of five double centuries of 160 men and the lead centurion was termed the primus pilus, or 'first spear'. This man was the senior centurion in the whole legion and would have led the first century, *centuria*, of the first cohort. He obtained equestrian class on retirement. In addition to the 5,120 infantry, the legion had a 120-man *alae*, cavalry, attached called the *eques legionis*, used as scouts and messengers.

There were therefore fifty-nine centurions in a legion, each with an *optio* as second in command. A century was made up of ten (or twenty in the first cohort) eight-man 'tent groups', *contubernium*, who shared a mess tent and a mule.[8] Each century had a signifier who carried the standard for the century. He was also responsible for the troop's pay and savings. Accompanying him was a *cornicen* or horn blower, and a *imaginifer*, carrying an image of the emperor to remind the men of their loyalty. One last point concerns battle standards. The *aquilifer* carried the legion's standard or eagle. The legions used three main types of military signals: the voiced; the 'semi-voiced', with bugle, horn

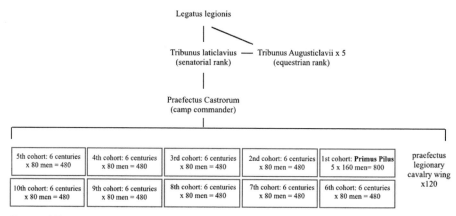

Figure 5: Legion command structure in the second century.

or trumpet; and the 'mute signals', with eagles, dragons, ensigns and plumes.[9] While the eagle was the standard of the Roman legions, later cohorts had their own 'dragon-bearer'.[10]

Auxiliaries

In battle the legions provided the heavy infantry but it was the auxiliaries who provided the bulk of the light troops and cavalry. As we shall see in contemporary accounts of battles, these forces were often deployed first and if the enemy broke the cavalry pursued them. By the mid-second century auxiliary troops had become a vital part of Rome's military force and under Marcus Aurelius there were 440 auxiliary regiments scattered across the empire, half of which were stationed along the Danube provinces.[11]

Auxiliary forces were generally divided into three types; A cavalry alae consisting of sixteen *turmae* of roughly thirty men each; an infantry cohort similar in size to a legionary cohort and also divided into centuries; and a mixed force of infantry and cavalry, the *cohortes equitatae*. Thus units of around 500 (*quingenaria*) were standard. Double-sized units, milliaria, of up to approximately 1,000 are also recorded. Commanding these units was an equestrian *praefectus* as one step on his career path. A praefectus alae was senior to an auxiliary infantry commander, *praefectus cohortis*. The period of service was not fixed, but was usually two to four years. In the early principate a primus pilus could move on to command an auxiliary unit. However, by the second century nearly all auxiliary commanders came from the established equestrian class, often beginning their careers as magistrates in Italian, and later provincial, municipal cities.[12]

Table one shows the various types of auxiliary units. Two things need to be borne in mind. Firstly, the numbers and composition shown represent the consensus opinion of historians regarding the composition of most units. This may not have been consistent across all units of the same type. Secondly, the paper strength of a unit may not reflect the reality in practice. As we shall see with evidence from Vindolanda a unit could have a significant proportion seconded to other duties or locations as well as sickness an injury.

Two other kinds of units are worth mentioning.[13] First, *numeri* was a term used for a body of irregular troops. One example was of a unit of Britons posted to the German frontier manning a series of watchtowers. Another example is a numerus of bargemen from the Tigris at South Shields on the Tyne in northern Britain. Second, *cunei* appears to be specifically a Germanic irregular unit. Literally meaning 'wedge', Tacitus refers to the Germanic tactic of attack and applies it to the Batavii in the civil war of AD 69.

Unit	Description	Number	Composition
Cohors quingeneria peditata	Infantry	480	6 centuries of 80
Ala quingenaria	Cavalry	480	16 turmae of 30
Cohors equitata quingeneria	Mixed	600	480 infantry, 120 Cavalry
Cohors milliaria peditata	Infanrty	800	10 centuries of 80
Ala milliaria	Cavalry	720	24 turmae of 32
Cohors equitata milliaria	Mixed	1040	800 infantry, 240 cavalry

Table 1: Types of auxiliary units.

Military forces in Britain in the second century

Leaving the fate of the Ninth Legion to one side the table below gives us the three legions which were stationed in Britain from the second quarter of the second century and beyond. These three legions would have placed approximately 15,720 troops, mostly heavy infantry, under the command of the provincial governor in London.

Legion	Emblem	Campaigns	Based
II Augusta	Capricorn, Pegasus	Cantabrian wars 26–19 BC Campaigns of Germanicus AD 9 Invasion of Britain 43 Scottish campaign of Septimius Severus 208–11	Isca Silurum, Caerleon.
XX Valeria Victrix	Boar	Cantabrian wars 27–19 BC Pannonian revolt AD 6–9 Germanic wars 15 Invasion of Britain 43 Campaign in Wales 43–60 Boudican revolt 60 2nd battle of Bedriacum 69 Campaign in Wales 77 Campaign against northern tribes 77–84 Battle of Lugdunum 196	Deva, Chester
VI Victrix	Bull	Perugia 41 BC Actium 31 BC Cantabrian wars 26–19 BC Batavian revolt AD 69–70 Saturninus revolt 89 Dacian wars 101–6 British revolt 155–8 Scottish campaign of Septimius Severus 208–11	Eboracum, York.

Table 2: Legions of Britain after c. 122.[14]

In the early second century we have evidence for the following distribution of auxiliary units:[15]

Units	Units size quingenarii	Units size milliariae	Total units	Total number of troops
Infantry, cohortes	12	2	14	7,360
Cavalry, alae	15	1	16	7,920
Mixed, equitatae	24	5	29	19,600
Total units	51	8	59	-
Total number of troops	27,360	7,520	-	34,880

Table 3: Auxiliary units of Britain.

We can see from this that there were over double the number of auxiliary troops compared to the legions. Many of these units were posted to northern Britain along with the Sixth and they could be called upon for support by the legatus at York. They often provided the first line of defence or offence against rebellious tribes either side of the Wall. They also provided the bulk of the cavalry. On paper, if we add the cavalry from the mixed units to the alae, the auxiliary troops could field 12,000 horsemen.

The Sixth would have worked and fought alongside the auxiliaries. We also have many instances of centurions of the Sixth taking temporary command of a unit. In some cases an auxiliary soldier would have been indistinguishable from a legionary of the Sixth. However in general the auxiliaries often wore chain mail rather than the *lorica segmentata* of the heavy infantry. They also tended to carry oval shields rather than the famous *scutum* and were armed with spears rather than a *gladius*. The next section will focus on the equipment of a soldier of the Sixth Legion.

Weapons

Polybius, writing in the second century BC, gave a good description of equipment carried by a Roman soldier.[16] The curved *scutum* measured 2½ feet in width by 4 feet in height. Constructed from two planks glued together, the outer surface was covered with canvas and calf-skin. The rims, strengthened by iron, protected it from blows and damage when rested on the ground. The iron boss could withstand 'the most formidable blows of stones, pikes, and heavy missiles in general'. Polybius describes the 'Spanish sword', hanging on the right thigh as 'excellent for thrusting, and both of its edges cut effectually, as the blade is very strong and firm'. In addition the soldiers carried two pila, a brass helmet, and greaves.

The main weapon of the legionaries of the Sixth in the second century was still the gladius. Recruits were taught to strike with the point rather than the edge; a cut rarely kills because the vitals are protected by armour, whereas 'a stab driven two inches in is fatal'.[17] It was ideally suited to the techniques and formations of the Roman army of the time. It was also capable of cutting as Livy, writing at the time of Augustus, records in his account of the Macedonian Wars: When they saw the style of weapon and type of men they were up against a 'shudder of horror' passed through the men, 'they saw bodies dismembered with the Spanish sword, arms cut off from the shoulder, heads struck off from the trunk, bowels exposed and other horrible wounds.'[18] In the republican era the *gladius hispaniensis* had a leaf-shaped blade 60–68 centimetres long and 5 centimetres wide, weighing just under a kilogram. This had evolved by the time the Sixth came to Britain to three main types: the Mainz gladius, with a shorter but wider blade, 50–55 by 7 centimetres, weighing 800 grams; the Fulham gladius, also at 50–55 centimetes, but slightly narrower and lighter at 6 centimetres and 700 grams respectively; and the Pompeii gladius, the shortest and narrowest blade, at 45–50 by 5 centimetres, also weighing 700 grams. All three swords had handles of 15 centimetres.

The soldiers of the Sixth also carried two pila, measuring about 2 metres long, with the top metre being made of iron with a hardened pyramidal-shape head of 5 to 17 centimetres weighing between two and four kilograms. Its effective range was 15–20 metres but could be thrown up to 33 metres. In the *Gallic Wars* Julius Caesar describes how an attack was defeated by a volley of pila. The Gauls suffered because several of their shields were 'pierced and fastened together by a single javelin-cast; and as the iron became bent, they could not pluck it forth, nor fight handily with the left arm encumbered'. This caused some to cast their shields aside while others struggled on with their shields severely compromised. Eventually they gave ground and retreated.[19] The Romans thus 'easily broke the mass-formation of the enemy by a volley of javelins'. They then drew their swords and charged. The front five cohorts of a single Roman legion could discharge 2,720 pila at a range of 30 metres and get a more accurate second volley in at half that distance, just as the rear five cohorts discharged their first volley.

Shorter javelins were also used as well as *plumbatae*, lead-weighted darts. Five such darts could be carried in the rear of a shield. Interesting experiments show they can penetrate exposed flesh by up to four inches.[20] Thrown underhand they reached 30 metres but were accurate only at short distances, as little as 6 metres. Shield and armour provided protection but unprotected limbs or heads would have been vulnerable and attackers would be forced to raise their shields just as they closed in on the enemy. The effective range of the shorter spears or javelins was around 12–15 metres.[21] Longer spears (*hasta*) were about 1.8 metres, or 6 feet in length and in the second century tended to be carried by auxiliary troops. Slingers with lead shot have been shown to penetrate 12 millimetres of plywood. Armour provided good protection, but tests on ballistic gel again shows unprotected areas to be highly vulnerable to severe injury. These are the slingshots found at Perugia with the Sixth's number inscribed.

The fourth century writer Vegetius suggests a percentage of each cohort were trained in the bow.

However, they also employed specialist units of auxiliary infantry *sagittarii* units. These outnumbered horse archers in the Roman army of the time by a ratio of two to one. The Romans used a composite bow with a maximum range of about 150–200 metres. Vegetius stated archers trained using targets up to a range of 180 metres.[22] They were less effective at over 100 metres, but became highly accurate at around 50–60 metres.[23] Archers, whether mounted or on foot, would have carried thirty to forty arrows.[24] Arrow heads had a variety of shapes with narrower bodkin-like heads better for piercing armour. However, the plates of the lorica segmentata offered good protection. As a comparison later medieval longbows were capable of up to 180lbs of pull. Earlier finds from the fourth century suggest Roman recurve bows were less powerful at 80–100lbs.

Thus Legio VI Victrix had a wide range of missile weapons available, even without help from auxiliary units. Aside from archers, slingers, smaller javelins and lead darts over 10,000 pila could rain down before an enemy even reached the first line of the front cohorts. Once there they were confronted with a highly-organised and disciplined formation. A wall of wood and iron with the short gladius swords stabbing out from behind shields inflicting horrific injuries.

Armour and shields

Contrary to many battle scenes on film armour was used for a very good reason. It worked. In particular it offered good protection against cutting or glancing blows.[25] Some armour was susceptible to spear thrusts and arrows, especially with narrow bodkin-type heads. However, even padded and leather armour offers reasonable protection against cutting blows.

In the late empire a *supermalis* consisted of two layers stuffed with sheep's wool. The fourth-century *De Rebus Bellicis* describes a *thoracomachus* designed to counteract the weight and friction of the armour.[26] It was made from 'thick sheep's wool felt'. The source also refers to 'Libyan Hide', which is thought to be goatskin. Re-enactors suggest some sort of under-armour is essential when wearing metal armour.[27] One modern test found five layers of material was enough to stop an arrow even at close range.[28] This wasn't just effective as an alternative to metal armour; shields, too, were covered in rawhide to give added protection.

There were three main types of armour used by the Roman army. The first is *lorica hamata*, or chainmail armour. This was constructed using metal rings riveted together. A central ring was riveted to the rows above and below. Tests using a gladius against riveted mail show a minimal amount of penetration of only about a centimetre, meaning any padding underneath will protect the body. A spear thrust performed at least as well as a gladius but required both hands for a significant amount of power. A *pilum* can penetrate mail by several inches, a fatal blow. But these tests were on static targets rather than a realistic flexible one that falls away when hit. Other tests show the pilum bouncing off. In general, this armour was excellent against cutting blows, a sword thrust and most missiles. However, a determined heavy spear or pilum throw delivered at the right angle could penetrate to sufficient depth.

Legionaries of the second century, and thus Legio VI Victrix, tended to wear lorica segmentata. Consisting of horizontal iron 'hoop' plates, bound together with leather straps to form a flexible, strong protection, this armour gives us the iconic image of a Roman soldier in many films. Appearing in the first century BC it faded out of use in the third century. This performed very well in most weapons tests. Even a determined spear thrust failed to penetrate although it's likely you would sustain some injury such as a broken rib.

The third common type of armour was the *lorica squamatae*, translated as 'scale of feathers', consisting of overlapping bronze or iron scales. It began to replace the lorica segmentata after the second century. The scales were normally of iron or bronze and approximately 0.6 by 1.2 centimetres to 5 by 8 centimetres, with a thickness of 0.5 to 0.8 millimetres. It was quick and easy to make. Similar types, such as lamellar armour, can be seen all over the world from Persia to Japan, made from a variety of material such as bone or leather.

Lastly, sculpted cuirasses were generally worn by officers.[29] By the late Roman period, muscle cuirasses can be seen on monuments as well as lamellar armour and segmented armour for the arms and legs of heavily armoured horsemen.[30] In the late Roman army, light units – infantry or cavalry – generally had no armour.[31] Many of their adversaries, whether in Germany or Britain, would have been armed with a spear and protected by a shield and a leather padded jerkin.

Helmets were made of bronze with iron trim. A large projecting piece protected the back of the neck and a small ridge ran along the front. Hinged cheek-pieces to protect the face could be tied together by leather straps. The main types in use when the Sixth arrived in Britain were the Imperial Gallic and Italic helmets. Some helmets had a crest holder for plumes of horse hair. Modern tests suggest they gave good protection from arrows as well as sword or even axe blows with the curved surface deflecting the force. However, a direct strike might still cause considerable injury even without the metal being penetrated.

The first line of protection was the shield. The rectangular Roman *scutum* was made of sheets of thin wood glued together with the grain at right angles to the ones both above and below. The edges were bound in iron or bronze and the centre hollowed out for a hand grip, which was in turn protected by a metal boss. The shield was then covered in leather, giving it extra protection from missile weapons. One example from Syria measures 105 by 41 centimetres allowing protection from chin to knees for a 6-foot-tall man. With greaves and a helmet, a shorter man with bent knees would only have his eyes visible to the enemy. The curved edges gave extra protection to the sides. At 10 kilograms it weighed as much as the armour a legionary wore. The covering of calf-skin reduced the penetration of arrows considerably.

Auxiliary infantry cohorts were often equipped with the same armour and weapons as legionaries, except that they tended to have oval rather than scutum shields.[32] Some units used specialised native tactics such as slingers and archers. Some light cavalry units were unarmored, whilst Gallic cavalry are depicted wearing a mail cuirass with leather jerkins, tight trousers, helmet and a knotted scarves round their necks. In armoured cavalry units, such as the *cataphracttarii*, both rider and horse were protected, the rider by mail, canvas or horn and thigh guards, and the horse with mail protecting front and sides. Whilst some heavy infantry units did wear lorica segmentata, both cavalry and infantry units, when armoured, tended to wear mail, *lorica hamata*, or scale, *lorica squamata*.

Formations and battle techniques

We get some idea of formations and tactics from Vegetius writing in the fourth century. He gives seven examples of deployment, many of which we can see used in contemporary accounts of battles:[33]

1. Rectangular formation with extended front. Should only be used with numerical superiority lest the flanks become enveloped. He describes this as the usual way to do battle in his day.
2. Oblique or angled formation engaging enemy's left flank with your stronger right and strongest cavalry to turn flank.

3. Same as 2 but engaging their right flank with your left.
4. Advance to 400–500 paces then spur on both wings having thinned out your own centre.
5. Same as point 4, above, but place light troops and archers in front of centre to protect from breach.
6. He describes this as the best: A letter 'I' formation, oblique with the right flank attacking first, and cavalry and light troops outflanking enemy.
7. Use of terrain: Simply by anchoring one flank against mountain, forest or river then placing all light troops and cavalry on the opposite wing.

The excellent HBO series *Rome* offered a highly entertaining and interesting tactic in the opening scene. The Romans' formation was several men deep with the front line facing the enemy. In the lines behind each man held the belt of

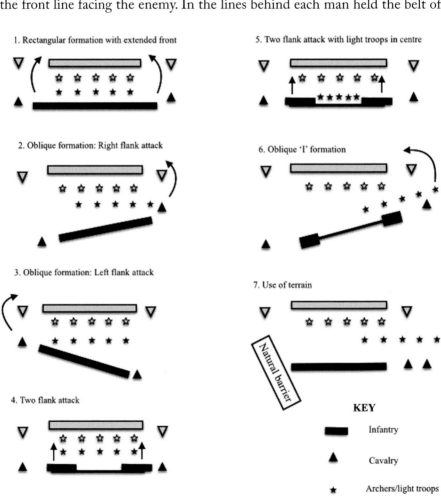

Figure 6: General battle tactics from Vegetius.

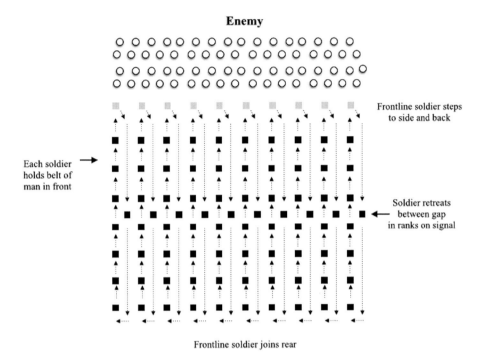

Figure 7: Roman century attacks in close formation 10 × 8.

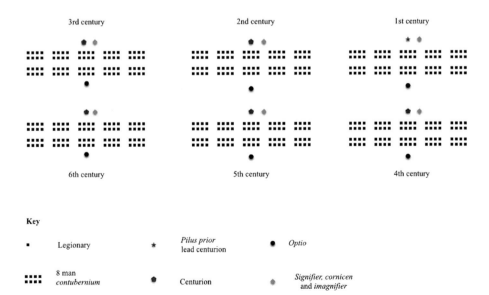

Figure 8: Roman Cohort in loose formation.

the man in front. In this way a century of eighty men could form a front ten-men wide and eight-men deep, with a small gap between each column. The front ten men received the initial charge of the enemy. Before they became exhausted the centurion blew a whistle and the second line released their grip. This allowed the front man to step right and backwards, retreating down the gap to the rear. The ten men of the second line now stepped forward to take their comrade's place at the front. This gave the men time to rest and maintained formation.

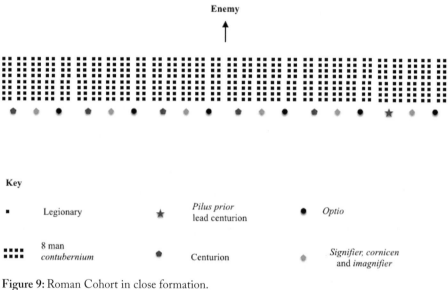

Figure 9: Roman Cohort in close formation.

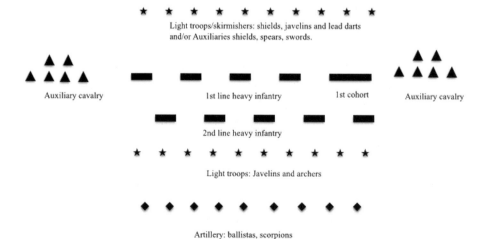

Figure 10: A typical Roman legion formation 2nd century AD.

The figures above show a possible formation of a cohort arrayed in both loose and close formation. The final figure depicts a typical Roman legion formation of the second century AD.

Batavian revolt 69–70

The Batavi were a Germanic tribe who had provided significant numbers of auxiliary troops to the Roman army, many of which had taken part in the invasion of Britain in 43. Relations between the Batavians and the Romans broke down during the civil war and 'Year of the Four Emperors' in 69. The Batavian leader, Julius Civilis, was also an experienced Roman officer and he led his Batavian cohorts and Gallic and Germanic allies to a series of victories against the local troops in Germania Inferior. He eventually was able to besiege two legions at Vetera, Xanten. It took the arrival of three Roman legions to relieve the camp. An attack further south forced the Romans to retire and Civilis was eventually able to take the camp and later destroy the two retreating legions.

The following spring Legio VI Victrix joined five other legions in a major offensive towards Castra Vetera. A wide marshy plain separated the armies and a day's confused fighting proved inconclusive. We then get an account from Tacitus. Fought near the fortress on a plain beside the Rhine, the Roman general Quintus Petilius Cerialis, formed up in two lines. Civilis had built a dam diverting the water onto the 'naturally marshy' plain. Tacitus tells us on the first day:[34] 'there was no fighting at close quarters, as is usual in an engagement between infantry, but the struggle was rather like a naval fight, for the men floundered about in the water'. The next day Cerialis posted his cavalry and auxiliary infantry in the front line with his legions behind, keeping 'picked troops' back under his own leadership for emergencies. The Batavians placed their troops in columns rather than an extended front, the Batavi and Cugerni were on his right; the left wing, nearer the river, was held by tribes from across the Rhine. Tacitus has the two generals talking to their troops and claims Cerialis reminded the Sixth that it was 'by their influence that Galba had been made emperor' and urged his troops to regain their former camp which the Batavians held.

The Germans, with 'clashing arms and wild dancing according to their custom' opened battle with a volley of missiles: stones, leaden balls and other missiles. But the Romans refused the provocation and were not lured onto the marshy ground. The Germans attacked and pushed back the auxiliary troops only for the legions, including the Sixth, to enter the fray and stop the advance. It was a Batavian deserter that apparently swung the balance to the Romans. He led two troops of Roman cavalry round the marsh and behind the Batavians. On a signal the cavalry attacked the rear and the legions charged, routing the enemy. Only heavy rain and nightfall saved them from complete destruction.

The victory was commemorated in an inscription that mentions the new emperor, Vespasian, and the commander of the sixth legion, Sextus Caelius Tuscus:[35]

> to the son of imperator Vespasian
> Augustus, with tribunician
> powers, imperator for the
> fourth time, twice consul, appointed
> for a third term, appointed as censors,
> to Aulus Marius Celsus,
> governor with the rank of propraetor,
> and to Sextus Caelius Tuscus,
> commander, [this was monument dedicated by]
> the Sixth legion
> Victrix

The Sixth remained in Germania Inferior, based at Neuss. At the end of the first century it was moved to Xanten, site of the famous victory a generation before. During the Dacian Wars of Trajan, units were sent to the Danube. In the early second century the legion was in Germania when Hadrian visited in person and organised construction of the Lower Rhine limes. The governor, Platorius Nepos, was a personal friend of Hadrian. It was perhaps this friendship, or the legion's work on the defences in Germany, that changed the course of history for the Sixth. For the following year Hadrian visited Britain, taking his friend and the Sixth with him.

As we shall see in the next chapter it is likely Hadrian's intervention was caused by unrest in the province. As such the Sixth may have taken part in the military response. To give some idea of the nature of warfare of this period we have two contemporary accounts of battles which demonstrate the effectiveness of Roman military training and organisation.

The Battle of Walling Street

The revolt of Boudicca in c.61 resulted in the destruction of Colchester, London and St Albans as well as an initial force sent against the Britons. The Roman governor of Britain, Gaius Suetonius Paulinus, had been campaigning on the island of Mona (Anglesey), a stronghold of the druids. General Suetonius arrived from North Wales with the Fourteenth Legion, detachments of the Twentieth and auxiliaries, numbering 10,000 troops. The Britons are said to have numbered as much as 230,000. This may be an exaggeration, but certainly it was many times that of the Roman force. Tacitus provides further details.[36] Suetonius chose a position 'approached by a narrow defile and secured in the rear by a wood'. The legionaries formed up in 'serried ranks', with light-armed troops on the side flanked by cavalry. The Britons' forces deployed in 'bands of foot and horse … moving jubilantly in every direction'. Clearly confident from their recent victories, Tacitus tells us they had brought 'even their wives to witness the victory', placing them in wagons on the edge of the plain which lay before the Roman front line.

Boudicca, 'mounted in a chariot with her daughters before her, rode up to clan after clan and delivered her protest': to avenge 'as a woman of the people, her liberty lost, her body tortured by the lash, the tarnished honour of her daughters'. She reminded them that Heaven was on 'the side of their just revenge' and that they had already destroyed a legion. Tacitus puts equally stirring words into the mouth of Suetonius. They should 'treat with contempt the noise and empty menaces of the barbarians' with 'more women than soldiers … unwarlike and unarmed, they would break immediately'. Shakespeare put similar words into Henry V's mouth at Agincourt: 'The fewer men, the greater share of honour … We few, we happy few, we band of brothers'. Tacitus claims the general advises his men: 'it was but a few men who decided the fate of battles; and it would be an additional glory that they, a handful of troops, were gathering the laurels of an entire army.'

We then read something of the formation and tactics: 'Only, keeping their order close, and, when their javelins were discharged, employing shield-boss and sword, let them steadily pile up the dead and forget the thought of plunder: once the victory was gained, all would be their own.' The Romans stood their ground, using the defile as protection. When the Britons came within range they exhausted their missiles and charged. We can imagine 10,000 pila from the fourteenth legion alone. If the auxiliaries were similarly armed we can double that. A pilum weighed on average between 0.9–2.3 kilograms. If we estimate just 10,000 pila at 1.5 kilo each that means the advancing Britons were met with about 15 tonnes of wood and iron raining down.

The Roman advance was a wedge-like formation, legions and auxiliaries alike. The cavalry, 'with lances extended, broke a way through.' This seems to have caused an immediate flight. However, escape was difficult and blocked by the cordon of wagons at the far end of the plain. The panic appears to have been total and the Romans gave no quarter. Women and even baggage train animals were 'added to the pile of bodies'. Tacitus tells us a little less than 80,000 Britons were killed and only 400 Romans died with a similar number wounded. Boudicca ended her days by taking poison.

Mons Graupius 83/4

Another contemporary account from Tacitus concerns the victory of his father-in-law, the general Agricola. Interestingly, he was a military tribune under Seutonius at Watling Street twenty years before. Now he was governor and leading a campaign into the north. The Caledonians had mustered a large army led by the chieftain Calgacus, with over 30,000 men. Tacitus again puts words in the mouths of his protagonists. In one of the best known lines from antiquity, the Romans are described as 'robbers of the world' and 'rapacious' with a 'lust for dominion'. Then: 'Alone among men they covet with equal eagerness poverty and riches. To robbery, slaughter, plunder, they give the lying name of empire; they make a solitude and call it peace.'[37]

Agricola laid out his troops in what would be a familiar formation with 8,000 infantry auxiliaries, in front, 3,000 cavalry on the wings and the legions drawn up behind. The Britons positioned themselves on high ground with their van on a plain in front of the Romans. The bulk of their army rose, arch-like, on the slope of a hill. Chariots and cavalry formed a screen on the plain. The battle began with a volley of missiles from the Britons and chariots attacks which the Romans repelled with arrows and javelins and cavalry.

The Britons were armed with their 'huge swords and small shields' and delivered 'a dense shower of darts' on the Romans. Agricola ordered three Batavian and two Tungrian cohorts forward (approximately 2,500 men) and 'come to close quarters' with their swords. The swords of the Britons are described as 'enormous … blunt at the point … unfit for close grappling, and engaging in a confined space'. They proved no match for the experienced Germanic troops who pushed the enemy up the hill, striking them with the 'bosses of their shields and stabbing them in the face'.[38] The remaining cohorts of auxiliaries joined the attack. A counter-attack by chariots failed to halt the Roman advance. The Britons on the summit of the hill looked 'with careless contempt' at the relatively small attacking force and began to descend. Agricola sent in 'four reserved squadrons of horse' which drove them back, then wheeled round to attack the rear. The Britons began to break and flee. Tacitus implies a rearguard action managed to blunt the pursuit, but only the forests and night saved the Britons from total destruction. It is estimated 10,000 Caledonians lay dead with Roman loses below 400.

Summary

As the Romans advanced north and west, so, too, did their culture and lifestyle. Tacitus tells how the general Agricola encouraged the sons of the leading men in 'the liberal arts'. The Latin language and Roman toga became popular as 'distaste' was replaced by 'passion' for Roman culture: 'In their innocence they called this 'civilisation, when in fact it was part of their enslavement.'[39] Tacitus was writing some years after Agricola's campaign in the north and makes an interesting reference to a King Togidumnus 'who maintained his unswerving

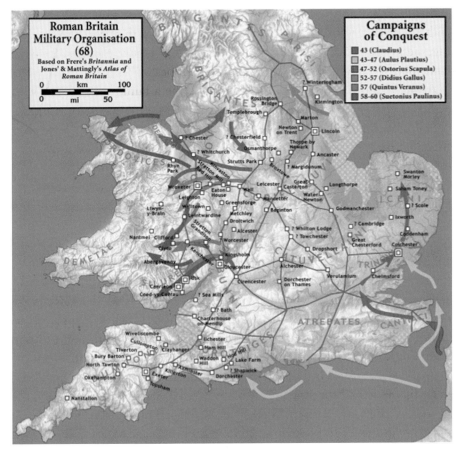

Figure 11: Map of Roman Britain c. 68. (*Wikimedia Commons*)

Figure 12: Map of
Agricola's campaigns 78–84.
(*Wikimedia Commons*)

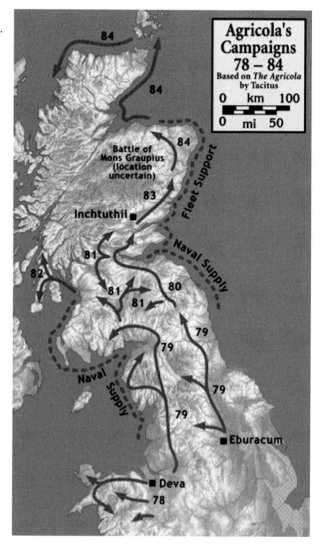

loyalty down to our own times, an example of the long established Roman
custom of employing even kings to make others slaves.'[40]

We shall conclude this chapter with three maps. The first shows the various
campaigns leading up to c. 68, just before the establishment of York, which we
will go into in detail in the next chapter. The second map shows the campaigns
of Agricola which culminated in the Battle of Mons Graupius described
previously. Thirdly, there is a map of northern Britain showing the military
forts and road network established by c. 84. Roman culture followed the
military machine. It is in this context, nearly eighty years after the Claudian
invasion, that the Sixth Legion arrives in Britain.

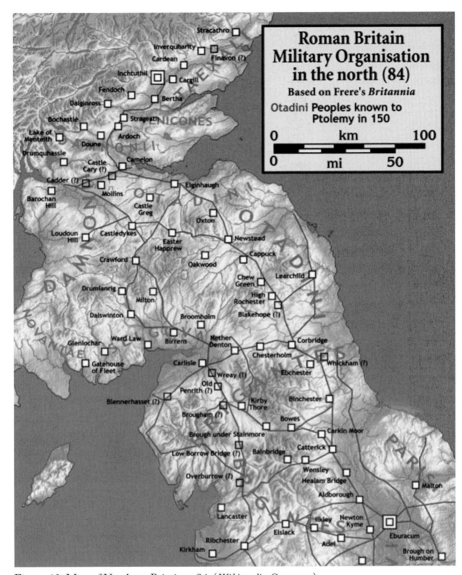

Figure 13: Map of Northern Britain c. 84. (*Wikimedia Commons*)

Chapter 2

The Coming of the Sixth Legion

Under Trajan, 98–117, the empire experienced both expansion and consolidation. In Britain we see an increase in urbanisation and, by the end of the first century, the establishment of several tribal *civitates*, each with its own town. Map 14 shows the expansion of Roman control as well as the towns and *coloniae*, settled by Roman veterans. In the north the Stanegate Road connected two Roman forts overlooking important river crossings. In the west Luguvalium at Carlisle on the river Eden and in the east Coria at Corbridge protected the Tyne. After Agricola's northern campaign the Romans withdrew further south and a line of forts was built along the Stanegate. It was built as a strategic road rather than a frontier and would have had forts at one-day-marching intervals along its length.[1] It was this line that eventually was roughly followed in the construction of Hadrian's Wall. Larger forts included Newbrough, Haltwhistle Burn, Magnis, Throp, Nether Denton, Castle Hill and Brampton Old Church. One of the most famous is perhaps Vindolanda. Before we discuss that it is necessary to look at the construction of camps and forts.

Camps and forts

The fourth-century writer Vegetius laid out the distances an army on the march could cover in a day. This usually began just after dawn and was completed in the afternoon, giving time for the construction of a camp. Using the 'military step', twenty miles took roughly five hours but at 'full step' they could cover twenty-four miles.[2] Vegetius complains that the necessity of building forts, along with the skills required, appeared to have been forgotten in his day.[3] He describes how camps should be built near a good supply of water, firewood and fodder, avoiding swampy areas and those overlooked by higher ground. Three types are listed:[4]

1. Where there's no immediate danger or for one night: A three-feet-deep fosse or ditch is cut five-feet wide with the turves stacked up on the inside edge.

Figures 14: Map of Roman Britain under Hadrian.

2. A 'stationary camp': A temporary fosse nine-feet wide and seven-feet deep.
3. When more serious forces threaten a twelve- to seventeen-feet wide and nine-feet-deep fosse is built. Then inside an embankment four-feet high overlooks the fosse making it thirteen-feett deep.

The legionaries carried stakes which they could place in a fixed line to protect the construction. If under threat, half the infantry and most of the cavalry would draw up in front to defend the rest of the men as they worked to complete the camp before evening. A well trained legion could build a fort in a few hours even under enemy pressure. Ramparts were reinforced with logs and battlements and turrets constructed to aid defence. At the siege of Alesia in 52 BC Julius Caesar took just three weeks to construct ten miles of fortifications to surround the hill fort occupied by Vercingetorix and 80,000 Gauls. With a relief force of 240,000 Gallic warriors on their way, this was followed by an outer ring fourteen miles long. Roman engineering skills were such that a legion could march up to twenty-four miles in five hours and then complete a camp by the evening.[5] Even a small marching camp would likely have some sort of palisade.

We get a more accurate picture of a camp in the first and second centuries from *De Munitionibus Castrorum*, 'Concerning the fortifications of a military camp', which was written a generation or two after the construction of Hadrian's Wall. It gives a detailed description of the typical camp layout of this period. This is supported by extensive archaeological evidence. The shape was generally a square or rectangular 'playing card'. Each side had a gate from which two main roads converged on the *principia*, at the centre of the camp. This contained the commander's headquarters and an open courtyard or forum with a raised platform to address the troops, and offices for day-to-day business. Within the headquarters was the *aedes*, or shrine, where the legion or unit's standards were kept. Under this was dug a strongroom for the fort's cash reserves' safe. Also here were armouries, *armamentaria*, and even rooms for officer recreation, *scholae*. Established camps would have had baths, granaries and even shops with local settlements growing up around them. However, a marching camp in enemy territory would have no such luxuries. Many early camps in the north of Britain would have been far more austere than their later and southern counterparts.

Whilst in Germany the Sixth would have been as competent in building such camps as the legions and auxiliaries in Britain. An outer ditch, the *fossae*, was dug about six-feet deep and five-feet wide. The soil was used to build a rampart, approximately six-feet high by eight-feet wide. This provided a fighting platform. On top a palisade was built, lined with six-foot hardened stakes carried by the legionaries and supplemented from local woods. Attackers were faced with a six-foot ditch, and a six-foot rampart topped with a six-foot wooden palisade.

The gates were forty-feet wide which allowed rapid deployment against an attacking force. As we shall see with Hadrian's Wall, the Romans preferred to engage in the open field and were not best suited to fighting from battlements. The gates were often protected by two towers. Inside the wall a road, the *via sagularis*, ran around the perimeter of the camp allowing access to the ramparts from any part of the camp. The size of camps differed due to the number and nature of units as well as terrain. A cavalry *ala* of 500 in the north of Britain would have to be larger than an infantry unit of a similar size to accommodate the horses. Both would have a different size and layout to the Sixth's eventual base at York. However, the consistency between surviving examples from Hadrian's Wall to others across the empire is striking. Aerial surveys have detected twenty 'labour' camps used in the construction of the Antonine Wall, built twenty year after its southern counterpart. We see similar dimensions from an anonymous Roman writer detailing slightly smaller dimensions compared to the later Vegetius:[6] A ditch, five-feet wide and three-feet deep surrounded a rampart nine-feet wide and six-feet in height. Most of the camps along the Antonine Wall are five acres in area.

Attached to the legions were a variety of specialists, *immunes*. Legionnaires with specific skills could also perform these vital functions; however, non-military personnel often accompanied the legions, adding considerably to the numbers. Larger and more established camps would have had a considerable number of these personnel. A list of some examples is instructive as to what a camp might have included:[7] surveyors, *mensores*; medical orderlies, *medici*; wound dressers, *capsarii*; veterinaries, *veterinarii*; master-builder, *architectus*; artillery makers/operators, *ballistrarii*; craftsmen, *fabri*; arrow makers, *sagittarii*; bow-makers, *acuarii*; blacksmiths, *ferrarii*; bronze-smiths, *aerarii*; lead-makers, *plumbarii*; carpenters, *carpentarii*; sword-makers, *gladiatores*; hydraulic engineers, *aquilices*; stonemasons, *lapidarii*; hunters, *venatores*; armourers, *custodes armorum*; and millers, *polliones*. Specialist builders, shipwrights, ships' pilots, bridge-builders and artillery specialists were also present, as were priests to officiate at ceremonies and staff to look after sacrificial animals. Repair shops and manufacturers needed officers, managers and a sizeable workforce of skilled labourers. Clerks of various kinds were also needed for the granaries, general book-keeping; and even one for the deceased.

We can see from the above how busy a large legionary camp or the headquarters at York might have been. In contrast, a cohort in enemy territory would have built a relatively small marching camp. An army consisting of one or more legions with a permanent camp would have had the equivalent of a small town accompanying them with bread ovens, granaries, stables, blacksmiths, doctors, infirmaries, kitchens and buildings for a whole variety of other activities. The forts along Hadrian's Wall ranged in size from two to nearly ten acres. The camp at Carnuntum on the Danube was home to four legions and covered about twenty-five acres. It became the provincial capital and grew into a city of 50,000 inhabitants. Figure 15 depicts an example of a typical camp layout for a legion-sized force.

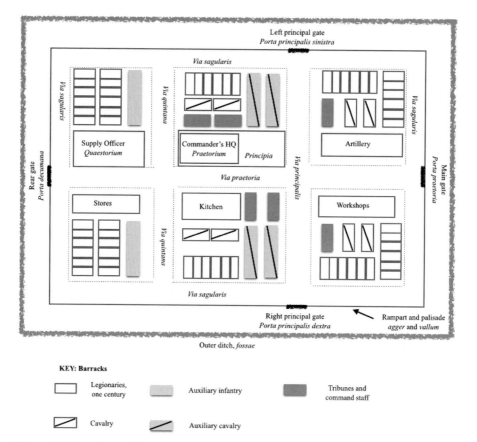

Figure 15: Map of typical Roman camp layout.

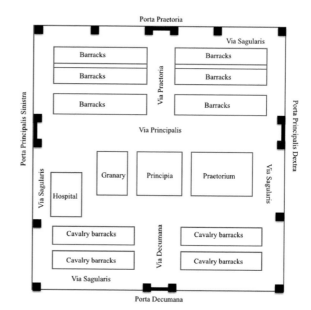

Figure 16: Plan of Wallsend Roman fort.

Figure 17: Model of Fort Housesteads on Hadrian's Wall. (*Wikimedia Commons*)

A good practical example is the fort at Wallsend, which can be seen in figure 16. Figure 17 shows a model of the fort at Housesteads on Hadrian's Wall.

Artillery

The outpost forts beyond Hadrian's Wall appear to have had some rebuilding work done after 216. At Bremenium, High Rochester, platforms for artillery were built or repaired after c. 226.[8] One type of artillery was known as an *onager*, or *scorpio* in the early empire, which consisted of a single throwing arm held under tension by twisted ropes. This could deliver a stone weighing 25 kilos 440 metres. Archaeological finds of artillery stones in the north of Britain weigh up to 50 kilos. The effects of these weapons were gruesome and armour provided little to no protection.[9] One example has a man's head being ripped off and thrown hundreds of yards away. Another has a pregnant woman being 'torn apart' and the unborn child tossed some distance away. Heavy artillery pieces such as these were difficult to manoeuvre and not easy to use on the battlefield. Vegetius describes how each legion had ten *onagri*, one for each cohort, transported on oxen-drawn wagons. This would slow down progress considerably. A legion could march twenty miles in a day but oxen drawing a heady carriage would be lucky to travel half that in the same time. Nor was it suited for battering down thick stone walls. It could break down wooden structures and thin stone walls. As an anti-personnel weapon in a fixed position it could create havoc and panic in an attacking force. It was very well suited as a defensive weapon and we see this at the fort at Bremenium where the stone platforms measuring 7.5 m by 10 m were attached behind its walls.

Ammianus describes one example as follows:[10] Between two posts a long iron bar is fixed which projects out 'like a great ruler'. To this is attached a squared staff 'hollowed out along its length with a narrow groove'. In this groove the gunner places a long wooden arrow tipped with 'a great iron point'. The arrow, 'driven by the power within, flies from the ballista … before the weapon is seen, the pain of a mortal wound makes itself felt.' He goes on to describe the scorpion or 'wild-ass'. A wooden arm, capable of holding a large stone, rises vertically (looking like a scorpion's sting) but can be pulled horizontally using iron hooks with tension supplied via the twisting of ropes. When released, the arm returns to the vertical with a violent kick (like an ass) and the wooden beam strikes a 'soft hair-cloth' cushion. Another name he gives is an 'onager'.

The Romans also used light artillery and these could more easily be utilised on the battlefield. The ballista could fire stones or bolts of up to a foot in length, with one example from Spain estimated to have had a range of 300 metres.[11] We can see examples of carro-ballistae on Trajan's column where the artillery is mounted on carts. Similar artillery pieces would have been utilised by the Sixth and been present at many of the forts and camps across the northern frontier.

Vindolanda

Vindolanda lay on the Stanegate Road a short distance to the south of where the later Hadrian's Wall was built. Approximately thirteen miles from Corbridge to the east and twenty-three miles from Carlisle in the west and about halfway between the North Sea and the Solway Firth. It can be found near the modern village of Bardon Mill in Northumberland. Located on an escarpment, the ground rises towards Hadrian's Wall a mile farther north. No trace of a British settlement has been discovered but the fort's name is Brythonic: vindo means 'white' or 'shining' and evolved into the Welsh gwyn or Irish finn.

The first fort was built c. 85 by the First Cohort of Tungrians, an infantry unit of 500. Later the Ninth Cohort of Batavians, a mixed unit of 1,000, rebuilt the fort around the year 95. The Tungrians returned, replacing the Batavians, and a larger wooden fort was built. This unit moved north when the Antonine Wall was built. Later a stone fort replaced the wooden one and an infantry unit of 500, Cohors II Nerviorum Civium Romanorum, is recorded as being present. In the third and fourth centuries the Cohors IV Gallorum Equitata, a mixed unit of 500, occupied a new stone fort built after the Scottish campaigns of Septimius Severus, 208–11.

Both of the first occupants, the Batavians and Tungrians, fought at the battle of Mons Graupius in 83. Six cohorts of auxiliaries, four of Batavians and two Tungrian, overwhelmed the Britons' front line. A Tungrian unit had joined the Batavian revolt of 69–70 and it was this revolt that the Sixth took part in crushing. Subsequently the first and second Tungrian infantry cohorts were stationed in Britain and remained for several hundred years. A cavalry *ala* joined them in 98.

The Batavians had fought for Julius Caesar in his civil wars. They often contributed to the subsequent emperors' mounted bodyguards, *Germani corpora custodes*. Augustus raised an *ala Batavorum*. The Batavian auxiliaries had played a major part in the Battle of the River Medway in Kent during the invasion of 43:[12] The Britons, feeling safe on the west bank, 'bivouacked in rather careless fashion on the opposite bank'. However, the Romans sent a unit of Germans 'who were accustomed to swim easily in full armour across the most turbulent streams … instead of shooting at any of the men they confined themselves to wounding the horses that drew their chariots'. Some of the Batavian elite remained loyal to Rome during the revolt of 69–70, including two cavalry commanders, Claudius Labeo and a Briganticus. The revolt was suppressed by Vespasian's son-in-law, Petillius Cerialis. Interestingly the Batavian commander at Vindolanda was named Flavius Cerialis and he may well be the son of one of the loyal Batavians, named after their benefactor.[13] It is this Cerialis who features in many of the written tablets found at the fort. The Batavians left in 105 to take part in Trajan's second Dacian War and never returned. The Tungrians, however, did.

Both the Tungrians and Batavians retained the name 'prefect' for their commander. This *praefectus* lived in the *praetorium* in the centre of the fort with his wife and family, slaves and freedmen. His salary was fifty times more than the ordinary soldier. Discharge after twenty-five years was introduced intermittently in the Flavian period and became regular after Trajan.[14] It is thought that the Tungrians were replaced in the mid-second century, c. 150–200, by a cohort of Nervians.[15] The final residents were the Fourth Cohort of Gauls, who remained until towards the end of Roman Britain.

Date	Unit	Comments
Period I c. 85–92	Cohors I Tungrorum	Established after Agricola's withdrawal from Scotland. Size approximately 3.5 acres. western ditch, 4.5m wide and up to 1.5m deep.
Period II c. 92–97	Cohors IX Batavorum equitata	Fort rebuilt and doubled in size to 7 acres.
Period III c. 97–105	Cohors IX Batavorum equitata	Fort renovated. Most writing tablets were excavated in this period, including Prefect Cerialis. Possibly also housed the 3rd Cohort of Batavians.
Period IV c. 105–120	Cohors I Tungrorum	Previous building demolished and site possibly temporarily abandoned. Reference to legionary soldiers in tablet might reflect temporary posting prior to building of Hadrian's Wall.
Period V c. 120–?	Cohors I Tungrorum Cohors II Nerviorum?	Site levelled and partly rebuilt. Possibly in time to house Hadrian in 122. The first cohort of Tungrians may have continued to provide the garrison since a discharge certificate, issued to a member of the unit in 146, has been found at Vindolanda. Possibly also 2nd Cohort of Nervians
Stone fort from c. 130–160	Cohors II Nerviorum? Cohors IV Gallorum Equitata	Fort remained occupied into early fifth century.
Early third century	Cohors IV Gallorum Equitata	Circular stone huts erected in neat rows. It is thought connected to Severus campaign in 208–11. These buildings levelled and a new stone fort built c. 213.

Table 4: The forts at Vindolanda.

Figure 18 shows the various stages of building over the centuries whilst figure 19 shows the final stone fort in the third century.

The Vindolanda Tablets

Many of the finds at Vindolanda are found up to four metres below the modern surface. Perhaps the most famous are the so-called 'Vindolanda tablets'. These tablets, thin pieces of wood (0.5 to 3mm), most about the size of a postcard (10 by 15cm), contained a range of fascinating insights into life in the Roman army of the first century. The 117 items, dated to c. 85–130, contain a number

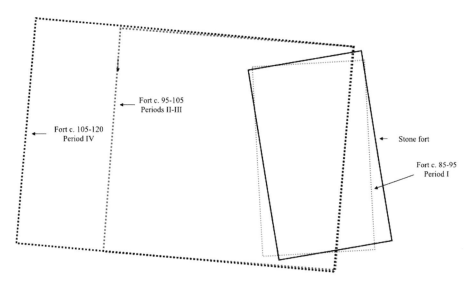

Figure 18: Vindolanda Fort plans from c. 85.

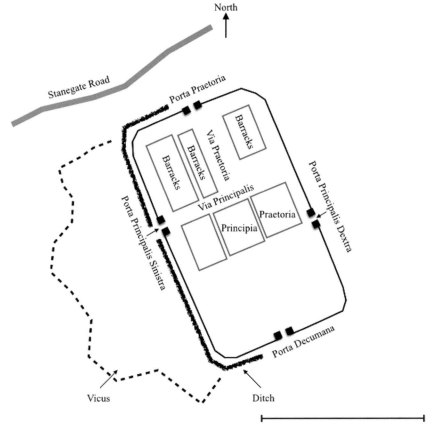

Figure 19: Vindolanda Fort in the third century.

of letters, documents, *descripta* tablets, and what are described as 'texts of uncertain nature'. Some are illegible or indecipherable.

Two tablets refer to the indigenous people, *Brittones*. One implies an economic relationship involving wagons and the supply of corn. The other is disparaging, using the word *Brittunculi*, 'wretched little Britons'. The use of the word 'unprotected is assumed to mean by armour rather than naked and so we read: 'the Britons are unprotected by armour. There are very many cavalry. The cavalry do not use swords nor do the wretched Britons mount in order to throw javelins' (tablet number 164).

Tacitus writes that the Britons 'submit readily to conscription' and also implies Britons were fighting in Agricola's army at Mons Graupius.[16] Units of Britons, *numeri Brittonum*, are attested to on the German frontier by 140 and are thought to have arrived as early as 100.[17] This implication is that it is probable that Britons were as likely to join auxiliary units as other tribal people across the empire. However, only citizens could join the Sixth Legion.

The tablets mention the two important bases at each end of the Stanegate, Corbridge and Carlisle. York and many of the forts to the south are referenced: Binchester, Catterick, Aldborough and Ribchester. London also features, and possibly Lincoln. To the north of the Wall High Rochester is mentioned but not Newstead, abandoned by 105.

We have seen the paper strength of various auxiliary units. One of the tablets gives us an insight into the reality. The strength report of the First Tungrians (tablet 154) lays out those available and absent citing various reasons:

Dated 18 May: 'net number of the First Cohort of Tungrians, of which the commander is Iulius Verecundus the prefect, 752, including centurions 6'. Recorded absent are: 'guards of the governor 46', presumably in London; 'at the office of Ferox at Coria (Corbridge) 337'; 'including centurions 2'; one centurion in London; a further 26 indecipherable; with a total number of 456 including 5 centurions. Present at Vindolanda are 296, including one centurion, 15 soldiers who are sick, 6 wounded and 10 'suffering from inflammation of the eyes'. Leaving one centurion and 264 men fit for active service at the fort.

A report of the ninth Batavians records 'All at their places who ought to be and their equipment intact'.[18] Similar reports are filled in today by military commanders all over the world. In the London Fire Brigade, before I retired, the duty person filled in the log book at the start of every shift. Certain pieces of equipment were counted and recorded as 'all present and correct'. Pole house doors, mats and lights were similarly recorded. Personnel were listed as riding the pump (one particular fire engine) or pump ladder with those on leave or sick recorded underneath. Interesting that this reads almost exactly the same as my duties as duty-person filling in the daily log book 2,000 years later.

Leave requests to Cerialis, Commander of the Ninth Batavians (tablet 169), are also as formulaic as similar requests I recall making in the Fire Brigade.

> Gannallius of the century of ... I ask, my lord Cerialis ...
> Tablet 172: 'I, Aventinus, of the century of ..., ask, my lord Flavianus ... a worthy person ...'
> Tablet 175: 'I, Messicus ..., ask, my lord, that you consider me a worthy person to whom to grant leave at Coria.' (Coria being Corbridge.)

Tablet 248 records a note to Flavius Cerialis, prefect of the cohort, presumably from persons who are close enough, perhaps in rank, to call the commander 'brother':

> Niger and Brocchus to their Cerialis, greeting. We pray, brother, that what you are about to do will be most successful. It will be so, indeed, since it is both in accord with our wishes to make this prayer on your behalf and you yourself are most worthy. You will assuredly meet our governor quite soon .... We pray, our lord and brother, that you are in good health.

Various tablets refer to travelling expenses. Tablet 185 refers to various items purchased: wine, barley, wheat, wagon-axles, a carriage, vests, salt and fodder. Locations included Isurium, Isurium, Cataractonium and Vinovia, all locations on the road from York to Corbridge. The grand total came to 94 *denarii*. Of the 200 persons named, around half, are Batavian or Tungrian and most have Celtic or Latin names.[19] Tablet 194 lists domestic items: 'shallow dishes, 2 (?) side-plates, 5 (?) vinegar-bowls, 3 (?) egg-cups, 3 on the purlin (?) a platter a shallow dish. (B) 'a strong-box (?) and a bronze lamp bread-baskets, 4 (?) cups, 2 (?) in a box bowls, 2 (?) in a box ...'.

Tablet 291 gives us one of the few insights into the wives of soldiers and commanders:

> Claudia Severa to her Lepidina greetings. On 11 September, sister, for the day of the celebration of my birthday, I give you a warm invitation to make sure that you come to us, to make the day more enjoyable for me by your arrival, if you are present (?). Give my greetings to your Cerialis. My Aelius and my little son send him (?) their greetings. (2nd hand) I shall expect you, sister. Farewell, sister, my dearest soul, as I hope to prosper,

and hail. (Back, 1st hand) To Sulpicia Lepidina, wife of Cerialis, from Severa.

This must be the same Cerialis who commanded the Batavians c. 92–105.

Another fascinating tablet hints at a story of corruption and violence. The presence of writing on the back suggests this was a draft and, given where it was found, not sent.

> he beat (?) me all the more ... goods ... or pour them down the drain (?). As befits an honest man (?) I implore your majesty not to allow me, an innocent man, to have been beaten with rods and, my lord, inasmuch as (?) I was unable to complain to the prefect because he was detained by ill-health I have complained in vain (?) to the *beneficiarius* and the rest (?) of the centurions of his (?) unit. Accordingly (?) I implore your mercifulness not to allow me, a man from overseas and an innocent one, about whose good faith you may inquire, to have been bloodied by rods as if I had committed some crime.

The writer, apparently a civilian trader, addresses the letter *maiestatem*, which translates as 'majesty'. It would appear soldiers poured his goods away and gave him a beating. The intriguing possibility is that the letter is to Hadrian himself when he was present in Britain which would date the letter to 122. Whatever the case, it shows the attitude of the complainant. He feels his treatment was unjust as he was an innocent man and 'from overseas'. Does this imply a Briton could be beaten with impunity? There is clearly an expectation that his complaint would be considered although he states he received no 'satisfaction from the *beneficiarius* or the centurions'. Was it eventually received and discarded by the commander at Vindolanda? We are left to wonder what became of our complainant. Perhaps he received redress and the soldiers were punished. Or perhaps the discarded letter found nearly 2,000 years later is evidence of a complaint dismissed and the trader was lucky if he received just the one beating.

Inscriptions at Vindolanda show continued occupation into the fourth century: 'To Jupiter, Best and Greatest, the Fourth Cohort of Gauls, under their prefect Sulpicius Pudens, set up this altar and willingly and deservedly fulfilled its vow' (RIB 1688). The early-fifth-century Notitia Dignitatum records the commander at Vindolanda as serving *per linear valli*, 'along the line of the Wall'. We will cover this document in more depth in the final chapter but it does indicate that Vindolanda was occupied right up to the end of Roman authority in Britain. A chapel was built within the commander's *praetorium* c.

400 and there is archaeological evidence of continued occupation.[20] Around c. 500 a high-ranking Briton, Brigomaglos, apparently a Christian, was buried there. In the sixth century a house was built over the south ditch, now filled in, where we have evidence of a stone slab with a form of the Christian *chi-rho* symbol.

Back in the first quarter of the second century the Tungrians looked north from Vindolanda, one of many forts stretched across the Stangate. The Ninth Legion was stationed at York while the Sixth was still in Germania Inferior. All this was about to change with the arrival of the emperor.

Emperor Hadrian

Publius Aelius Hadrianus was born c. 76. The family came from Picenum in northern Italy. His grandfather had married Trajan's aunt, Ulpia, which gave him important connections to the imperial family. His father died before his tenth birthday and he was entrusted to two guardians, Publius Aelius Attianus and Trajan, the future emperor. On reaching manhood he served as military tribune in various legions on the Danube and Rhine. When Trajan became emperor in 98, Hadrian accompanied him to Rome and in 100 married the emperor's niece, Matilda Augusta. Trajan was one of the more militarily aggressive emperors and extended the borders of the empire significantly. Hadrian served as a legionary commander during the Dacian Wars and as governor of Syria in the Parthian War of 114. He had received the consulship in 108 and was due a second term in 117 when Trajan died.

The day after Trajan's death it was announced the emperor had formally adopted Hadrian. Supported by the endorsement of the emperor's widow, Pompeia Plotina, but, more importantly, the army, the senate had few options but to accept. The new emperor addressed the senators, promising never to put any to death, a vow he was to break within a year after a plot was uncovered, although he claimed he was unaware of the orders.[21] One reason for the plot may have been disquiet over his abandonment of Trajan's expansionist policies. He pulled back from Parthia and left a client king in Armenia. But he retained Dacia and turned his attention to the northern borders. He became the 'greatest of all imperial travellers' by personally visiting the provinces and borders.[22] He was the first emperor to see the empire from anything other than a Roman standpoint. The new policy of avoiding external military action meant a strengthening of the border defences. It also meant legionary soldiers started to perform a number of other 'non-operational' tasks, one of which was large building and engineering projects.

Hadrian also took a keen interest in army discipline and even included it on his coinage, *Disciplina Augusti*.[23] He created a distinction between mobile and static troops which was similar to the later empire. We can see this later in Britain with auxiliary troops generally manning Hadrian's Wall and the Sixth being based at York, over seventy miles to the south. The only serious war in his reign was the Jewish War of 132–6. Reprisals were severe: nearly 1,000 villages were razed to the ground and Cassius Dio numbered those killed to over half-a-million Jews killed in battle alone. Aside from the severe reprisals to that insurrection, Hadrian is not considered overly heavy-handed by historians.[24]

Figure 20: Bust of Hadrian. (*Wikimedia Commons*)

He is recorded as being tall and well built, bearded and austere looking. He was also active and energetic, skilled with weapons and hunting. One favourite party tricks was killing a lion with a javelin.[25] He put on lavish gladiatorial and hunting displays and was especially keen on lions, once killing a hundred in one show. He also took a keen interest in Roman law and made important changes to governmental positions. Instead of freedmen, some positions now required an equestrian, which ultimately expanded and opened up career paths for those of this order.

However, the general view of his personality was negative. He could be unpredictable, envious, fickle and cruel. He reneged on his initial promise to the senate and killed off all his likely successors and once stabbed a slave in the eye with a stylus for a minor offence.[26] Soldiers and freedmen were executed for petty insults and he could be vengeful and vindictive. In contrast his policies prioritised peaceful, stable and controlled borders protected by a well-trained and disciplined army.[27]

There is some evidence of military problems in northern Britain at the start of his reign:[28] Hadrian's biographer records 'the Britons could not be kept under Roman control'; coins showing BRITANNIA issued in 119 suggest a successful campaign; and Fronto, writing in 162, refers to a large number of soldiers being killed under Hadrian. This had led some to speculate the Ninth Legion was destroyed by these troubles. An inscription from Italy from the reign of Hadrian shows that 3,000 men were sent from three different legions to Britain, suggesting that a significant number of men may have required replacing.[29]

Coins issued c. 122–3 allude to *expeditio Augusti*, when Hadrian was in Britain, which points to a possible subsequent campaign whilst the emperor was present.[30] All this suggests that, just after Trajan's death, significant unrest occurred in Britain which may initially have been put down around the year 119. This prompted Hadrian's visit in 122, after which there was possibly another successful campaign which was commemorated on coins. The importance of these events for our tale cannot be exaggerated. It was this which prompted the transfer of the Sixth Legion to northern Britain, the arrival of Hadrian and the wall which still bears his name today.

Arrival of the Sixth

In 121 the emperor Hadrian was in Germania Inferior, where he was overseeing the construction of the Lower Rhine limes. The local governor, Platorius Nepos, was a personal friend of the emperor. After the Batavian Revolt of 69–70 a new legionary base was built and in the first quarter of the second century it was occupied by the Sixth. It is likely that they were used for this engineering task and perhaps this experience convinced Hadrian to transfer Platorius and the Sixth to Britain in 122.

We read in the *Historia Augusta*: 'Then having reformed the soldiers in royal fashion [in Germany], he set out for Britain, where he corrected many things and, as the first to do so, built a wall for eighty miles, which was to separate the barbarians from the Romans'.[31] It is likely both the new governor and VI Victrix accompanied Hadrian when he crossed to Britain in the early summer of 122.[32]

Platorius was made governor of Britannia for at least two years and replaced certainly before 127. The sources tell us that, on arrival, Hadrian dismissed the guard prefect, Septimius Clarus, and the chief secretary, Suetonius Tranquillus, and 'many others', allegedly for disrespecting the emperor's wife.[33] Another anecdote tells us that Hadrian spied on many, even his friends. Coins refer to Hadrian's *adventus* and *exercitus Britannicus*, so it appears that some sort of campaign took place when he was present.[34] This can be dated to shortly after the arrival of Platorius, the new governor, with the Sixth.

The legionary commander of the Sixth in 122 in Lower Germany was a certain Marcus Valerius Propinquus Grattius. He may have travelled with it to Britain before handing command to Tullius Varro as he is attested as governor of Aquitania by 123.[35] Varro had also commanded XII Fulminata in Cappadocia and it was rare to command two legions. By 127 he had been proconsul of Baetica and Treasury Prefect and consul. So we can date him quite tightly to the first years of the Sixth's presence in Britain.

It would seem that they headed north and one is left to wonder if they landed at Richborough, the usual entry point into Britain, and marched the nearly 300 miles to York. Alternatively, they may have travelled by sea and landed at Petuaria on the Humber. Whatever the case, two altars found in the Tyne riverbed at Newcastle are thought to mark the site of a bridge. Dedicated to Neptune and the Ocean, both record the 'Legion VI Victrix Dutiful and Loyal'. as having 'set them up'.[36]

A dedication to Sabinus, an equestrian praefectus, suggests he led a number of units on a British expedition and this appears to be dated to c. 122.[37] If so, this supports the proposal that Hadrian's visit may have been in response to some unrest in the north. We also have a senatorial military tribune with a similar name dated exactly to the crossing from Germany to Britain, Marcus Pontius Laelianus Larcius Sabinus.[38] Forty years later, Fronto praised the 'old-fashioned discipline' of Laelianus which he may well have learnt from his experience under Hadrian. An altar found at Chesters was dedicated to 'the Discipline of the Emperor Hadrian'.[39] Laelianus was a *tribunus laticalvius* and as such would have been young at the time, perhaps 20, and of senatorial rank.

As second in command, Laelianus would have come to the attention of Hadrian. He later was to lead two armies under Antoninus, the first in Upper Pannonia and the second in Syria, between 138 and 161.[40] Marcus Aurelius appointed him as a senior advisor to Lucius Verus in the Parthian War of 161–6. He was reported to have been a strict disciplinarian when he took back control of his old Syrian forces. He was highly decorated and ended his career, aged approximately 70, fighting on the Danube in the 170s. Other examples of military tribunes from the early Hadrianic period include Quintus Licinius Silvanus Granianus Quadronius Proculus, and a partial inscription naming a Crassius.

It would seem then that Hadrian's visit was a direct response to unrest and his despatch of the Sixth to northern Britain places this unrest in the north. This has led some to speculate a serious incursion or uprising led to the Ninth Legion being destroyed. However, Birley lists the careers of a number of its officers after this time along with the following evidence.[41] Its last datable record is an inscription from York c. 108. At some point it was present at Nijmegen in Lower Germany and we have references to *vexillatio Britannica*. There is evidence from tile stamps that it was present at Carlisle, so it's also possible it was sent further north after the arrival of the Sixth at York. It may have remained in Britain for a further ten years or more and, possibly, was sent to the Jewish War of c. 134–6, or Cappodocia c. 137. An unnamed legion was destroyed at Elegia in the beginning of the Parthian War of 161–6. In summary, it would appear the Ninth remained in Britain for a few years before being removed to Germany. This left the Sixth based at York, the Second Augusta at Caerleon and the Twentieth at Chester.

Hadrian's Wall

In the first decades of Roman Britain the legions were positioned strategically to provide a swift mobile military response. Legionary bases at York, Chester and Caerleon were rebuilt in stone, most likely under Trajan,[42] and colonies for veterans created at Gloucester and Lincoln. The withdrawal from north of the Forth-Clyde isthmus came shortly after c. 86, with coin deposits suggesting it was complete by c. 88.[43] By the beginning of the second century they had retreated further to the Tyne-Solway isthmus. Tacitus was prompted to state 'Britain was totally conquered, and then immediately let go'.[44] We are left to speculate what the history of these islands may have been if Agricola had maintained his presence in the far north and extended it west to Ireland.

The decision to pull back was to prove fateful in later centuries. The Stanegate Road had been built by Agricola and connected Corbridge in the east and Carlisle in the west. The initial line of forts was likely set back from the Roman zone of influence. The information from the Vindolanda tablets found at one of those forts does not suggest serious military problems on the frontier in the years after Agricola's withdrawal.[45]

However, something clearly prompted Hadrian to visit and embark on the mammoth construction. The reason given was clear to one source: 'Hadrian was the first to build a wall, eighty miles long, to separate the Romans from the barbarians'.[46] The building work on the *Vallum Aelium* began soon after 122. The defensive structure consisted of three elements: a ditch running in front of the wall, the wall itself and, to the rear, another ditch, the Vallum. The dimensions were as follows:

1. The ditch was approximately 9–10 feet in depth and ranged from a usual 26 up to 40 feet in width. It was set roughly 20 feet in front of the wall.
2. The wall itself was approximately 14 feet in height and the width varied between 8 and 10 feet. The eastern two-thirds was constructed in stone whilst the remainder was constructed in turf, likely of the same

height. At intervals of about a mile fortified gateways, 'milecastles', were built, with double gates at front and rear. They were manned by eight to thirty-two men.

3. The Vallum was a flat-bottomed ditch, 20 feet wide and 10 feet deep. About 30 feet from the lip of both sides were two mounds, both 20 feet wide, thus creating a barrier 120 feet in total width. The Vallum was built after the forts and reduced access to the wall by half from nearly 30 to 14. Later in the second century it was partially filled in, suggesting its initial function was redundant and speed of access for the military was more important than potential defence.

The Stanegate ran to the south of the Vallum and eventually a new road was placed between the Vallum and the Wall. We can see a cross section of this arrangement in figure 21. The Vallum ran close to the Wall in some places but in others was as much as 700 metres away. One can imagine the difficulties attacking warriors might encounter in trying to navigate the front ditch before attempting to gain access over or through the Wall.

Three outpost forts were built north of the wall at Bewcastle, Netherby and Birrens. In the east, South Shields protected the south bank of the Tyne. In the west, Beckfoot, Maryport and Moresby and other smaller fortlets protected south of the Solway and the Cumbrian coast. Forts such as Corbridge and Vindolanda were a short distance to the south of the Wall.

Forts were added to the wall and ranged from approximately 3.35–9.32 acres in size. The smallest could hold an auxiliary unit numbering 500 men (with the exception of Drumburgh at 2 acres).[47] These forts were positioned astride the wall and built in stone with the earlier ones having their northern, eastern and western gates opening on the north side of the wall. This allowed rapid access of forces supporting the idea that the military preferred to engage in the open field rather than use the wall as a fighting platform. The lack of apparent

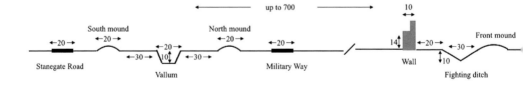

Key

20   All distances approximations in Roman feet.

Figure 21: A cross section of Hadrian's Wall, ditch and Vallum.

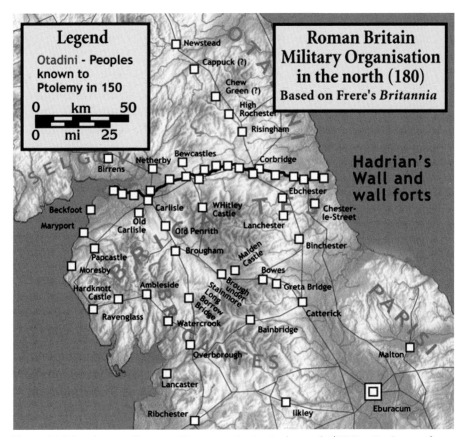

Figure 22: Map showing Roman military organisation in the north. (*Wikimedia Commons*)

access from the forts to the top of the wall supports this concept. The final forts were attached to the rear of the wall. The forts were positioned between six and just over nine miles apart, with the average distance about seven: Wallsend; Benwell; Rudchester; Halton Chesters; Chesters; Housesteads; Great Chesters; Birdoswald; Castlesteads; Stanwix; Bough-by-Sands; and Bowness-on-Solway.

A chain of towers and mileforts were placed twenty-six miles down the Cumbrian coast and there exists evidence of ditches and fences which likely controlled travel in a similar way to the wall. There is evidence for a fort at South Shields and smaller fortlets on the south bank of the Tyne, but none as yet for the eastern coast. Dedications to the goddess Brigantia at the latter fort suggest the tribal frontier extended beyond the wall. The construction took about six years to complete.

The question arises what was the purpose of the Wall? It was a huge expense of time, manpower and money. We get some hints from other parts

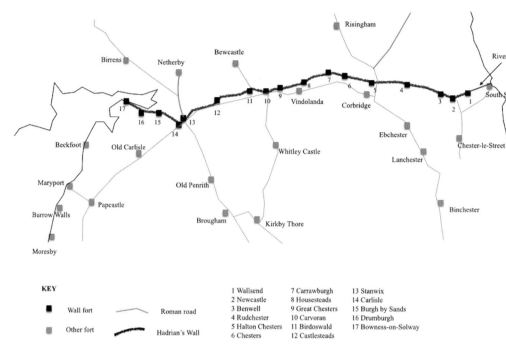

Figure 23: Hadrian's Wall forts.

of the empire. The regulations for the Rhine frontier laid down certain rules. One could only cross the barrier unarmed, under guard and on payment of a fee.[48] This has led Breeze and Dobson in *Hadrian's Wall*, to suggest the purpose of the wall was not to prevent movement but to control and tax it. Another important debate is whether the wall itself could be used as a fighting platform. With a parapet of about two-feet wide, this left only four to eight feet of space for perhaps two men at most, no room for artillery and no provision for protecting towers. Additionally, the Roman army was trained to fight in the open and, it is suggested, would move out from the wall to do so.[49]

It is thought that there were three cavalry units (at Chesters, Stanwix and Benwell), three infantry units (Housesteads, Great Chesters and Birdoswald) and the other mixed units, *cohortes equitatae*.[50] The fort at Stanwix held the largest cavalry unit in Britain, *ala milliaria*, and protected the main route north of the western part of the wall. The commanding officer there was the most senior on the wall but we cannot assume that he had command over the other units. For simplicity I have rounded the units up to 500 or 1,000 troops.

Fort	Size in acres	Estimated unit type and size under Hadrian
Wallsend	4	Mixed 500
Benwell	5	Cavalry 500
Rudchester	4.5	Mixed 500
Halton Chesters	4.3	Mixed 500
Chesters	5.75	Cavalry 500
Carrawburgh	3.9	Mixed 500
Housesteads	5	Infantry 1,000
Great Chesters	3.36	Infantry 500
Carvoran	3.6	Infantry 500
Birdoswald	5.33	Infantry 1,000
Castlesteads	3.75	Infantry 500
Stanwix	9.32	Cavalry 1,000
Burgh-by-Sands	4.9	Mixed 500
Drumburgh	2	Infantry 500
Bowness-on-Solway	7	Mixed 500
Beckfoot	2.55	Infantry 500
Maryport	5.8	Mixed 500
Moresby	3.6	Mixed 500

Table 5: Auxiliary units and forts under Hadrian[51]

These forts above are estimated to have been manned by 8,000 to 9,000 troops. Table 8 gives a snapshot of long term postings from the time of Hadrian to the end of the fourth century. It doesn't take into account temporary posting or detachments but it does give an idea of the main units and their primary postings. There are significant gaps in our knowledge as can be seen below. However interestingly there is a degree of consistency with some units remaining in certain bases across two centuries.

There is epigraphical evidence of the Sixth's building activity at various forts and part of the Wall. Two examples of stones at High House milecastle on the wall state the 'The Sixth Legion, Dutiful and Loyal, built [this]'.[52] Another stone at Halton Chesters states the Sixth were responsible for its construction and is dated to 'when Aulus Platorius Nepos was pro-praetorian legate' (122–4).[53] A stone at Castlehill declares that the Sixth were responsible to a very precise 3,666 ½ paces of the wall.[54] At quarries by the River Gelt near Brampton two masons, both soldiers of the Sixth, left their names, Eustus and Amnio, carved into the rock.[55]

We also have the names of various commanders of the Sixth for this period. Lucius Minicius Natalis Quadronis Verus, can be dated to c. 130. A native of

Fort	Hadrian	later 2nd century	3rd century	Notitia Dignitatum
Hadrian's Wall forts				
Wallsend	Cohors Quingenaria Equitata	Cohors II Nerviorum Civium Romanorum	Cohors IV Lingonum Equitata	Cohors IV Lingonum
Newcastle	-	-	Cohors I Ulpia Traiana Cugernorum Civium Romanorum	Cohors Prima Cornoviorum
Benwell	Ala Quingenaria	Cohors I Vangionum Milliaria Equitata	Ala I Asturum	Ala I Asturum
Rudchester	Cohors Quingenaria Equitata	-	Unknown (run down c. 270–370)	Cohors Prima Frisiavonum
Halton Chesters	Cohors Quingenaria Equitata	-	Ala Sabiniana	Ala Sabiniana
Chesters	Ala Augusta Ob Virtutem Appellata	Ala II Asturum	Ala II Asturum	Ala II Asturum
Carrawburgh	Cohors Quingenaria Equitata	-	Cohors I Batavorum Equitata	Cohors I Batavorum Equitata
Housesteads	Cohors Milliaria Peditata	-	Cohors I Tungrorum (Numerus Hnaudifridi & Cuneus Frisiorum)	Cohors I Tungrorum
Vindolanda	Cohors I Tungrorum	Cohors II Nerviorum Civium Romanorum	Cohors IV Gallorum Equitata	Cohors IV Gallorum Equitata
Great Chesters	Cohors VI Nerviorum	Cohors Raetorum	Cohors II Asturum	Cohors II Asturum
Carvoran	Cohors I Hamiorum	Cohors I Hamiorum	Cohors II Delmatarum Equitata	Cohors II Delmatarum Equitata

Fort	Hadrian	later 2nd century	3rd century	Notitia Dignitatum
Birdoswald	-	-	Cohors I Aelia Dacorum Milliaria	Cohors I Aelia Dacorum Milliaria
Castlesteads	Cohors IV Gallorum Equitata	-	Cohors II Tungrorum Equitata	-
Stanwix	Ala Petriana Milliaria	-	Ala Petriana Milliaria	Ala Petriana Milliaria
Burgh-by-Sands	Cohors Quingenaria Equitata	-	Cohors I Nervana Germanorum Milliaria Equitata, Numerus Maurorum Aurelianorum, Cuneus Frisionum Aballavensium	Numerus Maurorum Aurelianorum
Drumburgh	-	-	-	-
Bowness-on-Solway	Cohors Milliaria Equitata	-	Cohors Milliaria Equitata	-
Other forts				
Beckfoot	Cohors Quingenaria Peditata	Cohors II Pannoniorum	-	-
Maryport	Cohors I Hispanorum Milliaria Equitata	Cohors I Delmatarum Equitata, Cohors I Baetasiorum Civium Romanorum	Cohors Milliaria	-
Moresby	Cohors II Lingonum Equitata	-	-	cohors II Thracum equitata
Ravenglass	-	Cohors I Aelia Classica	-	-
South Shields	-	-	Cohors V Gallorum	Numerus Barcariorum Tigrisiensium

Fort	Hadrian	later 2nd century	3rd century	Notitia Dignitatum
Bewcastle	Cohors Dacorum Milliaria peditata	-	Cohors Milliaria	-
Netherby	-	-	Cohors I Aelia Hispanorum Equitata	
Birrens	-	Cohors II Tungrorum Milliaria Equitata	-	-
Risingham	-	Cohors IV Gallorum Equitata	Cohors I Vangionum Milliaria Equitata, Exilatio Raetorum Gaesatorum, Exploratores Habitancenses	-
High Rochester	-	Cohors I Lingonum Equitata	Cohors I Fida Vardullorum Civium Romanorum Milliaria Equitata, Explatores Bremensienses	-

Table 6: Auxiliary units from second to fourth century.

Barcino (Barcelona) in Tarraconensis, he served as tribune in three successive legions before becoming a legate to the pro-consul of Africa. He won the four-horse chariot race at the Olympic Games in 129.[56] Two late Hadrianic legates are Quintus Antonius Isauricus (c. 143) and Publius Mummius Sisenna Rutilianus (c. 146).[57] By this time the Sixth had been in Britain for a generation and no doubt some had already retired and settled in the growing new *vicus* appearing around the relatively new fort at Eboracum.

York

The origins of Eboracum, or York as we know it today, began with the arrival of the Ninth Legion c. 71. Around the year 120 the Sixth replaced the Ninth, with the latter possibly moving farther north to Carlisle. During the second century a major urban settlement developed around it and by the early third century it had become a provincial capital. The dual role of major military and civilian centre of authority was unique in Roman Britain. Two emperors died there, first Septimius Severus in 211 and then Constantius I in 306. It was there, at the headquarters of the Sixth, that Constantine the Great was proclaimed emperor by the troops after his father's death. The earliest written reference to York was around 100 from one of the famous Vindolanda tablets. It appears in both the Antonine Itinerary and the Ravenna Cosmography and in the works of Ptolemy, the second-century Greek geographer. By this time the Roman garrison had occupied the fort for over a generation.

Back in the year 69 Roman rule had extended north to a line roughly between the Rivers Humber and Mersey. Between this line and the Scottish

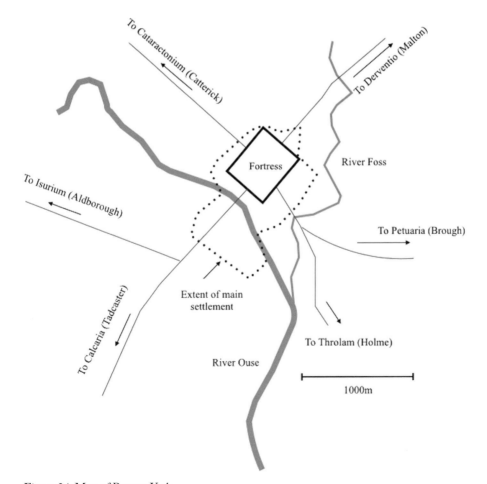

Figure 24: Map of Roman York.

lowlands were people known as the Brigantes. It is debatable if this was one tribal group or a confederation of tribes. The Brigantes were spread across small villages and farms with the exception of Stanwick which covered about 741 acres and was protected by a bank and ditch. Archaeological evidence suggests this was a major centre of Brigantian power with significant trade links to the Roman world. The events that brought, or allowed, the Romans into the region are an interesting snapshot of the local politics of the first century. Tacitus tells us of the civil and martial strife at the very heart of the Brigantian aristocracy. Queen Cartimandua favoured good relations with the Romans and had been responsible for handing over the British rebel leader, Caratacus some years before in 51. Her estranged husband, Venutius, however led an anti-Roman faction, a situation made worse when the queen took her former husband's armour-bearer as lover. Venutius seems to have got the upper

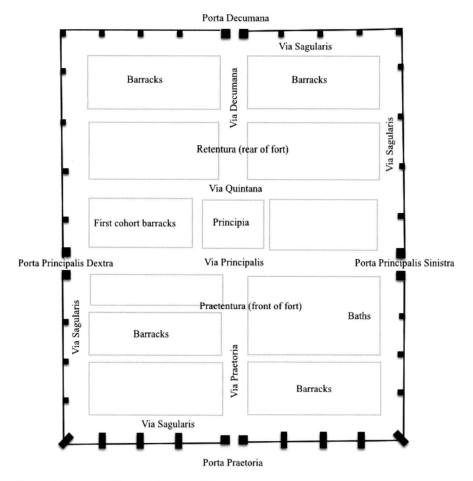

Figure 25: Layout of Roman Fortress of Eboracum.

hand as we read that it was only Roman interventions that rescued the queen around the year 69.

The Romans moved north. The site at York had a number of benefits:[58] It was on the boundary between the Parisi in the old East Riding of Yorkshire and the Brigantes to the west and north; it had good communications by road to Lincoln to the south and Tadcaster to the south-west; it also had good links via the River Ouse to the Humber and thus the sea; it was, well placed on a piece of high ground providing access through the marshy Vale of York; and it was protected on two sides by the rivers Ouse and Foss.

There is no evidence of previous native settlement on the site.[59] However, there is evidence for Roman military activity before the construction of the fortress.[60] The fort was laid out in the traditional 'playing-card' plan with the longer length running north-east to south-west at 1,600 Roman feet (slightly smaller than an imperial foot). The shorter side ran south-east to north-west and measured 1,360 Roman feet. This meant the diagonal was 2,100 Roman feet, suggesting that the surveyors were well aware of Pythagoras and thus could ensure reasonably accurate right angles at the corners.

The earliest fort consisted of a ditch and a rampart, approximately nine-feet high and nineteen-feet wide, strengthened by timbers and turf. An eight-feet-wide timber walkway was protected by a timber palisade. Evidence exists for timber towers and various points and the four gates, one of each side, would have also been of timber. Figure 25 shows the later stone fort with large towers built at intervals.

Roads

Prehistoric trackways existed in Britain long before the arrival of the Romans.[61] These networks would have been difficult for the Roman army to use outside the months of March to September. One estimate of the initial invasion estimates it would have taken 1,000 men fifteen weeks to clear the way ahead and build a temporary road from the Kent coast to the Thames near modern London.[62] Over 3,000 miles of main trunk roads connecting the various towns and cities were built. One testament to the quality of the engineering is that 40 per cent of the 3,000 miles survived into the medieval period.[63] Interestingly, nearly all the major battles on English soil can be located on or close to an old Roman Road.[64]

Examples include: Stamford Bridge and Hastings in 1066; Stirling Bridge 1297; Bannockburn 1314; Bosworth 1485; Marston Moor 1644, as well as most of the battles in the War of the Roses and English Civil Wars. Catterick on Dere Street between York and Corbridge may be the site of a sixth-century battle immortalised in the Welsh poem *Y Gododdin*. Penda fought the West Saxons at Cirencester, a junction of several Roman roads. In 633, Oswald of Northumbria defeated the British king, Cadwallon of Gwynedd, near Hexham along Hadrian's wall. This is worth bearing in mind when considering later incursions and the Roman response.

Back in the second century a cart travelling from Catterick to Corbridge, a little over fifty miles, might have taken five days.[65] Infantry could march that distance in two days at a forced march, whilst cavalry could cover the same distance in a single day. An example from the early fourteenth century has Edward III marching from Barnard Castle to Haydon Bridge in a day before retreating, a similar distance from Catterick to Corbridge.[66] One of the most remarkable feats of distance covered was in 1066 when Harold marched north to confront the Viking army at Stamford Bridge, averaging fifty-three miles a day.[67]

It is very likely Harold used some of the same roads laid down by Roman builders nearly 1,000 years before. The foundation consisted of coarse rubble

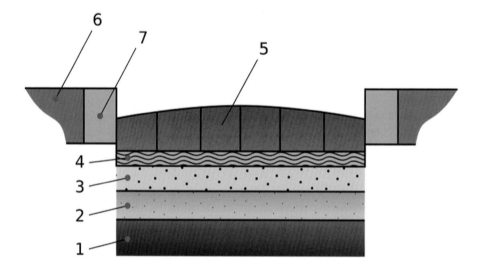

1 Native earth, levelled and, if necessary, rammed tight
2 Statumen: stones of a size to fill the hand
3 Audits: rubble or concrete of broken stones and lime
4 Nucleus: kernel or bedding of fine cement made of pounded potshards and lime
5 Dorsum or agger viae: the elliptical surface or crown of the road (media stratae eminentia) made of polygonal blocks of silex (basaltic lava) or rectangular blocks of saxum qitadratum (travertine, peperino, or other stone of the country). The upper surface was designed to cast off rain or water like the shell of a tortoise. The lower surfaces of the separate stones, here shown as flat, were sometimes cut to a point or edge in order to grasp the nucleus, or next layer, more firmly
6 Crepido, margo or semita: raised footway, or sidewalk, on each side of the via
7 Umbones or edge-stones

Figure 26: Section of a Roman street of Pompeii. (*Wikimedia Commons*)

or boulders covered with compacted sand or gravel. A camber enabled water to run off, bordered by drainage ditches. Cobbles were rare and the surface was often compacted gravel or flint. The width ranged from 1½ to 7 yards, the narrowest of which allowed the passage of the average wagon of the time, drawn by two yoked animals. The Dere Street road between York and Corbridge was 140 miles long and five yards wide. It has been estimated it would have taken 4,000 men a month to construct. However, Tacitus refers to pairs of centuries being used for construction. Thus 160 men would have taken 650 days to construct the same section.[68] If we consider a working season of about seven months, this would take three years to complete. However, a cohort of 480 men might be able to complete it in a single year.

A rule of thumb estimate is that it would have taken one man a day to build roughly 1½ yards of road at 5-feet wide.[69] We can use this to calculate various sections that might have been built by men of the Sixth. Corbridge to Vindolanda is approximately 15 miles which equates to 18,500 days of man power. A double-century of 160 men could complete this in 115 days. This seems like a very efficient use of manpower in times of relative peace. The 41 miles from Vindolanda to Carlisle might require another two double-centuries working in tandem. The entire stretch from Corbridge to Carlisle could be completed by a single cohort in one summer season. If the first cohort remained at base, cohorts two to ten could rotate working a month each.

Alternatively one could consider a legion of 5,000 men, each man working a month at a time on road building, at a rate of 4½ feet a day. This equates to just over 124 miles of road per legion each year. We can see how quickly a road network can be built. A double-century could complete a road linking York with the port at Petuaria on the Humber within 208 days. A cohort would take a little over two months.

The roads also had to be maintained, otherwise plants would rapidly colonise them, especially blackthorn. The margins required clearing to allow cavalry passage over softer ground. This also made ambush less likely. We can see how important this is in later medieval charters: The Statute of Winchester in 1285 requested manorial landowners clear up to 200 feet so that there was no 'ditch, *underwood or bushes where one could hide with evil inten*t.'[70] Henry I (1100–35) ordered that two wagons or sixteen knights could be able to pass side by side. Records from the time of Edward I leave one of the few examples of road building in the Middle Ages. In the North Wales campaign of 1274, just under 30 miles was cleared from Chester to Rhuddlan in about thirty-four days using 1,500 to 1,800 woodsmen.[71] We can compare this to our estimate for Roman legionaries. The same distance over the same thirty days would have required just 1,192 men. This may not be an exact comparison since other factors such as amount to be cleared and the nature of the ground affects it greatly. However, it does indicate how efficient and impressive Roman engineering was. Additionally, Edward I was only clearing a route and not laying a permanent road. It compares well with modern estimates such as the British Royal Engineers of one yard per man per day.[72]

We leave this section with a number of points: the Romans didn't invent the entire network but used existing trackways. Around 40 per cent survived into

Figure 27: Map of Roman roads of Britain. (*Wikimedia Commons*)

the early medieval period; the road network was built primarily for military purposes, but had unexpected benefits such as trade and a profound effect on medieval Britain. Forty per cent survived beyond the fifth and sixth centuries; Most post-Roman battles were fought on or near roads and it is likely any battles in the Roman period were similarly located. Figure 27 shows the major roads of Roman Britain.

Hadrian's death

His death appears to have been welcomed by some as the *Historia Augusta* records:

> Much was said against him after his death, and by many persons. The senate wished to annul his acts, and would have refrained from naming him 'the Deified' had not Antoninus requested it.
>
> Historia Augusta Hadrian, 27.1

Cassius Dio gives a more balanced account.

> Hadrian was hated by the people, in spite of his generally excellent reign, on account of the murders committed by him at the beginning and end of his reign, since they had been unjustly and impiously brought about. Yet he was so far from being of a bloodthirsty disposition that even in the case of some who clashed with him he thought it sufficient to write to their native places the bare statement that they did not please him. And if it was absolutely necessary to punish any man who had children, yet in proportion to the number of children he would lighten the penalty imposed
>
> Cassius Dio Book 69 23.2

Earlier in his reign Hadrian had adopted Ceionius Commodus as his son and renamed him Aelius Caesar but, unfortunately, Ceionius died. Soon after, the emperor's health deteriorated. His favoured successors were the seven-year-old Lucius Verus, a son of Ceionius, and the seventeen-year-old Marcus Aurelius. Considering them both to be too young, he surprised everyone by naming a relatively unknown senator as his successor. Aurelius Antoninus was reluctant, but it was his lack of ambition and age of 51 years old that influenced Hadrian's decision. He also had no siblings and only one surviving daughter. Antoninus was asked to adopt the seventeen-year-old Marcus and the seven-year-old Lucius Verus. If he considered refusing he may have been swayed by some of Hadrian's most recent excesses. Dio tells us Hadrian killed the ninety-year-old Servianus and his eighteen-year-old grandson: 'That I am guilty of no wrong, ye, O Gods, are well aware; as for Hadrian, this is my only prayer, that he may long for death but be unable to die'. As it turned out, Servianus got his wish and Hadrian died in considerable pain.

Marcus Aurelius is not reported to have been enthusiastic with these developments. Hadrian's last acts were to make Antoninus consul and Marcus a quaestor, seven years before the usual age limit of twenty-four. The emperor died aged sixty-two, 'hated by all' as the *Historia Augusta* records. In Marcus's later writing he praises Antoninus, but has little to say about the man who enabled him to become emperor.

In Britain the Wall had been completed for a decade and the Sixth Legion were firmly in place at York. By this time the Ninth Legion had likely left for the continent. The change in administration in Rome brought significant change in policy to the northern border in Britain. The Romans were to take the offensive once again and this time they were to build a new frontier further north.

Case study: A legionary and an auxiliary infantryman

We will now turn to two examples of Roman soldiers. The first is a legionary of the Sixth, Lucius Bebius Crescens. It is difficult to date him but we know he died aged forty-three after twenty-three years' service and his friend and heir dedicated the following inscription: 'To the spirits of the departed: Lucius Bebius Crescens, of Augusta Vindelicum, soldier of the Sixth Legion Pia Fidelis, aged 43, of 23 years' service; his heir had this set up to his friend' (RIB 671). Lucius Augusta Vindelicum was the capital of Raetia north of the Alps. To join the legion Lucius must have been a Roman citizen and we get epigraphical evidence for their various origins. An altar at Castlecary, dated to 140–90, has an inscription that reads: 'To the god Mercury soldiers of the Sixth Legion Victrix Pia Fidelis, being citizens of Italy and Noricum, set up this shrine' (RIB 2148).

Our second example, Amandius, was an infantryman in the First Cohort of Tungrians garrisoned at Housesteads from c. 130.[73] It was a unit of approximately 800 men recruited from the River Meuse region of Gallia Belgica, modern Belgium. A bronze discharge certificate dated to 146 was found in 1980. It was awarded by the commander, Pertnius. Amandius then retired to the civilian settlement a couple of miles to the west at Vindolanda. Assuming a twenty-five-year career, he would have joined up in c. 121, before Houseteads was built. At that time the First Cohort of Tungrians were at

Vindolanda where they had replaced the Batavians in 105. Amandius would have thus witnessed the visit of Emperor Hadrian and the construction of the Wall. He would have still been serving when Antoninus moved the frontier northwards and constructed a second wall.

In 120 there were seven cohorts of Tungrian auxiliaries:[74]

- First Tungrian Cavalry wing
- Fronto's First Tungrian Cavalry wing
- First Asturian and Tungrian Cavalry wing
- First Cohort of Tungrians
- Second Cohort of Hungarians, mixed infantry and cavalry
- Third Cohort of Tungrians
- Fourth Cohort of Tungrians

On retirement after twenty-five-years' service, legionaries received a cash payment and a land grant. The prize for auxiliaries was the granting of citizenship. This extended to their wives and children after they retired. They would also adopt a Roman name with some doing so on enrolment. Only 45 per cent of Amandius's cohort could expect to see retirement.[75] Some might be discharged early due to injury, others would succumb to disease or wounds. Amandius was luckier than our soldier of the Sixth. Lucius died two years before his retirement.

Whilst soldiers could not marry during service, they did form attachments and have children. These families would likely have lived in the town growing outside the fort. The soldier would have lived in one of two rooms with the seven other men of his *contubernium*, or 'tent group'. These rooms were part of a 'strip building' which formed the barracks within the fort. The smaller front room is likely to have been a storage area for equipment, but evidence of hearths in some suggest cooking took place there also.[76] In cavalry barracks, the rear room appears to have been home for just three men whilst the front room in some locations acted as stables:[77] At Wallsend and Carlisle there is evidence of clay-lined troughs.

Equestrians and other elites would have lived in more spacious buildings, often consisting of four wings arranged around a large courtyard. The senatorial legatus would have lived in such a building at the centre of the fort. One wing was devoted to kitchens, stores, stables and latrines. Another would have housed the important dining area and reception rooms. Some contained baths and underfloor heating. These courtyard houses were the best constructed with stone foundations and slated or tiled roofs. Many had upper storeys and the windows were glazed, although more opaque than the translucent type we are used to today.

Our two infantrymen, though, would have lived in two rooms with seven other men in one of the barracks. If they found a wife, the union would have been unofficial. If it was with a Briton, then she may have come from one of the farmsteads in the frontier zone. These were often enclosed by an outer ditch and wall.[78] The buildings of the Britons tended to be round with thatched roofs, wattle-and-daub walls and timber posts. Large farmsteads had a number of such buildings, likely for an extended multi-generational family group. Children were excluded citizen rights until their fathers were granted citizenship. This situation was swept away by the reforms of Severus at the end of the second century when soldiers were allowed to marry, thus legitimising any children and automatically making them citizens.

During the Republican era the Romans recruited citizens to raise armies in times of war. Under Augustus recruits had to state on oath that they were freeborn Roman citizens, and slaves and criminals were excluded. The importance of this is demonstrated in letters between Trajan and Pliny in the first century.[79] The emperor emphasised that it is necessary to find out first if certain slaves were conscripted or volunteered. If they volunteered and lied about their status they were to be executed. However, if they were 'substitutes' then those who swapped with them were to blame. Inscriptions in Britain show that recruits came from all over the empire from Syria to Spain, North Africa to the Danube.

In the first two centuries it is estimated 18,000 recruits were needed from across the empire.[80] These recruits were required to have good health, eyesight, a sound physique and understand Latin. The ability to read and write was prized, and necessary for officers. A strict medical examination ensured the potential recruit and the following attributes:[81] 'a clear eye, carry his head high, have a broad chest, his shoulders muscular, his arms long, his waist small, his legs and feet wiry and not too fleshy'. Each man had to prove his legal status as citizen and then take the *sacramentum*, or oath:[82] 'To serve the Emperor and his appointed delegates and obey all orders unto death and recognise the severe punishment for desertion and disobedience.' Both Amandius and Lucius would have taken this oath.

A common age of joining was eighteen to twenty-one years old, but they could be as young as seventeen to their late twenties. Lucius seems to have joined up at the age of twenty. The length of service was initially twenty years with an extra five as a reservist. However, there are many examples of those from centurion upwards serving much longer. Marcus Aurelius Alexander, camp prefect at Chester, died aged seventy-two and a Lucius Maximus Gaetulicus had served fifty-seven years in 184. If they served their time they received a *honesta missio*, a honourable discharge. However, bad behaviour could earn them *ignominiosa missio*, a dishonourable discharge. A discharge on medical grounds was termed *causaria missio*. Up to the reign of Hadrian, soldiers were often given plots of land usually in *colonia* such as Lincoln or Gloucester. After the reign of Hadrian land was often granted on an individual basis.

Non-citizens were termed *peregrini*, foreigners. As they were excluded from joining the legions, recruits from the many tribes, both inside and outside the empire, joined auxiliary units. They also served for twenty-five years, after which time they could be granted citizenship. Discipline was harsh:[83] Minor infractions resulted in flogging or monetary fines. But actions that endangered others, such as failing to guard the camp properly, could result in death. Even insubordination was subject to capital punishment. The methods used included being clubbed to death by your comrades, beheading, hanging or being burnt alive.

Polybius in the second century BC give the pay of various ranks:[84] Centurions earned double that of a legionary whilst a cavalryman earned half as much again. Soldiers had pay deducted for rations and equipment, and so it is difficult to compare across time, although in general pay did steadily increase.[85] Caesar had doubled the pay of legionaries and by the time of Augustus this had been tripled. To put this into perspective, a legionary soldier in the late second century could expect 1,200 sesterces.

There were high levels of inequality and a rigidly stratified social hierarchy based on property ownership and wealth.[86] The army was one of the few routes available to a poor freeborn citizen for advancement. It is estimated it costed 500 sesterces to feed a peasant family for a year. In contrast, a senatorial governor earned 400,000 a year whilst an equestrian procurator was ranked at 60,000, 100,000, 200,000 or 300,000 sesterces. At the end of the republic average wages were just four sesterces a day which we can compare to Cicero's 555,555 yearly salary from his legal work alone.[87] A moderately wealthy man had an income 714 times greater than a pauper, while for the very rich it was over 10,000 times.

In the Antonine period the legionary commander of the Sixth is thought to have been paid at least 200,000 sesterces.[88] The primus pilus was paid 72,000 sesterces.[89] Severus doubled these salaries and his son Caracalla increased them by around half as much again. A rough estimate of income inequality suggests the legate of the Sixth earned around 160 times that of the common soldier. A governor in London may have been paid double that. In contrast a brigadier in the British army of today, commanding about 4,000 troops, earns between five and six times that of a recruit.

During the Antonine period Severus doubled this to 144,000 and Caracalla increased this again to 216,000. A commander of a legion was paid around 200,000 under Marcus Aurelius and this, too, was doubled by Severus. Centurions of the Sixth earned around 13,000 sesterces under Augustus, rising to 18,000 by the second century. Severus doubled this and his son raised it again to 54,000 a year.

Pay (sesterces)	Arrival of Sixth in Britain c. 122	Reign of Severus 193–211	Mid-third century
Legionary soldier	1,200	2,400	7,200
Legionary cavalry	1,400	2,800	8,400
Auxiliary infantry	1,000	2,000	6,000
Auxiliary cavalry (cohortes)	1,200	2,400	7,200
Auxiliary cavalry (alae)	1,400	2,800	8,400
Legionary centurion	18,000	36,000	108,000
Auxiliary centurion	5,000	10,000	30,000
Auxiliary cavalry decurion	6,000	12,000	36,000
Primus pilus	72,000	144,000	432,000

Table 7: Roman army pay.

Amandius, as an auxiliary infantryman, was at the bottom of the pay scale. Lucius, if we can date him to the same time, earned 1,200 sesterces and was no doubt looking forward to a plot of land and cash payment to fund his retirement. Unfortunately for Lucius, as for many soldiers, he did not live to see it. Soldiering in Britain was about to get decidedly more dangerous. With the death of Hadrian came the reign of Antoninus Pius, one of whose first acts was to put aside his predecessor's non-expansionist policy. The Romans, and the Sixth, were on the march north again.

Chapter 3

Antoninus and the Wall of Turf

Hadrian's plan was no doubt for Antoninus to live just long enough for his two adoptive sons to come of age. As it turned out he reigned for twenty-three years, dying at the age of seventy-four. He came to the throne in 138 and very soon after there are indications of unrest in northern Britain. The *Historia Augusta* tells us, 'For Lollius Urbicus, his legate, overcame the Britons and built a second wall, one of turf, after driving back the barbarians.'[1] Lollius Urbicus had fought in the Bar Kokhba revolt, 132–5, under Hadrian, later becoming governor of Germania Inferior. In 142 the emperor took the title *imperator*, suggesting a previous successful campaign. Coins of the period bear the word 'Britannia', also implying a victory in the province. We thus have a relatively tight timeframe, 138–42, in which we can date a northern campaign.

Location	RIB	Date	Inscription
Balmuidy, north of Glasgow	2,191 & 2,192	139–43	For the Emperor Caesar Titus Aelius Hadrianus Antoninus Augustus Pius, father of his country, the Second Legion Augusta built this under Quintus Lollius Urbicus, emperor's propraetorian legate
Corbridge	1,147	139	For the Emperor Titus Aelius Antoninus Augustus Pius, consul for the second time, under the charge of Quintus Lollius Urbicus, emperor's propraetorian legate, the Second Legion Augusta built this
High Rochester	1,276	139–43	For the Emperor Caesar Titus Aelius Hadrianus Antoninus Augustus Pius, father of his country, under Quintus Lollius Urbicus, emperor's propraetorian legate, the First Cohort of Lingones, part-mounted, built this

Table 8: Lollius Urbicus, inscriptions in Britain.

The inscription at Balmuidy, bearing the name of the governor, Lullius Urbicus, suggests building of the first fort and part of the wall started here around 142.[2]

Two legates of the Sixth are known from the 130s. From the first, we learn his wife's name, Sosia Juncina. A stone altar at York reads (RIB 644): 'For the goddess Fortune [from] Sosia Juncina, wife of Quintus Antonius Isauricus, legate of the Emperor.' Isauricus was *suffect* consul in 140, which means he replaced a consul who had vacated office before his term had finished. Therefore we can date his post as legate to the mid-130s.[3] The second was P. Mummius Sisenna Rutilianus, legionary legate under the governor Quintus Lollius Urbicus (governor c. 138–44). We have a reference to Antonius praising Urbicus for 'completing the British war'[4] which ties in with the date for the commencement of construction of the Antonine Wall. A number of inscriptions place detachments of the Sixth Legion in the area from c. 139.

The new frontier moved approximately seventy-five miles to the north. Like Hadrian's Wall, it included a number of crossing points which Breeze, in *Edge of Empire: The Antonine Wall*, describes as 'Roman Checkpoint Charlies'.[5] Evidence at Corbridge, just south of Hadrian's Wall, shows significant rebuilding in 139 indicating preparations for a major campaign. It is estimated that governor Lollius Urbicus led a force of approximately 22,000, split equally between the legions and auxiliary units.[6] This force would have been protected by a screen of cavalry with auxiliary units in front and to the rear of the legions. Along with a baggage train towards the rear of the column it would have snaked approximately six miles through the northern countryside. The second legion appears to have been present along with vexillations of the Sixth and Twentieth.[7]

Fortunately, we have a number of sources that describe the order of march.[8] Polybius in the second century BC records it as follows:

> The elite troops at the head of the column; allied cavalry from right wing; allied infantry from right wing; pack animals and baggage; first legion; pack animals and baggage; second legion; pack animals and baggage; baggage of remaining allied troops; allied infantry from left wing; allied cavalry from left wing.

In the first century AD Josephus records Vespasian's march into Galilee: light armed auxiliary troops and archers, heavy Roman infantry and cavalry, ten men from each century with tools to prepare camp, baggage of Vespasian and senior officers, Vespasian with personal bodyguard (infantry and cavalry guards) legionary cavalry, mules carrying siege equipment, officers, legionary commanders, prefects and tribunes, eagles and standards; trumpeters, legionaries, six abreast, servants and baggage, auxiliary and allied troops, rearguard of light armed and heavy infantry and cavalry.

A few years before detachments of the Sixth marched north from Hadrian's Wall, Flavius Arrianus the governor of Cappadocia led a Roman army against an incursion by the Alani. His text is known as the *Ektaxis kata Alanoon* or as *Acies contra Alanos*, 'the order of battle against the Alans'. As with the Parthians at Carrhae the threat came from horse archers and heavy cavalry. Arrianus developed tactics and a formation to counter this threat.[9]

The army deployed in close order eight ranks deep. The first four ranks consisted of spearmen whilst ranks five to eight were armed with javelins. The front ranks then 'locked their shields and pressed their shoulders to receive the charge as strongly as possible in the most closely ordered formation bound together in the strongest manner.' To the rear were archers which, together with the javelin men, delivered missiles as the enemy became fixed onto the spears of the front ranks. Artillery pieces were placed on the flanks with a screen of heavy infantry and archers. To the rear the cavalry was placed in eight 'wings' with horse archers close enough to shoot over the battle line. This sounds very much like a shield wall from later centuries and shows how the Romans were willing to adapt. Ultimately, Arrianus was successful and the Alani defeated.

One of the Vindolanda tablets (164) dated c. 97–105 makes no mention of archers but hints at a significant cavalry element: 'the Britons are unprotected by armour. There are very many cavalry. The cavalry do not use swords nor do the wretched Britons mount in order to throw javelins'. It is probably more likely that the Sixth in the second century would use the same tactics as Agrippa at Mons Graupius a few decades before: auxiliary units in front, flanked by cavalry and the legionaries of the Sixth, Second and Twentieth forming a 'wall of iron and wood' behind. Specific battles are not recorded but the campaign itself must have been successful and the legionaries quickly began work on the new frontier

Antonine Wall

With Antoninus proclaimed *imperator*, conqueror, in August 142 and commemorative coins issued celebrating the victory, building work on the new frontier could begin. At the centre the Wall was to climb over two hills, Cray Hill and Bar Hill, and generally adapted itself more to the country than its southern counterpart which had a number of straight stretches. The central sector appears to have been constructed first followed by the thirteen miles of the eastern sector and lastly the western at three miles.[10] Distance slabs give very precise lengths such as the 3,660⅔ paces built by the Twentieth at Castlehill. Similar slabs are found on both the north and south faces of the wall and are unusually ornate compared to Hadrian's Wall or the German frontier. One example, at Bridgeness on the Wall, shows someone making a sacrifice on behalf of the Second Legion. Interestingly, evidence suggests the letters, LEG II AUG, had been painted red.[11]

A stone base, fifteen-feet wide, was laid to aid drainage and provide a firm base. Turf, earth or clay was laid on top. Vegetius specified turfs should measure 18 × 12 × 6 Roman inches, which is slightly narrower, but thicker, than a modern paving slab. The German frontier had a fence but no rampart walk and there is some debate if one was built into the Wall. Like its southern counterpart its purpose is thought to have been a 'demarcation line' rather being a defensive rampart.[12]

The rampart was fronted by a ditch between twenty to forty feet in width and eight-to-twelve-feet deep. A low bank was formed on the northern side from the deposits. At Watling Lodge in Falkirk the ditch is an impressive twelve-feet deep and forty-feet wide. To the rear of the wall, about 120 to 150 feet behind, ran the Military Way. A foundation of stones was topped with gravel and side ditches aiding draining.[13] At sixteen feet in width, it allowed soldiers to march up to four abreast which corresponds to the first century account of Flavius Arrianus, governor of Cappadocia a few years before the Antonine Wall's construction.

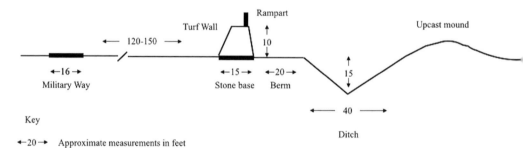

Figure 28: Cross section of The Antonine Wall.

At Dunchoter a detachment of the Sixth was responsible for 3,240 feet.[14] At Castlecary on the Antonine border we read: 'To the God Mercury soldiers of the Sixth Legion Victrix Dutiful and Loyal, citizens of Italy and Noricum, [by erecting] this shrine and statuette, gladly, willingly, deservedly paid their vow.'[15] Tomlin dates it to the reign of Commodus, which places troops back on the Antonine Wall twenty years after it was abandoned.

An altar on the Antonine Wall at Westerwood attests to the presence of officers' wives: 'Sacred to the celestial Silvanae and Quadriviae Vibia Pacata, wife of Flavius Verecundus, centurion of the Sixth Legion Victrix, with her family paid her vow willingly, deservedly.' This may be the same Verecundus who served in Upper Pannonia whilst the name Pacata suggests a North African origin.[16]

Location	RIB number	Date	Inscription (building inscription unless stated)
Duntocher	2,200	142–61	Distance slab: For the Emperor Caesar Titus Aelius Hadrianus Antoninus Augustus, father of his country, a detachment of the Sixth Legion Victrix Pia Fidelis did the construction of the rampart for 3,240 feet.
Old Kirkpatrick	2,205	142–80	Distance slab: For the Emperor Caesar Titus Aelius Hadrianus Antoninus Augustus, father of his country, a detachment of the Sixth Legion Victrix Pia Fidelis (did) the construction of the rampart for 4,141 feet.
Kirkintilloch	2,185	142–61	Distance slab: Victrix Pia Fidelis (built) for a distance of one mile
Castlehill	2,196	142–61	Distance slab: To the Emperor Caesar Titus Aelius Hadrianus Antoninus Augustus Pius, father of his country, a detachment of the Sixth Legion Victrix Pia Fidelis (built this) for a distance of 3,666½ paces.
Balmuildy	2,194	139–61	Distance slab: Victrix Pia Fidelis (built this) for a distance of 3,666½ paces
Castlecary	2,146	142–180	Dedication: To Fortune detachments of the Second Legion Augusta and Sixth Legion Victrix Pia Fidelis gladly and willingly set this up
Castlecary	2,148	140–90	Altar: To the god Mercury soldiers of the Sixth Legion Victrix Pia Fidelis, being citizens of Italy and Noricum, set up this shrine

Table 9: Building inscriptions of The Sixth Legion on the Antonine Wall.

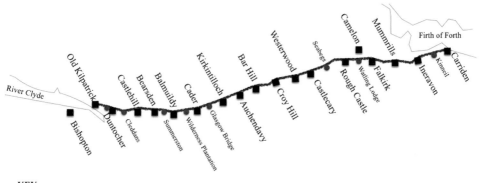

KEY

~ Antonine Wall

■ Fort

● Fortlet

Figure 29: The Antonine Wall.

Detachments of the Sixth may have remained posted to the new frontier throughout its existence. In the main, however, it was auxiliary units that manned the forts and fortlets and patrolled the land to the north. John Richardson from The Antonine Guard re-enactment group has helpfully listed the known units below.

Auxiliary units posted to the Antonine Wall

As with its southern counterpart the wall was mainly garrisoned by auxiliaries. Eight units are known to have been posted to one of the forts on the Wall.

1. First Cohort of Hamian archers
This unit consisted of 500 archers who originated from Hama in Syria. They are thought to have been present in the Claudian invasion in 43. It had served at Carvoran on Hadrian's Wall and moved north to the fort at Bar Hill after 142. When the frontier moved south evidence suggests they returned to Carvoran but also Fort Housesteads.

2. First Cohort of Tungrians
We met the First Cohort of Tungrians at Vindolanda in the Hadrianic period. They originated from what we call today Belgium and consisted of a force of some 800 infantry. Some evidence also places them at Carrawburgh before moving north under Antoninus to, possibly, Cramond by the river Forth (although the inscription may refer to the second cohort) and Castlecary on the Antonine Wall. By the third century it had returned to Hadrian's Wall at Fort Housesteads.

3. First Cohort of Baetasians
Originally raised in Germania Inferior in modern Netherlands, this unit of 480 infantry is thought to have been posted to the Manchester or Ribchester area prior to the building of the Antonine Wall.

Once there they are recorded at Old Kilpatrick on the western end by the River Clyde, and later at Bar Hill. On the withdrawal south this unit was sent to the Cumbrian coast and relocated to Maryport. It is recorded in the fifth century *Notitia Dignitatum* at Reculver in Kent

4. Second Cohort of Thracians
Raised in Thrace (modern Bulgaria) under Antoninus they were posted to Mumrill's Fort on the eastern end of the Antonine Wall. They were a mixed unit of 600 cavalry and infantry. By the third century they were on Cumbrian Coast at Moresby Fort, where the *Notitia* also places them.

5. Fourth Cohort of Gauls
A mixed unit of 600 thought to have arrived with the initial invasion in 43. Inscriptions place them at Castlesteads on Hadrian's Wall (RIB 1,979 and 1,980) before moving north to Castlehill Fort. It was from this Antonine fort that we know the name of the Roman commander, one Pisentius Lustus, who had an altar made to honour the Parade Ground Goddesses. Later evidence places them at Risingham to the south and by the third century they were at Vindolanda where the *Notitia* still places them.

6. First Cohort of Vardullians
This unit originated from Hispania Terraconensis in northern Spain. It was a mixed unit of just over 1,000, posted to Castlecary on the Antonine Wall. Its size may have meant it was stationed at other forts. Later evidence places it at Corbridge c. 161–3, Lanchester c. 175–6 and High Rochester and Cappuck c. 213.

7. Sixth Cohort of Nervians
The Sixth Cohort of Nervians, was a unit of 480 infantry from modern Belgium. Julius Caesar enlisted these soldiers into the Roman Army after he witnessed their military powers. Possibly at Great Chesters under Hadrian they were at Rough Castle on the Antonine Wall. In the third century they were at Bainbridge in North Yorkshire and the *Notitia* suggests they remained until the end of the fourth century.

8. First Cohort of Batavians
A unit of 600 mixed cavalry and infantry, they originated from modern Belgium and Netherlands area. The Cohort served under Agricola in his Scottish camping of the first century. Inscriptions from an altar at Castlecary Fort on the Antonine Wall place them there under Antoninus. In the third and fourth centuries they were posted to Carrawburgh on Hadrian's Wall.

Withdrawal

Construction took about twelve years and almost immediately we get evidence of unrest as coins dated to c. 155 refer to 'Britannia subdued'. Some sources suggest a revolt by the Brigantes in the unknown Genunian district whilst pressure from northern tribes is also possible. A new governor, Gnaeus Julius Verus, arrived c. 154–8 with soldiers from 'each of the three British legions' who had 'contributed to the two German armies'.[17] The archaeological evidence is that the Antonine Wall was abandoned soon after this time.[18] Further evidence indicates it was not occupied concurrently with Hadrian's Wall.[19]

It would appear therefore that Hadrian's Wall itself was abandoned in the early 140s when the border moved north. Twenty years later that, too, was abandoned and Hadrian's Wall re-occupied. We see some tentative epigraphical evidence of re-building work, some attributing detachments of the Sixth.[20] For example, a stone inscription at Corbridge (RIB 1132) dated to 155–9: 'A detachment of the Sixth Legion Victrix Pia Fidelis [set this up] under Gnaeus Julius Verus, pro-praetorian legate of the Emperor, [through the agency] of Lucius … military tribune … .'

Shortly after, during the governorship of Sextus Calpurnius Agricola (c. 163–6), we have the following inscription, also at Corbridge: 'To the Unconquered Sun-god, a detachment of the Sixth Legion Victrix Pia Fidelis made [this] under the charge of Sextus Calpurnius Agrippa, pro-praetorian legate of the Emperor.'[21]

The abandonment of this frontier began before the death of the emperor in 161, as rebuilding work along Hadrian's Wall appeared in 158. The buildings and forts were demolished and burned. Distance slabs were deliberately concealed by being buried in shallow pits. However, a coin dated 164–9 was found at Old Kirkpatrick, although this could easily be from trade or booty. It could simply be that it wasn't worth the effort. Yet Hadrian's Wall required more manpower and it is tempting to consider if resurgent British tribes were pressing the Romans from the north. We thus will now turn to military matters.

Weapons tests and re-enactors

We previously covered formations and contemporary accounts of battles at Watling Street and Mons Graupius. This section is more concerned with the individual soldier. It will concentrate on modern weapons' tests and the experience of re-enactors when using the weapons and equipment.

Swords and spears

When the Sixth arrived in Britain the average length of the gladius sword was just over 27 inches and weighed the equivalent of a bag of sugar. A legionary in a well-drilled formation could move forward purposefully. The size of the shield is such that if he leans forward slightly on his front foot and ducks his head a little he is protected from foot to chin. The curved scutum also protected the sides a little. The sword arm is largely hidden. An enemy warrior attempting to get at the legionary behind the shield risks two feet of steel punching out from the man in front or the two either side. Tests on ballistic gel show potentially horrific internal injuries easily penetrating more than the two inches Vegetius claimed would prove fatal.

Armour gives some protection, especially from a slicing blow. However, leather, linen and hide are susceptible to a determined sword thrust. Metal armour in contrast performs very well. Mail armour can occasionally be penetrated by a straight thrust if a rivet breaks but not deep enough to be fatal; thick undergarments can absorb most of the blow. In contrast, both lorica segmentata and lorica squamata holds up well. The Mainz gladius may have been designed to be a mail-ring breaker, as it had a longer point compared to the Pompeii gladius. In general tests showed a gladius had no effect from a slashing blow, but a thrust could penetrate lorica hamata – mail armour – on occasions.[22] We can conclude warriors without any armour were obviously vulnerable. Those with organic armour had some protection, especially from a slashing blow. Soldiers wearing metal armour had good protection with the iconic lorica segmentata performing best.

A pilum proved more powerful than a gladius, although in one test a mail shirt withstood a pilum throw from a few yards.[23] The mail was solid ring construction which is slightly tougher than the traditional riveted mail. Butted mail (unriveted 'split' rings joined together) is often used by films and re-enactors as a quick method that looks similar at first glance. However, it can be pulled apart by bare hands and performs very badly under tests. One can see from this that a badly maintained or poorly repaired mail shirt might fail completely from a sword or spear strike. One test on mail did burst through a rivet to penetrate a solid wicker target by two inches, enough to be potentially fatal.

In contrast a determined throw of a pilum from a distance of a few yards punched through a shield of wood and fabric. The ten inches of penetration was enough to injure the man behind or even fix his arm to the shield and we read examples of this at the Battle of Carrhae which we will come to later. Lorica segmentata again performed better. At most, a direct hit caused a small hole but usually the metal plates were just dented. This might well cause bruising or a broken rib, but you would be considerably better off than an unarmoured Briton at the Battle of Watling Street. Any shield would also have reduced the velocity, suggesting the combination with armour was sufficient. The curvature of the segmentata plates helped deflect strikes. Only a direct hit at 90 degrees would have chance of penetration.[24] Thus the effect of a spear or pilum was determined by a number of factors: strength, skill and accuracy of thrower, quality of the armour and the angle, power and speed of impact.

In another test a linen-covered shield stopped arrows but not a pilum, which penetrated shield, mail and ballistic gel.[25] Elsewhere, when comparing a

Roman pilum with a Celtic javelin, both were stopped by shields but only the pilum penetrated mail.[26] Roman re-enactors testing a number of pila found three, thrown from 21 to 27 yards, went through shields completely, eleven stuck in and nine bounced off, with the rest missing.[27] Heavier spears could reach up to 37 yards and lighter javelins nearly 60 yards. Thus a Roman cohort throwing 480 pila at about 30 yards might expect half of the enemy to be incapacitated or at least forced to drop their shields. They might even get a second volley of 480 pila in before any charge crashed into the front rank.

Swords vs spears:

A number of different YouTube channels depict sparring duels between spear, sword and other weapons from a range of different eras.[28] One particularly entertaining example focuses on duels between swordsmen and spearmen which give us the following results.[29]

Fighters and result			Comment
Spearman, no shield	9–3	Swordsman no shield	The longer reach of the spear was decisive. The swordsman had to get past the spearpoint and inside the longer reach to have a chance.
Spearman, no shield	4–2	Swordsman with buckler shield	Shield was easy to by-pass.
Spearman, no shield	7–6	Swordsman with medieval-type shield	Very even and depended on swordsman being able to get inside initial thrust
Spearman with shield	0–6	Swordsman with shield	The spear was less effective one-handed, especially when held over-arm.

Table 10: Spear vs Sword re-enactors duel.

In general the spear was effective in mêlée when held with both hands under-arm. The spear also works well in a defensive formation, a shield wall, where rear ranks can throw or thrust weapons over the top of the front rank. This is excellent in warding off cavalry as horses are loath to charge at a static body of men. However, once a formation is broken the odds even up and a swordsman with a shield is in fact at an advantage over a spearman with a shield. In practice, and perhaps counterintuitively, if the shield wall broke you might be better off dropping your shield and holding the spear two-handed. The question arises would you in fact do that? Most Britons at Mons Graupius carried a spear and shield. I would suggest in the mêlée some might instinctively cling on to their shields as a 'safety blanket' right up to the point a Roman stepped inside and thrust a gladius into their guts.

The shield in mêlée:

In later centuries the round shield became common on battlefields. There is one technique that has proved every useful. Interestingly, I discovered this myself independently having made two wooden shields, with a centre grip, out of plywood and mock fighting with my son in the garden. Two metal dog bowls sufficed as shield bosses and the shields were two feet in diameter. They were intended to be children's versions of the later Viking-type shields, usually three feet in diameter, but at the reduced size they were similar to fifth-century Germanic Anglo-Saxon type shields. I hadn't realised at the time this was exactly the same technique used by re-enactors.

The technique is to 'roll' the opponent's shield. Imagine two right-handed fighters, facing each other with left foot and shield in front. If you 'jab' out your shield like a boxer, holding it vertically, it strikes the left edge of your opponent's shield. Your enemy's shield is turned. Then, by 'rolling' the top of your shield to the left and down, your opponent's shield is underneath yours and he is forced to lean back. This opens up his entire left side. He is also off balance. His own sword is now further away from you as he is leaning back. But, as your shield pushes his down and you lean forward, your sword arm is within striking distance of his entire left side. His neck and thigh are open to attack and if he is unarmoured his whole left and torso as well. You can imagine a fighter moving fast, striking with shield, rolling his opponent's shield and then stepping in quickly to deliver a sword thrust, all within two or three seconds.

This shows two things. First one's initial instinct in how to use a weapon is likely to be similar to those who used it in the past. Secondly, whilst archaeologists and historians can show us physical and literary evidence, re-enactors can give a useful picture of *how* equipment was used.

The Roman scutum shields were very different. We recall Tacitus telling us that the auxiliaries used their shield bosses to strike the enemy at the battle of Mons Graupius. This may be more literary licence as in practice it's quite difficult to get that close and use a shield boss for this purpose.

However, the scutum can be lifted horizontally and jabbed forward, knocking the top of the opponent's shield. This opens a gap at stomach level allowing a thrust with the *gladius*. A more common tactic may have been to simply to keep the sword arm hidden from view. This allows two main methods of attack: first, over the top to the opponent's head and neck; second, a short movement of the shield to the left allows the sword arm to jab out at the torso. This can be quickly retracted and the shield covers the body again.

One re-enactor using scutum and gladius gives a very good example of such techniques.[30]

He stands slightly forward with the front foot turned parallel to the bottom edge of the shield and the head bent forward. The shield can quickly be brought to ground or a few inches up to protect lower leg or head. If the shield is held a little away from the body it protects from any arrows or spears that may penetrate. Raising it quickly reduces the possibility a sword or spear thrust will reach the defender. With just the eyes visible between the helmet and shield, turning the head is also enough to cause any sword thrust to slide off the curved surface of the helmet.

One can also 'jab' with the scutum using the bottom edge. If the enemy has no shield then an iron-rimmed scutum weighing 20 pounds could easily break someone's nose. A strike on an opponent's shield also creates an opening for a gladius thrust. What was very impressive when watching the re-enactor was the way the attack was hidden by the shield. When it came it was more like a boxer's right hand than a sword thrust. The shield obscured the movement of the body and the speed over the top towards the face or from the mid-section to the belly would be difficult to counter. It is easy to imagine how a well-trained formation would cut through a less organised and disciplined force, even more so if the enemy were mostly unarmored.

Bows and arrows:

Roman recurve bows of the period tended to be capable of approximately 80–100 pounds of pull.

In contrast medieval long bows were capable of up to 180 pounds of pull, although modern Olympic competitors are pulling between 40–50 pounds. A light 40-gram arrow can travel over 200 metres from a modern 80 pound bow. Interestingly this is only a little further than the distance which Vegetius stated targets should be set. Although the lighter arrows could reach 200 yards, they had less power for penetration and a heavier 70 gram arrow could be efficient at just 50 yards. So whilst bows could fire up to 200 yards, their effective range was 50–150 yards.[31] We will see what is meant by 'effective' in practice shortly, but factors included the draw weight of the bow; the weight of the arrow; the drag on the arrow; and the draw distance (usually around 27 inches). The early crossbows of the period also failed to penetrate mail.[32]

Lorica segmentata and squamata both give good protection against arrows. However, riveted mail can be penetrated by up 2 inches which could certainly cause severe injuries and prove fatal. A contemporary 45 pound Scythian bow, however, failed to penetrate mail but did go through padded armour and into ballistic gel by about an inch. Tests on such bows give a good indication of the effect of the Parthian archers at Carrhae.[33]

Various arrow types, targets and distances were used in the tests. Roman arrowheads were often tribolate-shaped – three-bladed – but bilobate and leaf-shaped heads were also common. Bodkin-type arrows were also used, especially in the east. Targets (4 inch, 3-ply wooden shields) set at 10 yards were penetrated by all metal-tipped arrowhead types. The three-bladed heads performed better than bodkin heads. Pork placed behind padding alone or unpadded mail was penetrated by about 4 inches, a likely fatal wound. An undergarment or padding of an inch reduced penetration into the meat to just one inch, still likely very painful but hopefully not fatal. At 60 feet shields were penetrated by 9 inches rather than clean through and padding, or mail without padding, by an inch. Mail with heavy padding was only penetrated by less than half an inch.

These tests were 'flat-shooting' horizontally when in practice they would more likely fire at an angle to rain down on an enemy and thus lose some power. If we double the Scythian bow strength from 40 to 80 pounds then the maximum range is between 80–160 yards. If the defenders wore padding of an inch then archers would need to get closer to be effective. At 20 yards an arrow might penetrate padded mail by an inch and the shield by 9 inches. Horse archers could come in and wheel away quickly, but infantry archers would be vulnerable at such short distances. At longer distances, only exposed flesh, such as arms and legs, would be vulnerable. Shield and armour gave excellent protection at long distances. A steady barrage of missiles from distance would mean you were well protected by shields and armour. But arms grow tired and if archers move closer and 'flat-shoot', shields start to be penetrated. Most armour stops injuries most of the time, but bare flesh is highly vulnerable. How then did the Romans lose against the Parthians at Carrhae in 53 BC?

Marcus Licinius Crassus led seven legions, over 40,000 men, across the River Euphrates into Parthia. The Parthians had a force of 9,000 horse archers and 1,000 heavy-armoured cataphract cavalry. Crassus foolishly advanced into open desert far from water when the Parthians struck. The Romans formed up in a hollow square with twelve cohorts on each side protected by 4,000 light cavalry and other 4,000 heavy cavalry. Plutarch recorded the effect of Parthian bows: 'the force of the arrows, which fractured armour, and tore their way through every covering alike, whether hard or soft.'[34] It is possible that the Parthian bows performed better than our tests above, or Plutarch is exaggerating. Light troops and archers were unable to drive them off, so the Romans formed a *testudo*. The Parthians positioned their 1,000 'mail-clad horsemen' in front, while the lighter cavalry rode around the Romans in loose formation, firing volleys of arrows. Plutarch again records the terrible effect; 'their hands were riveted to their shields and their feet nailed through and through to the ground.'

This seems at odds with our weapons' tests and requires some explanation. A percentage of 9,000 Parthian horse archers firing several volleys a minute could deliver tens of thousands of arrows in a relatively short space of time. The battle lasted some time, and Plutarch tells us the Parthians did not run out of arrows. Let us imagine they fired a leisurely two arrows a minute, wheeling forward and away each time. That would result in 18,000 arrows a minute raining down and being fired at nearly point-blank range. Armour and shield held up most of the time, but if just one per cent of arrows hit bare flesh or penetrated shield and armour then within ten minutes 1,800 men would be injured, some fatally. Within an hour Crassus would have lost a quarter of his force.

The battle lasted until nightfall so we can estimate fighting lasted several hours. Crassus retreated and left 4,000 injured behind who were killed by the Parthians the next day. We can attempt a very rough estimate if we ignore fatalities and injuries from other causes. The 9,000 Parthian horse-archers could fire around a million arrows an hour at two a minute. If only 0.1 per cent hit home that would equate to 1,000 men an hour being injured or killed. The seeming contradiction between Plutarch's description and modern weapon tests becomes clear. Shields and armour do indeed hold up well under such missiles. But a million arrows an hour at a static enemy has some affect. You may not recall the thousands of arrows that missed or were deflected by shields and armour. But you'd certainly remember the sight of those that 'riveted hands to shields' and 'nailed feet to the ground'.

Vegetius

The Epitome of Military Science, *Epitoma rei militaris*, was written in the fourth century by Vegetius. He gives us a valuable insight into recruitment and training of the Roman military. He emphasises skill and training over numbers and bravery as the key to victory: 'A small force which is highly trained in the conflicts of war is more apt to victory: a raw and untrained horde is always exposed to slaughter.'[35]

The rural population were 'better suited for arms' and adolescents were seen as the ones to recruit. A minimum height of 5 feet 10 inches was required for the cavalry or first cohort, preferably 6 feet. He lists a number of trades best suited: masons, blacksmiths, wainwrights, butchers, hunters. Pastry-cooks, weavers and fishermen should be avoided. Only once thoroughly tested should a recruit be 'tattooed with the pin-pricks of the official mark'. At this point they also swear an oath called *sacramenta*, the sacraments of military service.

In summer a soldier should be able to march 20 miles in five hours and 24 miles at 'full step' carrying a burden of 60 pounds. A day's march should begin before dawn, reaching their destination in the 'heat of the day'. They should not march at night or through snow and ice in the winter. He emphasises the need for adequate supplies of clothing, food and clean water and notes that armies are more often destroyed by these things than by the enemy. Jumping and swimming form part of the training, the latter for horses and grooms as well. They trained with sword and wicker shields against a 6-feet post, prioritising attacking with the point rather than the edge of the sword. It is here we read that a cut seldom kills as the vitals are protected by armour and bones whereas a 'stab driven two inches in is fatal'. The use of javelins, slings, lead-weighted darts (they should carry five *mattiobarbuli* each) and arrows all form part of standard training. A quarter to a third of recruits should be 'trained constantly' with the bow.

The role of the legion is neither to flee nor pursue easily but stand like a 'wall of iron'. The auxiliaries and light troops would advance and either defeat the enemy or draw them onto the legions behind. Vegetius laments if anyone 'desires the defeat of the barbarians in an open battle… the legions must be reinstated with new recruits … carefully selected and trained every day, not just in the morning but even in the afternoon'. He was writing at a time when Rome was beset by repeated incursions and harked back to a time when her army seemed invincible. It is precisely in this period that the Sixth were marching north to the new frontier and which many of the re-enactment groups below try to recreate.

Re-enactors

John Richardson of the Antonine guard:

The Antonine Guard is a re-enactment group from Scotland which specialises in Roman history of the late-first and early-second centuries. It appears at events and schools portraying auxiliaries and legionaries of the Sixth. John Richardson, the convenor for the group, and author of *The Romans and the*

Antonine Wall of Scotland, has many years' experience of re-enactments, and in the British Army.

We saw above that a legionary was expected to be able to march 20 miles in five hours, starting before dawn, and then set up camp in the afternoon. John Richardson makes the following interesting observations:

> I found the March to be the King of showing up any problems. This not only shows up any problems with equipment but just as importantly shows each member just how well they cope physically when doing a march. In the long term it sharpens up physical awareness and builds up stamina. Just as in ancient times there's no need to confront the enemy if you are unfit to do so.

Another point was the importance of having good foot care. John recalls the British Army lost a big part of manpower in one operation due to boggy ground and troops then suffering from athlete's foot. He thus ensures everyone in the group has good quality woollen socks. He points out that if we find something difficult now then the ancient Roman likely found it just the same adding, 'The Roman Army and Greek medics would have been well aware of the need for good foot protection.'

On one march, John found two members suffering from what the Romans called 'dead hands' and it took them about a week to get fully comfortable again with the hand:

> This proved that the need to have a shoulder strap, also quick release, would surely have been a necessity for the Roman Legionnaires. Which proved that shield carrying over even moderate distance could prove a real problem without the need of some means of support. In the above both members experienced the shield just slipped from their hand grip.

John's group often begins a training weekend with a march. This bonds the troop together quickly. On the kit side, if there are any weaknesses this quickly reveals what those may be: discomfort from poorly-fitting armour, loose footwear, and shield not hung properly or leather straps needing adjustment. This then allows people when they get back to sort out those matters before they become real problems. John states, 'Nothing I have found differs for re-enactors in our period for making sure all kit is up to the job and more importantly reliable. Just as in the forces of today and in ancient times having reliable kit could save your life.'

One problem that was resolved through experience and not found in any sources involved adding padding to shoulder areas under the lorica segmentata. Aside from abrasion, it became apparent that a hard strike on the shoulder plates would possibly result in a broken collar bone. Another area of discomfort was the constant rubbing on the lower armpit. This did not happen with the lorica hamata. But with the segmentata some protection would be necessary; otherwise, after several days of 20 mile marches, a percentage of soldiers would be less effective or out of action completely.

Regarding fighting, John's group was involved in an interesting exercise some years ago. A raised embankment, 6 to 9 feet in height, was topped with wooden stakes, lashed together: 'When the re-enactors on the outside being the foe tried to take this position not one, if I recall, even managed up the steep embankment that we were all manning, so that proved the effectiveness of that type of fortification would have been most difficult to penetrate.'

Next they carried out a number of engagements whilst forming a line:

We managed from my memory to hold the line but it was also pressure to do so, and we had one incident where a member of the opposing group lost the plot and started with his wooden hammer taking shots at us; he managed to hit my scutum and damage it and also cleanly knocked off the hand protective boss of another before his own group hauled him away. So holding the line was a tough experience in some ways.

Ultimately the line held and both exercises appear to support the effectiveness of Roman tactics and training.

Practical HEMA Group (Historical European Martial Arts):

There are several excellent Facebook groups devoted to history and many have some very knowledgeable members. One example is the Practical HEMA Group (Historical European Martial Arts). Whilst its focus is the medieval period, many members also are experts in the use of Roman weaponry. I asked Frederick Hopkins about the possibility of a cohort being able to discharge two volleys of pila before a charge struck home:

You'd want the enemy front rank stumbling over their wounded, dead and discarded shields as the charge was getting quite close because that way it'd be very ragged when it hit, allowing the front rank of a cohort a much better opportunity to mop up. Hit them too far out and unless you've got a high rate of fire they can recover, reform and continue the (thinner) charge. I'd say a couple of volleys are quite possible, especially once you factor in the charge stumbling as the first volley hits.

My next question concerned how far apart legionaries would stand in line. 'From experience when someone is in a line and still needs to be able to use a blade, you would have a gap of maybe a foot between legionaries.' He went on to describe using a gladius in such a close formation:

Thrusts from behind a door-sized shield are going to be hard to deal with, especially with comrades on either side. For maximum confusion I'd imagine the thrusts would probably be aimed at the foe stood at either 11 or 1 o'clock from 'our' point of view. Force the foe to fight and defend off their centre line while remaining relatively safe.

The gladius and scutum work well in this scenario but what about in a melee? "Solo fighting with a gladius, the balance and heft are great, they remain fast and good at both the cut and the thrust. The edge probably comes into things a little more. But its worth bearing in mind the scutum shield is what makes the gladius so dangerous as a pairing, because of the size of the thing it becomes impossible to see the gladius because rotating the shield arm to the fore now means my entire body from jaw to shin is behind the board. I can thrust around it, over it or use the damn great boss in the centre to smash the senses out of someone before jabbing with the blade. It's single biggest disadvantage is the length and reach-when compared to later swords. But again, the shield largely made up for this by giving excellent protection".

Richard Hughes of Practical HEMA also runs the Order of the Blade, a medieval martial arts group from the Midlands. Regarding the discharge of two pila he had this to say:

Theoretically yes, yet the tactics employed meant this was rarely done. Given each trooper had both a heavy and a light pilum, and the rest of their kit, I can see the desire to get rid of these early in the engagement. The light one first for distance throws, then the heavier one to go in second to drop a charging adversary. Given effective drilling, a hallmark of the professional standing army, I could see an effective launching of both volleys within a typical charge. As for the whole cohort letting rip, this I doubt as it's better to let the first three centuries discharge and tank the first wave, with the next three centuries holding back for the call to switch. When that happens, a discharging of javelins to make the gaps and then drive in with the reserve legions could well shatter the enemy in a simple switch.

Similar to Frederick Hopkins, Richard sees the gladius and scutum as a 'weapon set, designed and optimised for unit work, able to work in close formation'. Interestingly, he echoes John's earlier words about footwear:

Bad ground is something that trips up your average HEMA fighter, but that's mostly down to bad preparation. Footwear is king. The standard attire would be hobnail sandals. So leather strapped tight to the foot embedded with metal studs, akin to rugby boots. This helps with grip on poor terrain and allows you to dig into the group and push back easily.

Alexander Iles, a re-enactor and tour guide, walked the Wall in February 2022 to highlight the Hadrian's Wall 1900 event. Wearing the period costume of a second-century auxiliary soldier, he averaged fourteen to fifteen miles a day, which on the face of it compares badly to Vegetius's twenty miles in five hours. However, it is worth pointing out that Alexander did not use the military road and the rough ground close to the Wall made going tough. Travelling at 4 miles an hour on a flat straight surface is entirely possible. Moving across uneven ground with significant inclines is another thing entirely. He found it 'exhausting' and felt it was worse being alone. One interesting observation was the wind: 'It was a nightmare and it turned my shield into a kite and knocked me over at one point. This could be my user error but I will have to study that further and really understand how best to use the shield with carrying straps.'

His helmet was an imperial gallic helmet and his shield an oval type called a *clipeus*, used by auxiliaries. It carried the name of the unit, in this case the *Cugernorum Ulpia Tariana Civium Romanorum*. He carried a *Spatha* sword after one found at Vindolanda, a *hasta* spear based on one from Housesteads and a shield from depictions on Trajan's column. The armour was chainmail with quarter-inch links. Padding was used under the armour and helmet. Under the padding was a thick woollen tunic with long sleeves. Trousers were also of thick wool and slightly 'baggy'. Another interesting point was the position of his sword. It is thought the sword baldric should be under the military belt but he found that this did not work at all. He took it out from underneath and found it sat much better causing no trouble for the rest of the walk. Most importantly, his boots – *calcei* – were similar to ones found at Vindolanda and had hobnails to protect the soles.

Summary

Modern weapons' tests and re-enactments can sometimes be difficult to interpret. Not all materials, either today or in the Roman period, were of consistent quality, manufacture or maintenance. However, some general points can be made. Firstly, some protection was better than no protection – even fabric or leather armour worked up to a point, especially from slashing or glancing blows. Metal armour generally worked very well with segmentata performing the best. A determined sword thrust could penetrate leather armour and, at times, some chainmail. Missile weapons caused most problems but depended on the distance, draw-weight of the bow and type of arrow head. At close distance the pilum could penetrate shields and chainmail. What is clear is that the portrayal of battles in films is often misleading. A sword strike against lorica segmentata or hamata is unlikely to cause injury. In reality a fighter would go for the exposed parts of his opponent. Thrusts to the face, arms and legs would have been common.

For a large-scale battle scene let us imagine a standard football field. The pitch at Wembley stadium measures 114 × 75 yards. A Roman cohort of the Sixth Legion, numbering 480, could line up eight deep at one end with perhaps some left over to act as archers or light skirmishers. At the other end stand our Britons, perhaps outnumbering the Romans as they did at both Watling Street and Mons Graupius. Whilst arrows can reach nearly twice this distance, at this range they start to have an effect. This, along with the actions of skirmishers, causes a decision to be made. If the Britons attack, once they pass the halfway line, arrows, lead darts and sling-shot become effective. As the advance passed the centre circle into the opposition's half light javelins and the first wave of pila hit home. Shields would be dropped and the attackers would experience significant casualties. This might disrupt the charge as those behind tripped over fallen comrades. A possible second volley of pila would deliver more wood and iron towards the enemy.

As the attackers enter the penalty box a rain of missiles from the rear ranks would disrupt the charge. Javelins, pila, arrows and sling shot would all hit home with devastating effect. Any unarmoured warrior, or those who had dropped shields, would be horribly exposed. They might well stop to discharge their own spears, which could make them vulnerable. As most would be carrying spears they would need to be a spear-length from the Roman front line before they could bring their weapons to bear. What percentage of their comrades had fallen we can only speculate, but our previous tests showed a far greater number would have discarded their shields as unusable. Now the real work began as they were confronted with a wall of wood and iron. The Roman front rank would stab out with two feet of steel and withdraw behind their shields which protected virtually their entire bodies. Celtic and Germanic tactics relied heavily on the success of this initial charge. If it failed they would be forced backwards over fallen comrades. At a signal the cohort would advance, turning a failed charge into a rout. Fallen warriors could be despatched easily as they advanced.

The disparity in casualties at Watling Street and Mons Graupius suggests the above is a likely scenario, perhaps repeated on a smaller scale multiple times as the Sixth advanced with the Roman forces. Ultimately they were successful and the Antonine frontier held for a generation. Yet by the death of Antoninus Pius the Romans were already preparing to withdraw back to the Solway-Tyne isthmus. It is to the reign of Marcus Aurelius that we will now turn.

Chapter 4

From a Kingdom of Gold to One of Iron and Rust

Marcus was forty years old when he became emperor and, like his predecessor, he was a conservative man who disliked change. He allowed the senate a level of sovereignty in theory at least. Cassius Dio records that Marcus was genuinely reluctant to be emperor, preferring his intellectual studies instead. His first act was to appoint his thirty-one-year-old adoptive brother, Lucius Verus, as co-emperor and this innovative decision seems to have been his own. Lucius was in many ways the polar opposite of Marcus. He had little interest in books, preferring physical pursuits. Unlike his brother, he loved chariot races and was a fanatical supporter of the Greens against the Blues, Reds and Whites.[1] He was described as tall, good-looking, vain and unpredictable. Marcus, in contrast, was said to have been unconcerned about outward appearance to the point of being careless and wore plain clothes in keeping with his stoic beliefs.

We have three inscriptions referencing the Sixth, all potentially from this period. Quintus Camurius Lemonia Numisius Junior was a legate of the Sixth before his consulship in 161. He had been a tribune in the Ninth Hispana and served a variety of posts after. Birley suggests he may have been legate in Germania Inferior before moving to Britain in the dangerous situation in the mid-150s.[2] From an altar near the western end of the wall we read: 'Lucius Victorinus Flavius Caelinus, imperial legate of the Sixth Legion Victrix Dutiful and Loyal, [set this up] because of successful achievements beyond the wall.' A late Antonine date is thought the most likely.[3] An undated inscription at Corbridge reads: 'To Apollo Maponus, Quintus Terentius Firmus, son of Quintus, of the Oufentine voting-tribe, from Saena, prefect of the camp of the Sixth Legion Victrix Pia Fidelis, gave and dedicated this.'[4] The stone reads 'praefectus castrorum', suggesting a second century date since castrorum was often dropped from inscriptions from the beginning of the third century.

The reign of the two adoptive brothers started badly. First, in the autumn of 161 the Tiber burst its banks and caused a severe flood in Rome. There followed an earthquake in Cyzicus, modern Turkey. These events severely drained treasury funds, but worse was to follow. Parthia had taken over parts of the Seleucid Empire, formed after the conquests of Alexander the Great. As Rome expanded east and Parthia westwards, friction became inevitable. It was this friction which caused Marcus Crassus to lead seven legions to disaster at Carrhae in 53 BC. Yet peace had held for forty years since the time of Trajan.

Perhaps sensing weakness in the new emperors, Vologases IV of Parthia invaded the Roman client state of Armenia, installing his puppet-king, Pacorus. The Romans responded immediately and Severianus, governor of Cappadocia in eastern Turkey, led a legion to restore Roman rule. His force became trapped at the city of Elegeia and destroyed. Another force in the south, led by Lucius Attidius Cornelianus, governor of Syria, was also defeated. Marcus turned to the recently appointed governor of Britain, Marcus Statius Priscus. He took over the vacant spot of governor of Cappadocia, Severianus having committed suicide at Elegeia, and began preparations for a northern campaign into Armenia.

It is worth speculating at this point if Priscus took any troops from Britain. It is certainly unlikely he travelled alone and with the northern frontier recently re-established further south it is possible this had freed up some troops. We have one tantalising piece of evidence. An inscription on a memorial stone for Lucius Artorius Castus found in Croatia marks him as a praefectus of the Sixth Legion based at York. It states he commanded a force against an enemy beginning with ARM or possibly ARME. We will discuss this in greater depth later, but it is clearly possible this represents a movement of troops from Britain to Armenia. There were other Armenian campaigns in 213 and 233 but the Parthian War of 161–6 is certainly a possibility. The absence of vexillations on the inscription isn't thought by historians to be problematic. Given we know the Sixth did not leave Britain, one likely interpretation is that he commanded detachments of the Sixth, and other legions, accompanying Priscus to Cappadocia. If so, they would have been part of a successful campaign in 163 that culminated in the taking of the Armenian capital at Artaxata.

Verus took credit for this, receiving the title Armeniacus, despite never swinging a sword in anger. A new capital, Kaine Polis, was built thirty miles closer to the Roman border and a new king was installed, a Roman senator of Arsacid descent. The Parthians had also replaced the Roman client king of Osroene on the eastern border of Syria. By 165 Verus had captured its capital at Edessa. Meanwhile, farther south, Avidius Cassius captured the Parthian cities of Seleucia and Ctesiphon on the Tigris. By 166 the Parthians were completely defeated and a triumph was held in Rome on 12 October. Marcus had a 'deep loathing' for games and public spectacles and insisted the gladiators used blunted weapon.[5] The co-emperors were accompanied by the young son of Marcus Aurelius, Commodus, then aged five, along with his three-year-old brother, Annius Verus. Commodus was made Caesar, demonstrating the early intention of grooming him for the throne.

It is during the Parthian War that a future tribune of the Sixth rose to prominence. Publius Helvius Pertinax was born on 1 August 126, the son of a freed slave in Liguria, north-east Italy. He initially worked as a teacher but, relatively late in life, in his mid-thirties, he began a career in the army with the help of patronage. He gained access entry into the equestrian class and served as a cavalry officer in the Roman-Parthian War. Pertinax distinguished himself and was soon promoted to tribune of the Sixth, followed by praefectus of an auxiliary unit (First or Second Tungrorum, also in northern Britain) before later taking command of an ala in Moesia.[6] At this point he was still an equestrian. Cassius Dio describes him as an 'excellent and upright man'.

Meanwhile some Germanic tribes had taken advantage of the Parthian war to increase raids across the Danube and Rhine. It is those events that led to the conflict known as the Marcomanni Wars that resulted in 5,500 Sarmatians being sent to Britain. A major incursion in c. 166 involved 6,000 Langobard and Lacringli warriors crossing the Danube into Pannonia Superior before being defeated at a battle near the River Danube.[7] In 167 the Marcomanni advanced on the city of Aquileia before being pushed back. Some sources point to a major Roman defeat soon after, with casualties of 20,000.[8] However, by 171 the Romans were on the offensive and a series of victories followed.

By this time Pertinax was in charge of a unit in Moesia and a new patron, Tiberius Claudius Pompeianus, resurrected his career. Pertinax served with distinction on the Danube and went on to be promoted to senatorial rank and served as suffect consul in 175. This was a remarkable achievement for the son of a freedman. More was to follow as he was appointed governor of Moesia, Dacia and Syria in succession. Later he was to return to Britain when it would seem the legions, and the Sixth among them, were in near open mutiny. First though, we must detail the events leading up to the Sarmatian defeat.

As the war on the Danube dragged on the Romans continued on the offensive. By the end of 174 they had subdued both the Marcomanni and Quadi tribes. In 175 they advanced deep into Sarmatian territory, inflicting a series of defeats as they went. The Sarmatian king, Zanticus, surrendered. At this point the sources hint that the normally magnanimous emperor was thoroughly fed up with the numerous broken treaties and promises. He was determined to wipe them out and even annex their territory and create a new province. Fortunately for the Sarmatians, events hundreds of miles away saved them. In the East, Avidus Cassius revolted and declared himself emperor. The emperor was forced to 'make terms with the Iazyges very much against his will' and was so alarmed by events he didn't even inform the senate of the conditions of the peace treaty, as was usual.[9]

The Sarmatians were treated far more harshly than the German tribes: they were 'required to dwell twice as far away from the Ister [Danube] as those tribes. Indeed, the emperor had wished to exterminate them utterly.' He mistrusted the Sarmatians so much he refused rights to the Quadi, 'for fear that the Iazyges and the Marcomani, whom they had sworn not to receive nor to allow to pass through their country, should mingle with them'. Harsh restrictions prevented them from even using the islands on the Danube: 'from all save those affecting their assembling and trading together and the requirements that they should not use boats of their own and should keep away from the islands in the Ister.' They were allowed passage across Dacia, but only for the specific task of dealing with the Roxolani and only then with permission of the Roman governor of Dacia.

A hundred-thousand captives were returned by the Iazyges, supporting Dio's statement that the Iazyges were 'still strong at this time and had done the Romans great harm'. The defeated Iazyges 'furnished as their contribution to the alliance eight thousand cavalry, fifty-five hundred of whom he sent to Britain.'[10] This, unfortunately, is the last we hear of these Sarmatians. We don't know if they all arrived, what they did or where they were posted to if indeed they got there.[11] In the early second century there were approximately fifty-nine auxiliary units in Britain.[12] Of these, fifteen were cavalry units of 500 and only one was of 1,000. There were twenty-nine mixed units and it's possible the Sarmatians were divided among these as well. But at face value the 5,500 would provide eleven units of 500 or nine units of 500 and one *milliariae*.

The little evidence of their presence that does exist is confined to Chesters on Hadrian's Wall, Ribchester and Chester, where there is the tombstone of an unnamed cavalryman.[13] The Chester carving is hugely debatable and more likely a Dacian than Sarmatian. An inscription from Ribchester, dated to c. 241, records a unit of Sarmatian cavalry of Bremetennacum. Units often retained their original name and give no indication of the ethnicity of troops later assigned to that unit. A reference to *numerus* rather than *ala* suggests a smaller unit instead of a regiment. The fourth-century *Notitia Dignitatum* uses the title *cuneus* or squadron which suggests a steady reduction in size over time: (cuneus Saramatarum, bremetenraco, based likely at Ribchester in Lancashire). What we don't have is any evidence of Sarmatian units posted anywhere on or near either Hadrian's or the Antonine Wall.

However, let us assume all 5,500 did indeed reach Britain. Given wars on the Danube erupted two years later and again at the beginning of the reign of Commodus, it is unlikely that these auxiliaries would have been kept close together. Instead, they would have been split up and spread across the province. A normal posting would have been for twenty-five years. However, as we will see, tumultuous events lay ahead. Even without the threat of death in combat, life expectancy was low; twenty-two for men and twenty for women,[14] although infant mortality skews the figures significantly. A third of the population died before the age of three, and nearly half by the age of eight. For men serving in the military, life expectancy was significantly lower and it's uncommon to find tombstones for soldiers in later middle age. For a Roman joining the army at age twenty, 78 per cent would reach the age of thirty-five and just 60 per cent to forty-five. In peacetime, roughly two-thirds might survive a twenty-five-year career. Uprisings, incursions and mutinies, followed by a vicious civil war, would very likely have reduced these numbers considerably. Whatever the case, at the end of their posting many would have returned home. It wasn't until the edict of Caracalla in 212 that everyone received citizenship.

If a Sarmatian unit was posted to Ribchester in 175 then the inscription from c. 241 gives a clue concerning links to the Sixth. Here we have a centurion 'acting-commander and prefect', no doubt a temporary posting in place of an equestrian praefectus commander (RIB 583):

> To the holy god Apollo Maponus for the welfare of our Lord (the Emperor) and of Gordian's Own Unit of Sarmatian cavalry of Bremetennacum Aelius Antoninus, centurion of the Sixth Legion Victrix, from Melitene, acting-commander and prefect, fulfilled his vow willingly, deservedly. Dedicated 31 August in the consulship of the Emperor Our Lord Gordian for the second time and of Ponpeianus.

A slightly earlier inscription dated c. 225–35, also from Ribchester gives another clue (RIB 587):

> To … for the welfare of our Emperor Caesar Alexander Augustus and of Julia Mamaea the mother of our Lord (the Emperor) and of the army, under the charge of Valerius Crescens Fulvianus, his pro-praetorian governor, Titus Floridius Natalis, legionary centurion and commandant of the unit and of the region, restored from ground-level and dedicated this temple from his own resources according to the reply of the god … .

The unit isn't named but, if we assume it's the same Sarmatian unit, we see another legionary centurion in charge of a single unit and 'the region', which likely refers to the territory surrounding the fort. Whilst auxiliary units had their own command structures, it would seem that the legion provided temporary commanders from their centurions. Additionally, the Sixth had some authority over the units in their area as the senatorial legate at York outranked all the equestrian commanders of those units.

In March 180, five years after Sarmatians units were sent to Britain, the emperor fell ill at Sirmium in Pannonia, on the verge of victory in the second Marcomanni War. The symptoms match those recorded for the Antonine plague, most likely smallpox. Marcus summoned Commodus and requested the German war to be continued. Marcus soon stopped eating and drinking and on the sixth day must have suspected his death was close. He summoned his generals and Commodus and formally announced his succession. He asked his advisors to be 'guides' and 'fathers' to Commodus, so that he could become 'an excellent emperor'.[15] This proved to be a forlorn hope. Cassius Dio had this to say:

> I admire him … that amid unusual and extraordinary difficulties he both survived himself and preserved the empire. Just one thing prevented him from being completely happy, namely, that after rearing and educating his son in the best possible way he was vastly disappointed in him … our history now descends from a kingdom of gold to one of iron and rust, as affairs did for the Romans of that day.
>
> Cassius Dio, book 72.36

The following decades were to prove a tumultuous time for the Sixth in Britain. A major incursion was followed by mutinies and revolts. This, in turn, was followed by a civil war and a climactic battle before Severus lead a massive invasion of northern Britain.

Incursions and revolts

Commodus began his reign with a successful continuation of the war on the northern frontier.[16] Cassius Dio records wars in Dacia but that his 'greatest struggle' was in fact in Britain early in his career.

> When the tribes in that island, crossing the wall that separated them from the Roman legions, proceeded to do much mischief and cut down a general together with his troops, Commodus became alarmed but sent Ulpius Marcellus against them … and he ruthlessly put down the barbarians of Britain.
>
> Cassius Dio book 73.8

The phrase 'cut down a general' might suggest a legionary commander was killed, which in turn would most likely be the legatus of the Sixth. However, the word could just as easily mean a praefectus of an auxiliary unit based on one of the forts along Hadrian's Wall. Lucius Ulpius Marcellus is recorded as governor in 178 and was sent to quell the incursion before being recalled to Rome around 184. There is some debate about whether there were two persons of the same name or Marcellus served twice as governor with an unknown senatorial figure in between. However, on balance Birley finds it likely the general killed was the legionary legate of VI Victrix and Marcellus served from 178–84 and was sent from London rather than elsewhere.[17] The war was evidently finished by 184 and the title Britannicus appears on coins with Commodus. We can thus date this major incursion to the first years of Commodus's reign, c. 182.

How severe it was is open to debate. Archaeological evidence of destruction can be found along the eastern section of the Wall and at the following forts:[18] Halton Chesters, Rudchester and Corbridge. Several other forts appear to have been abandoned: Birrens, Newstead, High Rochester and Risingham. This suggests an invasion down eastern Northumberland and the lower Tweed

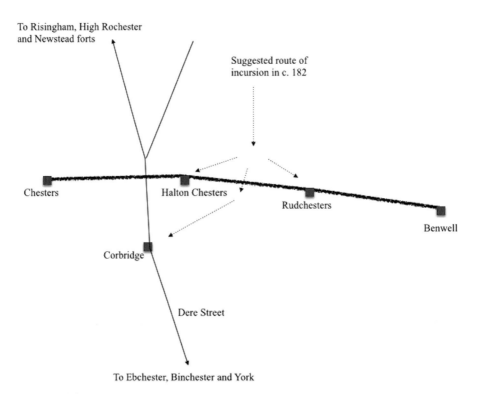

Figure 30: The incursion of 182.

Valley and then down Dere Street, although there's no indication they reached anywhere near the legionary base at York.

By 184 Ulpius Marcellus had restored order, but he was 'strict, arrogant and unpleasant' and the army mutinied.[19] Pertinax, by now a senator, was sent to replace him and is thought to have served from 185–7. There is then a gap in the records until c. 191–2 when Decimus Clodius Albinus was appointed governor by Commodus. As Britain in this period was an imperial province with a senatorial governor any gap must have been someone of senatorial rank. We do have an example of the provincial *iuridicus* in London acting as governor. The inscription of Marcus Antius Crescens Calpurnianus reads: 'vice legati legato pro praetore, acting legate, propraetorian legate.' It is likely, therefore, that he, or his equivalent, acted as governor in any short temporary breaks.

Whilst these events were playing out in Britain an assassination attempt was made on the emperor.

Around 182 Commodus was entering the 'hunting-theatre' where a senator lay in wait.

> thrusting out a sword in the narrow entrance, he said: 'See! This is what the senate has sent you.' This man had been betrothed to the daughter out of Lucilla, but had intimate relations both with the girl herself and with her mother.
>
> Cassius Dio book 73.4

The emperor's sister Lucilla was implicated and relations with the senate deteriorated significantly Unsurprisingly, Commodus became wary of the senate and he promoted freedmen such as Saoterus and Cleander which made matters worse. Saoterus was caught up in the reprisals and killed. This allowed the rise of the Praetorian Prefect Perennis whose actions may have instigated the unrest in the army in Britain.

Corbridge Roman fort

A fort was built at Corbridge in c. 86 to guard the crossing over the River Tyne. To the south, Dere Street led from York, to the north the main invasion route into southern Scotland. The Stangate led to Vindolanda and further west was Carlisle. These two roads met in the centre of the fort outside the headquarters and commander's house, buildings that were later replaced by a large courtyard. The *via principalis* followed the Stangate whilst the *via praetoria* ran north to south, following Dere Street. For four decades it protected this strategic position until Hadrian's Wall was built a short distance to the north. A civilian settlement formed to the west of the fort.

The original fort is thought to have been large enough for a 500-strong unit, possibly the Cohors I Vardullorum from Spain. The Vindolanda tablets suggest it was an important base. Fire damage dated to c. 105 may have been a result of enemy action as some other forts were abandoned at this time. A new fort was built over 6.7 acres. In 122 work started on Hadrian's Wall 2.5 miles to the north of Vindolanda. When Antoninus began extending the frontier to the Clyde-Firth isthmus, Corbridge underwent substantial improvements with stone buildings replacing former timber ones. At some point after Hadrian's Wall was recommissioned the northern part of the fort was converted into a large courtyard building still housing the *principia* and *praetorium*. Two large military compounds were constructed south of the Stangate with substantial granaries to the north. Detachments of the Sixth appear on inscriptions dated to c. 160. At this time the barracks themselves appear to have been rebuilt in stone, possibly by and for the men of the Sixth.

The town now became a legionary base and the auxiliary unit was sent elsewhere. Detachments of the Second Augusta and Twentieth Valeria were also present. Corbridge became a major supply depot and base for operations further north. Further fire damage in the second half of the second century might be a result of the incursion during the early years of the reign of Commodus. Cassius Dio recorded tribes crossed the wall who did 'much mischief', killing a general and his troops. The eastern section of Hadrian's Wall shows archaeological evidence of destruction as well as at specific forts:[20] Halton Chesters, Rudchester and Corbridge. Several other forts appear to have been abandoned: Birrens, Newstead, High Rochester and Risingham. A 'general' could simply mean a commander of an auxiliary unit. The legate of the Sixth would likely be at York but if he led a response up Dere Street he could have been ambushed. However, he would likely have led a legion- sized force along with various auxiliary units, and we have no record of such a loss or defeat.

Given the relatively localised damage, if it is synonymous with Dio's incursion of c. 182, we can suggest the following scenario. An attack down the Tweed Valley and to the east of, but parallel to, Dere Street, required the neighbouring forts of Rudchester and Halton Chesters to be neutralised. Perhaps the supply base at Corbridge was the target. The forts at Rudchester and Halton Chesters both probably had mixed units of 500, cohors quingenaria equitata. It would make sense to attack them simultaneously and a traditional rule of thumb is that an attacking force requires a ratio of three to one to take a defensive position. Of course, we simply cannot know the circumstances or how long the unrest lasted. But the Britons must have had at least numbered in the low thousands to take two forts and then attack a site like Corbridge.

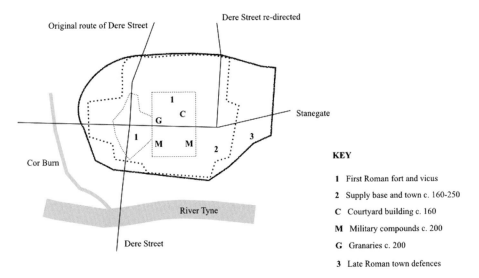

Figure 31: Map of Corbridge Roman Fort.

The plot of Perennis and 1,500 javelin men

Just before Pertinax arrived in Britain we read of a curious incident involving a contingent of javelin men leaving Britain to confront the emperor. Cassius Dio gives us the following narrative:[21] Commodus had taken little interest in governance and Perennis began to act as *de facto* head of state. In Britain the army rebelled, perhaps partly due to the harshness of the governor, Marcellus. The soldiers declared 'Priscus, a lieutenant' as their emperor. Birley identifies him as possibly Junius Priscus, legate of the Sixth.[22] He declined, stating, 'I am no more an emperor than you are soldiers.' If the date of 184 is accurate, it would explain why Marcellus was recalled and Pertinax sent the following year.

Dio continues: The still rebellious soldiers chose 'out of their number fifteen hundred javelin men and sent them into Italy'. It is interesting to note that an auxiliary unit of light infantry attached to a legion numbers 500. Three such units, possibly one from each legion, would give us approximately 1,500 men. They reached Italy and Commodus met them personally on the road outside Rome. Dio, writing shortly after, claims their reason for coming was that 'Perennis is plotting against you and plans to make his son emperor'. The emperor handed his praetorian prefect over to be killed, allowing the rise of a certain Cleander to prominence. Dio reports that 'Commodus was wholly devoted to pleasure and gave himself up to chariot-racing, caring nothing for anything …'.

Herodian, writing a little later, confirms much of this: Cleander encouraged Commodus to give up Perennis and he was handed over and 'struck down by those men'. His wife, sister, and two sons were also killed. We also read that unrest in Britain continued until Pertinax quelled it a couple of years later. We learn more details of the plot involving Perennis and his son to take the throne. Commodus had been persuaded to put the prefect's sons in command of the army of Illyricum. Perennis had 'amassed a huge sum of money' in order to bribe the army to revolt. But the plot was uncovered and Perennis and his sons 'perished miserably'.[23] As Perennis died in c. 185 we can be fairly certain these events involving the Sixth occurred in 184–5.

The much later, and less reliable, *Historia Augusta* gives a slightly different account. It claims that, because of the war in Britain, Perennis had dismissed 'certain senators' and placed equestrians 'in command of the soldiers'. This can only mean the senatorial tribunes or legates of the legions although whether it means all three legions or just two is unknown. However, in this version it is the legates in command of the army who reported the matter. Were these the same legates Perennis had dismissed? Were these the legates in Britain complaining that the senatorial tribunes under them had been replaced? Whatever the case, the senatorial governor remained in overall command in London. All the known and attested governors of Britain were of senatorial rank and most had experience of governorships in other provinces. Given the importance of Britain it is extremely unlikely all three legates would have been replaced by equestrians. Dio and Herodian would almost certainly have mentioned such a breach in protocol. Dio especially, with a deep dislike of Commodus, would have noted such a huge departure from tradition. Bad enough that equestrians and freedmen had more access to the emperor than senators. Ultimately Perennis paid with his life in c. 185. He was 'delivered up to the soldiers to be torn to pieces' as soon as the matter was reported to Commodus.[24]

After the death of Perennis a frenzy of denunciations and executions coupled with tax rises for the rich made Commodus a hated man among many senators. It's probably safer to dismiss the *Historia's* account and accept Dio and Herodian concerning a plot. However, if equestrians were replacing senators and the soldiers weren't happy about this it almost certainly wasn't the legate of the Sixth as, in all the accounts, it is the legates who report the matter. Additionally, we have a likely candidate for a commander of the Sixth. The practice would have also been short lived as, even if we trust the *Historia*, it tells us Perennis was executed precisely because of this in 185.

This Priscus, described as a 'lieutenant', is not the Statius Priscus of the AD 160s.[25] It is possible his full name was Junius Priscus Gargilius Quintilianus who we later find as legion commander of V Macedonia. Sequential posts as legate were uncommon and might be explained by a problem with the previous post. An attempted mutiny would certainly count as a problem even though he demonstrated an apparent show of loyalty in turning down the soldiers' requests.

We can attempt to reconstruct a rough time line. The northern tribes crossed the wall c. 182 and caused damage to two forts on the Wall, Rudchester and Halton Chesters. The main base at Corbridge was the most significant casualty. A body of troops and their commander were 'cut down'. This is more likely the commander at Corbridge or one of the auxiliary commanders. But it is possible the Sixth responded from York and suffered a defeat along Dere Street. Marcellus was sent north to deal with it and this was achieved by 184. A combination of his harsh discipline and decisions by Perennis in Rome caused a mutiny and Marcellus was recalled, perhaps after the arrival of the 1,500 javelin men in Rome. The next governor was Pertinax who was to experience similar levels of unrest.

The revolt under Pertinax

Dio, we recall, stated the soldiers in Britain remained restless 'until Pertinax quelled them'. The *Historia* gives a little more information. After the death of Perennis, Commodus sent a letter asking him to be governor of Britain. We read that he kept the soldiers from revolt:

> for they wished to set up some other man as emperor, preferably Pertinax himself ... . And certainly he did suppress a mutiny against himself in Britain, but in so doing he came into great danger; for in a mutiny of a legion he was almost killed, and indeed was left among the slain. This mutiny Pertinax punished very severely. Later on, however, he petitioned to be excused from his governorship, saying that the legions were hostile to him because he had been strict in his discipline.
>
> *Historia Augusta, The Life of Pertinax,* 5–9

We are left to wonder which legions were hostile? Given the previous incident involving Priscus, it is quite possible it was the Sixth. If so, this was his old legion, having served as tribune in the 160s. Pertinax was governor for a relatively short time, c.185–7.

The Deserters' War

While Pertinax was in Britain dealing with rebellious legions a major problem appeared in Gaul. Maternus, a former soldier, deserted and gathered a band of followers. He plundered villages and farms and amassed a large sum of money. More men joined him and even began to threaten large urban centres. Herodian describes the threat as 'no longer brigands but rather enemy troops'. They attacked 'the largest cities… all over Gaul and Spain'. Many were abandoned or destroyed by fire and Maternus swelled his ranks with released prisoners, slaves and deserters.

Commodus was enraged and sent threatening letters to the governors 'charging them with negligence and ordering them to raise an army to oppose the bandits'.[26] It is possible one letter reached Pertinax and troops from Britain were sent to help, though we have no evidence.

We recall Junius Priscus, the likely legatus of VI Victrix at York in 184, who refused to be made emperor.[27] At this point he appears to have been legatus of V Macedonia on the Danube. Interestingly, he commanded detachments of Britanniciarum, his inscription reads:[28] *praeposito vexillationum legionum III Britanniciarum*, Commander of the vexillations of three British legions.

It is possible this is a reference to the 1,500 javelin men mentioned by Cassius Dio. Alternatively, he may have been sent to help suppress the war against Maternus.

By 186 the rebellion had nearly been wiped out, but Maternus attempted one last desperate throw of the dice. During the festival of Hilaria in March 187 he planned to infiltrate the festivities in Rome and assassinate Commodus.[29] It is interesting to read that 'the majority of the Roman people were still well disposed toward Commodus', unlike the senators and most of the sources. Importantly, the emperor retained the support of the Praetorian Guard. Maternus was betrayed, captured and beheaded. After this latest assassination attempt Commodus was rarely seen in public.

Back in Britain Pertinax was requesting he leave his post due to the hostility of the soldiers. The next attested governor was Clodius Albinus in c. 192. It is possible Pertinax stayed a little later and Albinus arrived earlier, but it does seem likely there is a gap in our records. This may have been filled by the senatorial iuridicus acting as governor and we do have an inscription of just that for a certain Calpurnius in Britain, although his date is uncertain. Given nearly all governors of Britain had previous experience of governing another province, it is likely Commodus turned to a senior experienced senator.

The death of Commodus

By 188–9 Pertinax, having suppressed the mutinous legions in Britain, was appointed governor of North Africa to deal with unrest there, but by 190 he was back in Rome. A plague struck Italy, followed by a famine and Commodus left Rome for Laurentum, a few miles to the south-west on the coast. Cleander, the new power behind the throne since Perennis was executed, remained in Rome, entrusted to secure the grain supply. Cleander, well known for corruption and selling privileges, took full advantage.

Shortages of labour had pushed up wages and reduced tax receipts. Herodian states that Cleander bought up most of the grain supply and put it in storage, hoping to control the people and army with future generous distributions of grain. However 'the Romans … hated the man and blamed him for all their difficulties; they especially despised him for his greed.'[30] Cleander made a fatal mistake when he reneged on a promise to a certain Papyrius Dionysius, who was praefectus annonae. The prefect of the grain supply was one of the four great prefectures of Rome, but the plum prize was prefect of Egypt. When Cleander rescinded this appointment, Dionysius looked for an opportunity for revenge.

The population of Rome was nearly 1 million, and 200,000 households were entitled to free grain. This required 300 million tonnes of grain a year to be transported and stored. Dionysius restricted the supply and then stirred up the mob against Cleander, blaming him for the shortages. A horse race at the Circus Maximus developed into a protest against Cleander and the crowd marched towards the emperor's palace shouting 'bitter words' about Cleander who made his second fatal error. Soldiers were sent against the crowd and many were killed or injured. The soldiers were likely the 1,000 Equites Singulares Augusti who reported directly to Cleander. But they were not the only force in Rome.

Dio reports the Praetorian Guard joined in on the side of the crowd. The sources agree the anger was directed at Cleander and not Commodus. Confronted with near anarchy and an angry mob baying for blood, the emperor once again threw his closest advisor to the mob, just as he'd done with Perennis. We read Commodus was so terrified, 'he was ever the greatest coward', that he immediately ordered Cleander and his son to be killed. The boy was 'dashed to the earth and so perished'. The body of Cleander was dragged away and abused and his head carried 'all about the city on a pole'. We also read that many who had 'enjoyed great power' under Cleander were also killed.[31]

Herodian states this was a turning point for Commodus, giving himself over to 'licentious pleasures'. Men of 'intelligence and … even a smattering of learning' were replaced by 'the filthy skits of comedians and actors'. He turned his attention to the games, taking lessons in driving the chariot and training for beast fights.[32] Cassius Dio records that one of his many titles was 'The Roman Hercules', and statues were erected depicting him in this way. A lion skin and club were paraded before him and placed on a chair in the amphitheatre. Commodus would enter the arena in the 'costliest finery available'.[33]

As a gladiator he liked to perform as a *secutor*. In beast hunts he killed hundreds of animals, on one occasion a hundred bears using spears from a walkway.[34] Lions, elephants, rhinoceroses and even a giraffe were despatched. The crowd loved it, but the deeply conservative senators were outraged. Cassius Dio himself witnessed one event: Commodus killed an ostrich and held its head aloft in front of the senators, grinning as he did so. Dio states: 'many would have died by the sword, there and then, for laughing at him', a fate they avoided by chewing on some laurel leaves.

The sources may well be biased but executions and despotic behaviour increased. He ordered Rome be renamed Commodiana, the legions Commodian, and a day of Commodiana to celebrate this 'elevation'. He titled himself Emperor Caesar Lucius Aelius Aurelius Commodus Augustus Pius Felix Sarmaticus Germanicus Maximus Britannicus, Pacifier of the Whole Earth, Invincible, the Roman Hercules, Pontifex Maximus, Holder of the Tribunician Authority for the eighteenth time, Imperator for the eighth time, Consul for the seventh time, Father of his Country. Not content with that he insisted the months be renamed in honour of this, thus calling them: Amazonius, Invictus, Felix, Pius Lucius, Aelius, Aurelius, Commodus, Augustus, Herculeus, Romanus, Exsuperatorius. Dio remarks 'so superlatively mad had the abandoned wretch become'.

With Cleander gone another freedman, Eclectus, rose to prominence and his friend Laetus was appointed praetorian prefect in 191. Key events now occurred which were to have a dramatic effect on Britain and the Sixth. Three senators, each of whom were to play a part in The Year of the Five Emperors, were appointed to important governorships: Clodius Albinus in Britain, Pescennius Niger in Syria and Septimius Severus in Pannonia Superior on the Danube.

The last year of his life started badly with a devastating fire in Rome in 192. Many were left destitute and at the same time the emperor introduced higher taxes for the rich, taking two gold pieces from each senator and his family each year on his birthday in August. Statues dedicated to Commodus appeared in Rome, often in the garb of Hercules. Despite his public displays against animals, he had so far confined gladiatorial bouts to a private audience. However, he now planned something extraordinary. The emperor arranged a public display for the festival of Saturnalia in mid-to late December.[35]

His former lover and confident Marcia pleaded with him not to debase the imperial image and he angrily dismissed her, calling for Laetus and Eclectus. They, too, protested and he angrily threw them out. Commodus retired to bed but not before writing down 'the names of those who were to be put to death that night'.[36] Top of the list were Marcia, Eclectus and Laetus, followed by a number of senators, elder statesmen and advisors appointed by his father. Fortunately for Marcia, a young boy picked up the wax tablet and by a momentous stroke of luck walked off with it and happened into the arms of Marcia.[37]

We can only imagine the panic as the three advisors made hasty plans. Eclectus and Marcia were rumoured to have been lovers, and it may be telling that they married shortly after the murder. There is some debate whether this event occurred the night of the murder or two weeks previously, before the planned festivities. On the evening of 31 December Marcia attempted to poison his food. Cassius Dio claims she put it in his beef while Herodian says it was the wine. It failed and Commodus vomited. In some pain he went to the bathhouse where he was sick for a second time. This no doubt created more panic in our would-be murderers. They approached Commodus's personal wrestling partner, Narcissus, and he agreed to finish the job. Herodian states: 'Narcissus rushed in where the emperor lay overcome by the poisoned wine, seized him by the throat, and finished him off.' While Dio has Commodus suspecting the truth: 'he indulged in some threats. Then they sent Narcissus, an athlete, against him, and caused this man to strangle him while he was taking a bath.'

Two slaves wrapped the body up and carried it through the palace past guards who were sleeping or drunk from the festivities. There is a suspicion that this story hides a conspiracy that sources such as Cassius Dio were only too happy to forget. Laetus and Eclectus went to see Pertinax who was still up. It's claimed he expected the late visit to augur his arrest by Commodus. After being re-assured, he sent out a trusted man to view the body. This being done, Laetus and Pertinax then sent messengers to all the senators, most of whom were still in Rome. Even the old favourite of Marcus Aurelius, Claudius Pompeianus, husband of Lucilla, absent for some time was in Rome, as Dio noted. The senators were assembled that very night and supporters of Pertinax, such as Pompeianus, just happened to be in the city.

Herodian and Cassius Dio both claim the people and senate were 'in a frenzy of joy', although especially the wealthy and those in particular danger from Commodus. However, the Praetorian Guard were still loyal to Commodus and their support was vital. A promise of 12,000 sesterces placated them and Pertinax was soon proclaimed by the senate with Commodus suffering *damnatio memoriae*, erasing his name and tearing down his statues. A remarkable rise for a freedman. The former equestrian tribune of the Sixth and auxiliary praefectus in northern Britain was now Emperor.

Case study: Pertinax

Cassius Dio describes Publius Helvius Pertinax as an 'excellent and upright man'. He was born on 1 August 126, the son of a freedman Helvius Successus, in Liguria, north-east Italy. Pertinax initially worked as a teacher but relatively late in life, in his mid-thirties, began a career in the army with the help of the patronage of Lollianus Avitus, a former consul. This allowed him access to the equestrian class. He served as a cavalry officer in the Roman-Parthian War, 161–166. His next appointment was as a military tribune in Legio VI Victrix, based at York in Britain. The next step was as a commander of an auxiliary unit, I or II Tungrorum, also in northern Britain, and then in charge of a unit in Moesia in the Marcomannic Wars. It was at this point he obtained a new patron, Tiberius Claudius Pompeianus. Pompeianus himself rose from equestrian status to become one of Marcus Aurelius's most trusted advisors, even marrying his daughter Lucilla.

It was during the first Marcomanni War on the Danube that Pertinax came to prominence. In c. 174 he led one army against the Quadi and it is during this campaign that we hear of the 'Battle of the Thundering Legion', also known as the 'miracle of the rain'.[38] A legion became trapped and surrounded by enemies. Suffering from thirst they were saved by a sudden thunderstorm. The scene is depicted on the Column of Marcus Aurelius in Rome. Pertinax, still an equestrian at this point, served as procurator of Dacia. Palace intrigue nearly ended his career before Pompeianus recalled him to his staff and he served with distinction on the Danube.

Soon he was a senator and on its own this would have been an extraordinary achievement for the son of a freedman. In 175 he received a suffect consulship followed by governor in three provinces, Moesia, Dacia and Syria. He had been forced out of favour by Perennis, but after the latter's death Commodus wrote to Pertinax asking him to serve in Britain. The posting nearly cost him his life but he remained in the emperor's favour as he subsequently was appointed proconsul of Africa. He served as consul for a second time alongside Commodus and then was appointed praetorian prefect.

This remarkable career brought him into contact with many of the inner circle of the old confidants of Marcus Aurelius. One can only imagine what men such as Pompeianus thought when they compared their former beloved emperor with his son, Commodus. We know more details about Pertinax' career from an inscription that was found in Brьhl, near Cologne.

PVBLIO HELVIO PERTINACI
EQVO PVBLICO PRAEFECTO COHORTIS IIII GAL-
LORVM EQVITATAE TRIBVNO LEGIONIS VI VICTRICIS
PRAEFECTO COHORTIS I TVNGRORVM PRAEFECTO
ALAE .... PRO-
CVRATORI AD ALIMENTA
PRAEFECTO CLASSIS GERMANICAE PROCVRATORI
AVGVSTI AD DVCENA III DACIARVM IDEM
MOESIAE SVPERIORIS
AGRIPPINENSES
PVBLICE

To Publius Helvius Pertinax, who was enrolled in the equestrian order, prefect of the Fourth (?) Regiment of Mounted Gauls, tribune of the *Sixth Legion Victrix*, prefect of the First (?) Tungrian Regiment, prefect of the .... Squadron, procurator of the food supply, prefect of the German Fleet, imperial procurator ducenarius in the Three Dacian Provinces and in Moesia Superior, have the inhabitants of Cologne erected this from public means.

The sources are generally very kind to Pertinax and it would seem he attempted to return to the government of Marcus Aurelius and away from the madness of Commodus. Unfortunately, the Praetorian Guard did not share this good opinion as they feared a reduction in their privileges and an increase in discipline. The first attempt to remove him came quickly as he visited the nearby port at Ostia. He was informed of a plot by praetorian officers to replace him with the consul Quintus Sosius Falco. Pertinax rushed back to Rome and Falco was arrested. The emperor kept his promise not to execute a senator and banished him to his estates. On 28 March unrest in the praetorian camp caused Pertinax to send his father-in-law and Urban Prefect, Sulpicianus. There he was held while 300 armed Praetorians marched on the palace. The sources claim that some of the palace servants favoured Commodus and allowed the guards in. Laetus, still the praetorian prefect from the last days of Commodus, refused to intervene.

Pertinax had the opportunity to escape, but bravely chose to leave his rooms and meet the guards face to face. Eclectus, Commodus's right-hand man and murderer, was at the new emperor's side. In a dramatic stand-off, Pertinax confronted them. The praetorians were shamed and sheathed their swords, all except one man. A certain Tausius from Gaul was not so cowed by the emperor's words. He attacked and struck the emperor down. Many of the others were now spurred to join in the carnage. Eclectus bravely wounded some of the assailants before he, too, was killed.

So ended the reign of our former tribune of the Sixth Legion. Son of a slave, war hero and former governor of Britain, his head was placed on a spear and marched back to the Praetorian camp where Sulpicianus was still waiting. There seems to have been nothing planned about the murder as there was no candidate waiting in the wings. This led to what was described as one of the most disgraceful episodes of Roman history, and the cause of the 'year of the five emperors'. It was to result in a climactic battle involving the legions of Britain at Lugdunum in Gaul, possibly the only time the Sixth left the province until the last days of Roman Britain.

Chapter 5

Septimius Severus, the Hammer of the Scots

As the headless corpse of Pertinax lay on the floor, word of his murder spread. Those senators fearing reprisals from an angry Praetorian Guard left the city or laid low. Meanwhile, back at the Praetorian camp Sulpicianus, who had been sent by Pertinax to calm things down, must have been shocked to see his son-in-law's head paraded through the gates. Any grief he may have felt was quickly put to one side and he offered the soldiers a large sum of money to secure their support for the throne. However, he wasn't the only one to see an opportunity in a crisis.

Nearby, a certain Didius Severus Julianus was having dinner when the news broke. His guests urged him to seize the moment and he rushed to the Praetorian camp. Having been refused entry, he was forced to shout his offer through the gates which elicited a higher bid from Sulpicianus inside. The Praetorians no doubt quickly realised their new position as middle-men could prove fruitful. They went back and forth with bids and counter-bids. Sulpicianus got to 20,000 sesterces but Julianus reminded the soldiers that the son-in-law of Pertinax might take revenge on his murderers, promised he would restore the name of Commodus and their privileges. He raised his offer to 25,000, promising the cash immediately. This sealed the deal and the soldiers escorted their new emperor to the senate. With little option in the face of several thousand armed Praetorians, they declared Julianus emperor, no doubt through gritted teeth. Laetus was removed from post and, along with Marcia, soon executed, leaving only one of the murderers of Commodus left alive, the wrestler Narcissus.

The elevation of Julianus did not go down well with the citizens and he was called a thief and murderer in the streets. But it wasn't lack of support in the senate or the mob which proved fatal. Rather it was the army. On learning of the death of Pertinax, three contenders all declared themselves emperor, each with a powerful army consisting of several battle-hardened legions: Pescennius Niger in the East, Septimius Severus on the Danube and Clodius Albinus with the three legions of Britain, including the Sixth. Severus was closest and moved first. He quickly secured his western flank, agreeing to make the governor of Britain Caesar in return for support, and marched on Rome.

Julianus started to panic and asked the respected Pompeianus to share the throne, which he declined. His proposal to lead the senate and meet Severus on the road, presumably to negotiate a way out of his predicament, was also refused and he lost all support from his fellow senators. Worse was to follow; on returning to the palace he found the Praetorians unwilling to support him either. He was forced to recall the senate and declare Severus as joint emperor. This, however, did not save him.

Severus sent a message promising no harm to the guard so long as the murderers of Pertinax were handed over. The senate was recalled by the consuls without Julianus being present and they declared Severus sole emperor and condemned Julianus to death. A single tribune found the emperor cowering alone in the palace. His last words were: 'But what evil have I done? Whom have I killed?' The new emperor hunted down and executed all the conspirators in the murders of both Pertinax and Commodus. Narcissus the wrestler was thrown to the beasts in the arena. He then turned his anger towards the Praetorians and forced them to assemble in their ceremonial dress without their armour and weapons. Severus lectured them about their disloyalty and their actions in murdering Pertinax and selling the empire. They were disbanded and dismissed, forbidden from coming within 100 miles of Rome on pain of death.

As events unfolded in Rome, Niger began advancing from the east. Within a year, and several defeats later, he was captured and beheaded after the battle of Issus in 194. The pivotal moment for the legions of Britain came when Severus declared his son Caracalla as his heir. Clodius Albinus realised he'd been duped and prepared his response.

The battle of Lugdunum

Cassius Dio was a member of the senate when Niger was defeated and Albinus was made consul alongside the emperor in 194. He states that after his victory in the east Severus would no longer allow Albinus the title of Caesar whilst Albinus 'aspired even to the pre-eminence of emperor'. Cassius describes the tense situation as 'the entire world was disturbed by this situation' and 'we senators remained quiet, at least as many of us as did not, by openly inclining to the one or the other'.

Herodian records that 'the aristocracy much preferred Albinus as emperor because he belonged to a noble family and was reputed to have a mild nature'.[1] Severus planned to send messengers with 'secret orders' to be given in private. Once there, they were to kill him. Herodian also reports they had 'deadly poisons' as a back-up plan. However, the emperor's behaviour towards

Niger's supporters did not help create trust. He used their children to force the provincial governors to betray Niger yet still put them and their children to death afterwards, revealing a 'despicable character'. Albinus increased his bodyguard and the messengers were stripped and searched before being seized and tortured to reveal the plot.

A cold-war situation developed and Herodian records that the emperor gave a rousing speech to his soldiers. Albinus, he claimed, had 'violated his pledges and broken his oaths, and … chosen to be hostile rather than friendly and belligerent instead of peaceful … so let us now punish him with our arms for his treachery and cowardice.' The legions of Britain also came in for similar rhetoric:

> His army, small and island-bred, will not stand against your might. For you, who by your valour and readiness to act on your own behalf have been victorious in many battles and have gained control of the entire East, how can you fail to emerge victorious with the greatest of ease when you have so large a number of allies and when virtually the entire army is here. Whereas they, by contrast, are few in number and lack a brave and competent general to lead them.

More insults included Albinus' 'effeminate nature' and his way of life suited 'more for the chorus than for the battlefield'. Perhaps crucially, we also read of 'generous gifts to the soldiers' before publicly announcing the expedition against Albinus. The first move was to seize the Alpine passes.

Dio tells us of a certain Numerianus, 'a schoolmaster', who set out from Rome to Gaul and, pretending to be a Roman senator sent by Severus, collected a small force and began to attack Albinus' troops, killing a few of the enemy's cavalry and 'other daring exploits in Severus' interest'.

This could be the 'few minor skirmishes' Herodian records. He claims Albinus was in 'a state of complete confusion' but crossed over to Gaul and established his headquarters there. Messages were sent to local governors for supplies, food and money, but we hear nothing from Herodian about extra troops. Those who did obey the call later faced 'destruction', such was the price for choosing the wrong side.

The *Historia Augusta* follows much of what Herodian says. It includes not just the attempted assassination plot, but the text of the letter the messengers brought to Albinus:

> The Emperor Severus Augustus to Clodius Albinus Caesar, our most loving and loyal brother, greeting. After defeating Pescennius we

despatched a letter to Rome, which the senate, ever devoted to you, received with rejoicing. Now I entreat you that in the same spirit in which you were chosen as the brother of my heart you will rule the empire as my brother on the throne. Bassianus and Geta send you greetings, and our Julia, too, greets both you and your sister. To your little son Pescennius Princus we will send a present, worthy both of his station and your own. I would like you to hold the troops in their allegiance to the empire and to ourselves, my most loyal, most dear, and loving friend.

We get further details: 'five sturdy fellows were to slay him with daggers hidden in their garments.' However, instead of panic we read that Albinus 'assembled a mighty force and advanced to meet Severus and his generals'. Albinus was victorious in the first engagement although where and who was involved is not said. Severus then had the senate declare Albinus a public enemy and he set out for Gaul. It is likely these events occurred in 196 as Niger was defeated in 194 and the following year was spent mopping up in the east. A supporter of Albinus would no doubt claim Severus naming his son Caracalla as heir broke an agreement and gave him no option.

Albinus brought much of the garrison from Britain which, of course, included the Sixth Legion. Britain had over 15,000 legionaries and 30,000 auxiliaries. It is likely he left a skeleton force behind but, with Severus having over 70,000 troops available, Albinus needed all the men he could get. Things started out well as Dio records 'in an earlier battle Albinus had defeated Lupus, one of Severus' generals, and had slain many of his soldiers'.

Herodian tells us the final battle was fought near the 'large and prosperous city of Lugdunum' on 19 February 197. Albinus remained behind in the city as his army set out. Dio numbers the combatants to 150,000 soldiers on each side.[2] This perhaps is an exaggeration or possibly a mistake as 150,000 in total is more likely. Severus is described as 'superior in warfare and was a skilful commander'. Both Herodian and Cassius Dio agree that the battle was a close-run thing as a 'major engagement developed, and for a long time each side's chances of victory were equal' and there were 'many phases and shifts of fortune'. Herodian gives our first hint that soldiers from Britain, and thus the Sixth, played a crucial part: 'for in courage and ruthlessness the soldiers from Britain were in no way inferior to the soldiers from Illyria. When these two magnificent armies were locked in combat, it was no easy matter to put either one to flight'.

The left wing of Albinus was driven back and fled to their camp, pursued by the Severan right. Meanwhile, on the opposite side, things were going bad for the emperor: The enemy had dug trenches and pits covered over with earth.

They advanced to the edge of this defensive line and hurled javelins before quickly retreating, luring the Severan army. It worked and the left wing of Severus's army charged to near disaster. The front rank plunged into the trap causing those behind to stumble also. The rear ranks panicked and were driven into a 'deep ravine'. Showers of missiles and arrows caused a 'great loss of life', horses and men 'perished in wild confusion'.

Seeing this, Severus led the Praetorians to stop the retreat but came close to destruction as well. Worse was to follow as the emperor himself lost his horse and the future of the Roman empire hung in the balance. His left flank began to disintegrate and the enemy sensed victory and pursued the Severans. Rather dramatically we read:

> When he saw all his men in flight, he tore off his riding cloak, and drawing his sword, rushed among the fugitives, hoping either that they would be ashamed and turn back or that he might himself perish with them. Some, indeed, did stop when they saw him in this attitude, and turned back; and brought in this way face to face with the men following them, they cut down not a few of them … and they routed all their pursuers.

At this point another turning point occurred. Laetus, commanding the cavalry for Severus, was, according to Dio, waiting and hedging his bets to see who was winning. With the left wing already defeated and seeing Severus turning the Clodian right wing back, Laetus chose this moment to charge into the flank of the retreating enemy.

Where then were the British legions in this bloody battle? Herodian, who lived through these great events, once again tells us:

> the division of the army stationed opposite the sector where Severus and his command were fighting proved far superior; the emperor slipped from his horse and fled, managing to escape by throwing off the imperial cloak. But while the soldiers from Britain were pursuing the Illyrians, chanting paeans of praise as if they were already victorious, they say that Laetus, one of Severus' generals, appeared with the troops under his command fresh and not yet committed in the battle.

Laetus was accused of 'watching the progress of the battle and deliberately waiting'. It was claimed that the affair 'substantiates the charge that Laetus coveted the empire himself'. Severus later rewarded his generals and only Laetus was executed, adding it seemed 'reasonable under the circumstances, considering the general's past performances'.

On the battlefield 'Severus' soldiers, taking heart, wrapped the emperor in the imperial cloak again and mounted him on his horse'. The Britons now found themselves beset on two sides and their pursuit stopped in its tracks. A brief resistance turned into a retreat and then a rout, while Severus' soldiers 'pursued and slaughtered the fugitives until they drove them into Lugdunum'.

Severus had won a great victory but 'countless numbers' had fallen on both sides and we read even

> the victors deplored the disaster, for the entire plain was seen to be covered with the bodies of men and horses; some of them lay there mutilated by many wounds, as if hacked in pieces, and others, though unwounded, were piled up in heaps, weapons were scattered about, and blood flowed in streams, even pouring into the rivers.

Dio records Albinus took refuge in a house that stood beside the Rhone and, when he saw there was no escape, committed suicide. The emperor viewed the body personally 'giving free rein to his tongue as well'. Herodian records the emperor's troops captured Lugdunum and burned it and when they caught Albinus they cut off his head and sent it to Severus. The body was cast away but the head was sent to Rome and stuck on a pole. Dio remarks on the emperor's cruelty, but he released thirty-five prisoners charged with siding with Albinus. Others he killed, especially those who he discovered had privately sent letters of support. One notable death was Sulpicianus, father-in-law of Pertinax, and would-be emperor in 193.

The *Historia Augusta* also records that countless soldiers fell and many fled or surrendered. We are left to guess how many of the Sixth perished. In this version Albinus stabbed himself or, 'according to others', was stabbed by a slave and was brought to Severus where he was beheaded still 'half alive'.

Severus then rode on horseback over the body and 'when the horse shied, spoke to it and loosed the reins, that it might trample boldly'. The emperor exacted a terrible revenge, breaking a promise of safe passage, and killed the wife and child of Albinus, casting them into the river. A letter to the senate accompanied the head to Rome whilst the body was allowed to rot for days before also being thrown in the river. He even ordered the bodies of the senators who had been slain in the battle to be mutilated. Countless people were put to death, numerous leading men, many distinguished women and many nobles of the Gauls and Spain. Their goods were confiscated and sent to swell the public treasury.

Herodian makes an interesting reference to Britain: 'After settling affairs in Britain, he divided this region into two provinces, each under its own governor

… he put all the friends of Albinus to death and confiscated their property, indifferent to whether they had supported the man by choice or by necessity'. Leaving the cruelty to one side, there are two points worth noting. Firstly, as we shall see later, it is thought the first division of Britain actually occurred under Caracalla. One reason is that we have continued references to governors of a single province throughout the reign of Severus. It is thought Herodian has mistaken the division of Syria for that of Britain. However, 'settling affairs in Britain' could mean many things. Clearly the province continued to be garrisoned and we know the Sixth was present after these events. There was likely a major culling of anyone considered disloyal.

Herodian claims that after Albinus' death 'many who remained loyal to him were defeated by Severus in battle'. A legion in Arabia had also gone over to Albinus. Unfortunately, we have no evidence of what occurred in Britain immediately after 197. One likely scenario is as follows: much of the Sixth left with Albinus in 196, leaving a skeleton force behind at York. What was left of the legions after Lugdunum was led back to Britain with new legates. Severus likely killed all the senior officers and any others considered potentially disloyal. The sources make it very clear how ruthless he was towards the defeated legions under Niger: 'Many who had never even seen Niger and had not joined his faction were dealt with harshly on the ground that they had favoured his cause.' When Byzantium fell, the Romans 'put to death all the soldiers and magistrates'. Herodian also reports that Severus 'now put to death without mercy all the man's friends, whether they had supported him by choice or by necessity'. Returning soldiers however he granted a full pardon.

The remnants of the Sixth returning to Britain may well have been confronted by their former comrades at York. Unfortunately, we have no evidence of what transpired, but life evidently carried on as we have inscriptions referring to building work at Corbridge under a new governor, Virius Lupus (c. 197–200): 'A detachment of the Sixth Legion, Victorious, Dutiful and Faithful, [built this], under the charge of Virius Lupus, senator of consular rank.'[3] Still 'dutiful and faithful' the Sixth were now Severus's men.

Inscriptions during the reign of Septimius Severus

In the early third century improvements and repairs were made to various northern forts:[4] New aqueducts were built at Chester-le-Street and South Shields, a granary at Great Chesters; cavaliers 'exercise hall' at Netherby, a gate and towers at Vindolanda and a catapult platform at High Rochester, along with renovations at various other sites such as Birdoswald, Carrawburgh and Old Carlisle. Pay was raised under Severus and again under Caracalla.

Herodian records that Severus allowed soldiers to marry, although this may simply be an acknowledgement of 'unofficial' wives and children.[5] An inscription at Westerwood, on the Antonine Wall, shows that a centurion of the Sixth brought his wife and family with him from York.

One centurion had a particularly interesting career.[6] He lived for seventy years after forty-five years of service and married a very British sounding Lollia Bodicca. He had two sons, Flavius Victor and Flaviius Victorinus. His centurion posts included all three legions in Britain before he retired to North Africa. His memorial stone is dated to c. 222–35 placing his birth c. 152–165. A similarly long career was enjoyed by Petronius Fortunatus.[7] Rising up from the ranks he served in fourteen centurion posts including VI Victrix and was awarded various honours. He served fifty years and was aged eighty when the work was completed. His 'dearest wife', Claudia Marcia Capitolina' was aged sixty-five. The stone was to honour their son, Marcus, aged thirty-five, who had served six years as centurion, the last post being with II Augusta. Through his posts Tomlin calculates he was born c. mid-130s and joined up in the 150s retiring after c. 200. His son was born perhaps in the mid-170s, placing his death at the end of the reign of Severus.

An inscription at York has a legate called Claudius Hieronymianus dedicating a temple to the god Serapis and this might be the same Hieronymianus killed by Caracalla in 211–2:[8] 'To the holy god Serapis Claudius Hieronymianus, legate of the Sixth Legion Victrix, built this temple from the ground.' The youngest person for whom we have an inscription is a ten-month-old girl:[9] 'To the shades of the dead [and] of Simplicia Florentina, a most innocent soul, who lived ten months. Felicius Simplex her father made this, centurion of the Sixth Legion Victrix.' Another centurion of the Sixth, Aurelius Super, also from York, was remembered by his wife Aurelia Censorina, having died aged thirty-eight.[10]

The invasion of Caledonia 208–11

Cassius Dio gives us a detailed account of the campaign of Severus in northern Britain.[11] The reasons he gives are that the legions and his sons, Caracalla and Geta, were becoming idle. The emperor apparently believed he would not return on account of prophecies and his seers. We also get an interesting picture of early third century Britain from the Roman point of view. The two principal races are named: the Caledonians and the Maeatae. The account suggests other known tribes may have been merged into two 'confederations'. The Maeatae were located in central Scotland and the Caledonians are said to live 'beyond them'. Cassius stated the Romans held a little less than half the island and the Maeatae lived 'next to the cross-wall which cuts the island in half'. We can conclude at this point that he is referring to Hadrian's rather than the Antonine Wall.

The Britons inhabit 'wild and waterless mountains and desolate and swampy plains'. Cassius claims they had no cities or walls and did not even till their fields, but instead lived on 'flocks, wild game, and certain fruits'. According to the writer, the Britons lived in tents, 'naked and unshod' and 'possess' their women and children in common. They have a love of plunder and thus choose their 'boldest men' to lead them. They use chariots and 'small, swift horses'. The infantry were swift in running and 'very firm in standing their ground'.

Their principal weapons were shields, daggers and short spears. The latter has a 'bronze apple' at one end to bash against their shields to terrify their enemies. They had a reputation for enduring extremes of hunger and cold, although it's doubtful they could 'plunge into the swamps and exist there for many days with only their heads above water'. A certain food is described, only a small portion of which prevents hunger or thirst.

After a detailed description of Britain we are told Severus wished to 'subjugate the whole of it' and invaded Caledonia. As he advanced he found he could not force an open battle. Instead he 'experienced countless hardships in cutting down the forests, levelling the heights, filling up the swamps, and bridging the rivers.' The Britons confined themselves to guerrilla tactics, using sheep and cattle to lure them into ambushes. Lack of clean drinking water caused a major problem too.

The campaign must have been vicious as we are told that the Romans would rather kill their own wounded rather than leave them behind and 50,000 men perished in the war.

Severus reached the 'extremity of the island' although already sick enough at this point to be carried much of the way in a litter. The Britons were forced to come to terms and abandon a 'large part of their territory'. We learn the name of one chieftain of the Caledonians, Argentocoxus. During negotiations his wife was conversing with the empress Julia Augusta. The latter was jesting with the Briton about the free intercourse the women of Britain had with their men. Cassius seems rather impressed with the reply: 'We fulfil the demands of nature in a much better way than do you Roman women; for we consort openly with the best men, whereas you let yourselves be debauched in secret by the vilest.'

Whilst military affairs were eventually coming to a seemingly satisfactory conclusion domestically things were far from rosy. Caracalla, now twenty-two, caused his father 'alarm and endless anxiety by his intemperate life', not least because he wished to kill his own brother, the twenty-one-year-old Geta.

Worse was to follow. Caracalla had accompanied his father in the campaign north and on one occasion attempted to kill him. We are told they were riding forward to discuss terms with the Caledonians. Caracalla suddenly reined in his horse and 'drew his sword, as if he were going to strike his father in the back'. Others cried out in alarm, causing Caracalla to hesitate and re-sheath his sword, but not before the emperor turned in time to witness it.

One can only imagine what went through Caracalla's head as his father waited until the end of the day to summon him. The events as Cassius tells them are dramatic. He placed a sword within easy reach and then when his son arrived confronted him for not only daring such a 'monstrous crime' but for attempting it in front of army and the enemy.

> Now if you really want to slay me, put me out of the way here; for you are strong, while I am an old man and prostrate. For, if you do not shrink from the deed, but hesitate to murder me with your own hands, there is Papinian, the prefect, standing beside you, whom you can order to slay me; for surely he will do anything that you command, since you are virtually emperor.

Cassius laments that Severus had often criticised Marcus Aurelius for not dealing with his own son, Commodus, and had always promised he would have killed him if in the same position. But his love for his son betrayed him and condemned Geta for Severus knew full well what would happen when he was gone.

But events quickly intervened as once again the Maeatae rebelled. The emperor's response was decisive and ruthless as his orders demonstrate: 'Let no one escape sheer destruction … not even the babe in the womb of the mother, if it be male; let it nevertheless not escape sheer destruction.' The Caledonians joined the revolt and preparations were made for another war. This must have been in early 211 as we are told Severus fell ill on 4 February 211 and died in the city of York. Cassius reports the words he spoke to his sons on his death bed: 'Be harmonious, enrich the soldiers, and scorn all other men.'

Herodian adds important evidence while confirming much of what Cassius Dio said.[12] Whilst his sons were causing Severus much distress a message arrived form the governor of Britain: the barbarians were in revolt and 'overrunning the country, looting and destroying virtually everything on the island'. Severus, we are told, was delighted with the news: 'glory-loving by nature', he also wished to remove his sons from the pleasures of Rome and teach them a bit of military discipline. Despite his age and being 'crippled with arthritis', the emperor prepared the expedition to Britain, and 'in his heart he was more enthusiastic than any youth'. The Britons immediately sued for peace but Severus, eager for a victory and to avoid a quick return to Rome, dismissed them.

Like Cassius, Herodian describes the Britons as 'savage and warlike' and 'strangers to clothing', wearing 'ornaments of iron' around their waists and necks. Their bodies were tattooed with coloured designs and picture of animals. The land is described as marshy and flooded with the barbarians accustomed to swimming or wading through, carrying a spear and narrow shield but also a sword suspended from a belt hanging 'from their otherwise naked bodies'. Herodian pointedly says that they wore no helmets or breastplates which must have put them at a disadvantage in combat against the heavily-armed legionaries. The Romans won 'frequent battles and skirmishes', but the Britons slipped away easily using their knowledge of the woods and marshes.

Geta had been left at York whilst Caracalla was at one point placed in control of the army while his father was ill. He tried to persuade the soldiers to look to him as sole leader and even attempted to bribe the doctors to poison his father. Herodian adds grief to the cause of the emperor's death: he left 'an invincible army and more money than any emperor had ever left to his successors.'

The *Historia Augusta* erroneously states he built a wall across the island of Britain 'from sea to sea', but this likely means he simply rebuilt certain sections. The title Britannicus is said to have been 'the crowning glory of his reign'. After his death at York the *Historia Augusta* tells us his body was brought from Britain to Rome whilst 'some men say that only a golden urn containing Severus' ashes was so conveyed'. Whatever the case, whether cremated in Britain or Rome, his ashes were laid in the tomb of the Antonines.

A number of inscriptions suggest elements of the Sixth took part in the campaign whilst others remained at Corbridge and York. Stamped tiles found at Carpow in Scotland read 'victrix Britannica pia fidelis'.[13] A legate of the Sixth, Lucius Junius Victorinus Flavius Caelianus, has a dedication for 'successes beyond the wall' which could be dated to Antonine or early Severan period.[14] Another find at Corbridge is undated: 'To eternal Jupiter of Doliche and to Caelestis Brigantia and to Salus Gaius Julius Apolinaris, centurion of the Sixth Legion, at the command of the god (set this up).'[15]

An inscription found at Corbridge is dated to the reign of Caracalla. 'To Jupiter Dolichenus Best and Greatest, for the welfare of the detachments of the Sixth Legion Victrix and of the army of each Germany under the charge of Marcus Lollius Venator, centurion of the Second Legion Augusta. They paid their vow willingly, deservedly'.[16] It is to Caracalla's reign that we will turn to next. As bloody and vengeful as his father could be, Caracalla was able to surpass him in wanton cruelty. This turning point in Rome's history began at the home of the Sixth Legion as the emperor lay dead in the first days of February in 211.

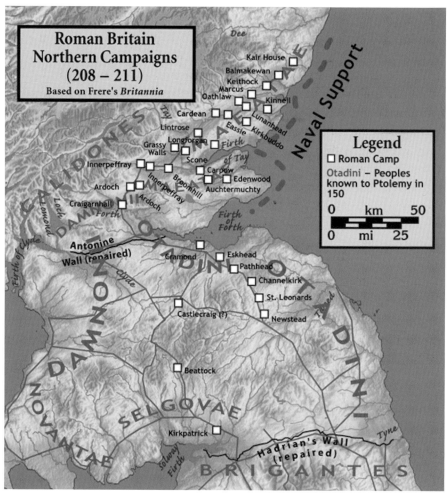

Figure 32: Map of northern campaign of Septimius Severus c. 208–11. (*Wikimedia Commons*)

The reign of Caracalla

Herodian records the immediate events before they returned to Gaul.[17] We can thus assume these occurred at York. Caracalla seized control and began a spree of murders: the physicians who had refused to poison his father; those who had raised both his brother and himself because they urged him to live in peace with Geta; and all those who attended his father 'or were held in esteem by him'. He tried to bribe the army commanders and we can assume the legates of the Sixth were among them. It would seem this all happened with the campaigning army still in the north as, when the army refused to back him against his brother, and his father's wishes, he immediately signed a treaty with the Britons and headed south to his mother and brother. Cassius tells us he 'withdrew from their territory, and abandoned the forts' which suggests a withdrawal back to Hadrian's Wall. At this point he agreed to live with Geta 'in peace and friendship' although Herodian doubts his sincerity.

The new co-emperors left Britain 'with the army' and returned to Rome with their father's remains. The Sixth, however, remained at York. Much to the consternation of their mother they each 'took up residence in his half of the palace. Barricading the inner doors, they used in common only the public outer doors'. An uneasy cold-war-type situation prevailed with Caracalla and Geta stationing their own private guards and avoiding each other. An agreement was reached to divide the empire. But the enmity grew and both plotted to poison the other. In the end it was Caracalla who proved successful. In a rare private meeting in front of their mother Caracalla stabbed his brother and rushed to the Praetorian camp claiming he was the intended victim. Cassius gives further details of the murder:[18] Caracalla tricked his mother into summoning them both to her apartment, unattended by guards. But Caracalla had some centurions standing by to rush in and attack. Geta was hacked down and his mother wounded her hand as she tried to protect him when he 'clung to her bosom and breasts'. Caracalla would not even allow her to mourn or weep for her son, even in private.

The praetorians, given only one side of the story, plus an offer of 2,500 denarii and increased rations, proclaimed Caracalla emperor and declared Geta a public enemy. Another murder spree ensued: Geta's friends and supporters, all those living in his half of the palace, his attendants. No one was spared, not even the infants. Even mere acquaintances were butchered: athletes, charioteers, singers and dancers of every type were killed. Senators, too, were killed, even if the charges were unsupported and the accusers unidentified. Their bodies were unceremoniously dragged out of the city in carts and piled up, burned or simply thrown in the ditch. Even Cornifica was executed, the now elderly daughter of Marcus Aurelius, merely for weeping at Geta's funeral. The sons of Pertinax and Lucilla, Commodus's sister, even Caracalla's own wife Plautilla and 'anyone who belonged to the imperial family and any senator of distinguished ancestry, all were cut down to the last one'. The killing did not end there as governors and procurators friendly to Geta were executed. Vestal Virgins were burnt alive and people from every walk of life were killed.

The *Historia Augusta* gives the same murderous narrative as does Cassius Dio, who gives an estimate of the number killed: 'Of the imperial freedmen and soldiers who had been with Geta, he immediately put to death some twenty thousand, men and women alike, wherever in the palace any of them happened to be; and he slew various distinguished men also.' With the throne now secured and the murderous Caracalla on the rampage it is unlikely Britain was untouched. It is possible that the division of Britain into two provinces came about to prevent a similar situation as occurred under Albinus: a powerful province with three legions and twice as many auxiliary troops was too dangerous to leave in one piece.

The first division of Britain

Cassius Dio, writing after the event, describes Lower Britain, in the north, as possessing one legion, the Sixth. Upper Britain, in the south and west, were home to the Second Augusta at Caerleon and the Twentieth Valeria Victrix

Figure 33: Map of Roman Provinces of Britannia from c. 212.

at Chester. A similar change occurred in Pannonia, dividing it into Upper and Lower Pannonia between 212 and 217. Birley suggests 214 is a likely date for the division as we have epigraphical evidence for a governor of northern Britain by 216, so it was certainly completed by then.[19] Both provinces would still have had senatorial governors with the distinction of the northern province having a propraetorian governor whilst Britannia Superior had a consular governor.

The reference in Herodian placing the division under Severus is thus thought to have been a mistake – perhaps for the division of Syria at that time. Three attested governors under Severus are recorded as being governors of a single province of Britannia and not of Upper or Lower Britannia. Additionally, an equestrian procurator dated to 208–11 is recorded as a procurator of Britain rather than of Upper or Lower or 'of the Britains'. In addition, Herodian himself refers to a single governor and single province of Britain leading up to the northern campaign of 208–11. Leaving the exact date of this division to one side, we do have a reasonable idea as to where the dividing line was. Chester was in the southern province and the border east towards the Humber looped south to place Lincoln in the northern province.

Three inscriptions survive from this time: the first details the construction of a bathhouse and water supply at Chester-le-Street; the second, from High Rochester, details a cohort of Vardulli, 'Roman Citizens, part mounted, one thousand strong'; and the third is dedicated to the 'welfare and victory' of the emperor, but also 'Julia Augusta mother of our Lord and of the camps' of the legate. An undated tombstone at York suggests a family tragedy for a veteran of the Sixth: '

To the spirits of the departed (and) of Flavia Augustina; she lived 39 years, 7 months, 11 days; her son, Saenius Augustinus, lived 1 year, 3 days, and […], (her daughter), lived 1 year 9 months, 5 days; Gaius Aeresius Saenus, veteran of the Sixth Legion Victrix, had this set up for his beloved wife and himself.[20]

Life expectancy was relatively low, although the high infant mortality skewed the figures considerably. For men it was twenty-two and women twenty.[21] One in three died before their third birthday and only half reached the age of eight. If you were lucky enough to be born into the senatorial class, your chances of reaching old age were considerably higher with an average life expectancy of thirty. Soldiers fared surprisingly well with 78 per cent of twenty-year-old recruits surviving to their mid-thirties, and 60 per cent reaching their mid-forties. Disease and poor nutrition were greater dangers than enemy action. Roughly two thirds of recruits might survive a twenty-five year career to reach retirement. Just as dangerous were the battles women fought. The average Roman woman bore six children in her lifetime.[22] Haemorrhaging and sepsis contributed to 2.5 per cent of women dying in childbirth. A fifth of pregnancies resulted in stillbirths and miscarriages. A woman experiencing two such tragedies followed by two of her children dying before their eighth birthday was norm rather than the exception; if she was lucky two more survived to adulthood. When Marcus Aurelius married Faustina, daughter of Emperor Antoninus, there was a 25 per cent chance that one or both would be dead within five years.[23]

The new men of the Sixth, and their wives and children living around York, may have had little interest in the changing provincial structure or who was emperor in Rome, over 1,000 miles away by sea and road. Lower Britain continued to be governed by senatorial legates until c. 260 when Emperor Gallienus began to appoint equestrian prefects to command legions and later governors with the title *praeses*.[24] Below we can see a list of governors of Britannia Inferior after the first division. As governors they would also have probably been based at York and commanded the Sixth Legion.

216	Marcus Antonius Gordianus Sempronianus Romanus
219	Modius Julius
220	Tiberius Claudius Paulinus
221–2	Marius Valerianus
223	Claudius Xenophon
225	Maximus
226–34	Valerius Crescens Fulvianus and Calvisius
237	Tuccianus
238–44	Maecilius Fuscus, Egnatius Lucilianus, Nonius Philippus

We have some information concerning one of these men, Tiberius Claudius Paulinus, propraetorian legate of the Sixth c. 219–22.[25] He had also been legate of II Augusta and so we see here a promotion from legate to governor. A letter survives from Paulinus to a certain Sennius Solemnis.[26] He sends him a number of gifts, including a 'British rug' and the promise of a tribunate lasting six months, presumably in the Sixth, along with the salary of 25,000 sesterces. Caracalla had doubled legionary pay to 2,500 so this was a considerable amount for a short-term post, which perhaps demonstrates how mentors could use state funds to reward loyalty.

Around the same time at York an equestrian and ex-praefectus of the Sixth, Antonius Gargilianus, died aged fifty-six. His son-in-law and town council dedicated a memorial stone to his father-in-law.[27] A tombstone found near Chalons in Gaul is dedicated to Vegetinia Romana, wife of Memmius

Rusticus, a soldier of the Sixth Legion Victrix Antoniniana, 'an innocent wife when she died in a foreign place'. Tomlin dates this to c. 211–22 and suggests Rusticus was on the road to a different post in Rome. We see here an example of how soldiers could be posted across the empire, something we will see in our case study just below. Meanwhile the city of York, a *municipium* when Severus died in 211, became a *colonia* in the early third century.[28]

Case study: Lucius Artorius Castus

A funerary inscription from Epetium, near Salona (Dalmatia), in modern Croatia, preserves the military career of a Roman equestrian. Lucius Artorius Castus served in a number of posts across the empire in the second to third centuries. One of his posts was as *praefectus castrorum* of the Sixth Legion at York. There is some debate about the date of the stone and interpretation of the inscription. Two stones were found, the first a sarcophagus inscription broken into two pieces and found set in the wall of a churchyard. The second was a memorial plaque, also broken, found nearby.

Some of the letters are ligatured, i.e. two or more letters are joined together. This is similar to 'AE' when written as 'Æ' in the Anglo-Saxon name Æthelberht. To represent this, the relevant letters are underlined. The figure '7' indicates the post of centurion. The dots indicate where the text has been lost to damage. It must also be remembered abbreviations were common in inscriptions, such as leg for legionis, or P P for primus pilus.

```
    L ARTORI..........................................STVS 7 LEG
        III GALLICAE ITEM .......................G VI FERRA
    TAE ITEM 7 LEG II AD I............TEM 7 LEG V M
    C ITEM P P EIVSDEM ................. PRAEPOSITO
    CLASSIS MISENATIVM ................AEFF LEG VI
    VICTRICIS DVCI LEGG ............M BRITANICI
        MIARVM AD VERSVS ARM....S PROC CENTE
    NARIO PROVINCIAE LI................... GL AD I VI
    VVS IPSE SIBI ET SVIS ....................ST..........
```

The second inscription is as follows:

```
            L * ARTORIVS
            CASTVS * P * P
            LEG * VMAC * PR
            AEFEC..VS * LE..
            VI * VICTRIC *
```

Filling in the damaged section might reveal the following (missing letters and expanded abbreviations in brackets):[29]

L(ucius) Artori[us Ca]stus centurioni leg(ionis)
III Gallicae item [centurioni le]g(ionis) VI Ferra-
-tae item centurioni leg(ionis) II Adi[ut(ricis) (P{iae} F{idelis}) i]tem
centurioni leg(ionis) V M[a]-
-c(edonicae) item p(rimo) p(ilo) eiusdem [leg(ionis)] praeposito
classis Misenatium [pr]aef{f}(ecto) leg(ionis) VI
Victricis duci legg(ionum) [triu]m Britan(n)ici-
-{an}arum adversus Arm[enio]s proc(uratori) cente-
-nario provinciae Li[burniae iure] gladi(i) vi-
-vus ipse sibi et suis [... ex te]st[amento]

One possible translation of the sarcophagus is as follows:[30]

To the divine shades, Lucius Artorius Castus, centurion of the Third Legion Gallica, also centurion of the Sixth Legion Ferrata, also centurion of the Second Legion Adiutrix, also centurion of the Fifth Legion Macedonica, also chief centurion of the same legion, in charge of (Praepositus) the Misenum fleet, prefect of the Sixth Legion Victrix, commander of three British legions against the Armenians, centenary procurator of Liburnia with the power of the sword. He himself (set this up) for himself and his family in his lifetime.

Proposed translation of the second inscription (and expansion) is as follows:

Lucius Artorius Castus
Primus Pilus legionis V Macedonia
Praefectus legionis VI Victrix

I covered the debate and various options concerning interpretation in my previous book, *The Roman King Arthur? Lucius Artorius Castus*. I will discuss this unlikely theory briefly at the end of this case study. The debate around interpretation can be summarised as follows: the style of the stone suggests an Antonine period (c. 160–193) whilst the wording suggests a possible Severan period (c. 193–235). One of our best clues is the phrase *adversus Arm-*. A campaign against internal enemies was referred to as against rebels or public enemies (e.g. *adversus rebelles hostes publicos*) in both literary and epigraphical sources. One against an external enemy would normally name the nation or tribe, such as Parthia or the Marcomanni.

This led some initially to read it as *armoricanos*, meaning Armorica or modern Brittany. However, not only is there no record of significant unrest we don't have a record of this regional name (or derivatives such as *armoricani* or *amorici*) in this period. Additionally, the gap is not big enough to allow the word. The only other enemy that starts with arm- is Armenia and we do indeed have three examples of wars in Armenia, albeit part of a wider Parthian War: in c. 163 under Marcus Aurelius and Lucius Verus, 215 under Caracalla and 233 and Severus Alexander. In support of this, the earliest reading of the stone by the Croatian archaeologist Francesco Carrara in 1850 is as ADVERSUS ARME- with a ligatured ME. The stone is now weathered and by the early twentieth century the E was gone and the ligature disputed.

The proponents of a link with King Arthur suggest therefore that *Armatos*, 'armed men', is the correct reading. However, there is no example of such a phrase being used on a similar inscription. Its presence in literary sources and on one inscribed law code (one of twelve bronze tablets, the *Lex Ursonensis* is the founding text of the colonia Iulia Genetiva, modern Urso near Osuna, province of Seville) is not strong evidence since it is a common Latin word.

There is thus a consensus amongst historians that Armenia is the correct interpretation unless we find an alternative tribal name beginning with arm-. A debate about the date however continues, with Tomlin[31] and Higham[32] favouring the Armenia campaign of c. 163 and Davenport,[33] Loriot,[34] and Birley[35] suggesting an early third-century date and thus one of the two later Armenian wars.

Perhaps significantly the word castrorum began to be dropped from inscriptions in the late second century, the last example being from 202. The double FF on the main inscription, for praefectus legio VI, is thought to be a stone cutter's mistake; however, it could indicate multiple camp prefects or camps. The words *dux* and *praepositus* were descriptors meaning 'commander' and did not evolve into official titles until the third century. However, whilst Severus preferred to maintain the traditional precedence of senators over equestrians, Caracalla often appointed ad hoc positions such as his freedman Theocritus leading an army to defeat in Armenia. We also have a Roman *dux* in Armenia a year after the death of Caracalla. In the reign of Macrinus, 217–18, the *Historia Augusta* states there was a 'dux Armeniae erat et item legatus Asiae atque Arabiae'.

All this led me to suggest a rival theory to the leading contender proposed by Higham. Instead of Castus leading detachments with Priscus during the Armenian campaign of 163, I put forward the following possible time line. Having served under Severus as a legionary he was promoted to the eastern legions after the defeat of Niger in 194. He later returned to the Danubian legions and rose to primus pilus with V Macedonia. This was possibly after the climactic battle of Lugdunum against Clodius Albinus. Coincidently, the Sixth, or detachments thereof, also likely took part in the fighting although on the opposite side to Legio V Macedonia. If his four posts as centurion lasted about twelve years his following two posts might take him up to c. 208. This would place him, as a praefectus castrorum of the Sixth, at York as Septimius Severus arrived and prepared for his campaign against the Maeatae and Caledonians, a campaign which involved numerous camps and multiple camp prefects.

The sudden death of Severus at York in 211, the hasty peace treaty with the northern tribes by Caracalla and the uncertainty of the short joint reign with Geta would have left a large number of troops in northern Britain. Perhaps here we have an explanation for the suggested interpretation of the inscription, 'Commander of legions from Britain'. The absence of the letters vex (vexillations, meaning part of) does not mean it was all three of the legions stationed in Britain in their entirety. Thus, it could mean detachments which would likely include the Sixth, especially as he was camp prefect. However, if it was the Armenian campaign of 215 it is quite possible Caracalla would have chosen an officer he probably got to know in Britain a few years earlier. Severus had taken a huge army to Britain in 208. If some of these troops had remained, with the province pacified, the troops could be withdrawn to the east.

With Castus we get a good example of a military career spanning several decades and the entire length of the empire from east to west. If he started life as a legionary at eighteen then he probably obtained his promotion to centurion around thirty. To achieve primus pilus he must have been a competent and battle-hardened soldier. By his posting to Britain he was likely over fifty years of age and it is possible he did not see active fighting. He may have spent the entire time at York or Corbridge, or any one of the forts or camps in the north. But if he did take part in the northern campaign of Severus then he would have seen a vicious war of extermination and overseen camps and forts built into the heart of the northern tribes. His last posting across the rugged hills of Armenia would have gained him a well-earned retirement as an equestrian procurator on the Dalmatian coast, in the great scheme of things a relatively minor position. However, if he started life as a plebeian then this would have been a remarkable achievement.

What then of the alleged links to King Arthur? I have covered this in great depth in my previous book, *The Roman King Arthur? Lucius Artorius Castus*, which focuses on the theory behind the 2004 film *King Arthur*, starring Clive

Post and rank	Details
Centurion Legion III Gallica	For most of the second and third centuries this was stationed in Syria.
Centurion Legion VI Ferrata	From middle of second century to early third, this was stationed in Judea.
Centurion Legion II Adiutrix	From early second century based at Aquincum (Budapest). Took part in campaigns against the Marcomanni and Quadi (north of the Danube) in the second century. Also the Parthians, and, in the third century, the Sassanids.
Centurion and Primus Pilus of Legion V Macedonia	Based in Dacia in second and most of the third century. Took part in campaigns against the Marcomanni, Sarmatians and Quadi (north of the Danube) in the second century. The rank of Primus Pilus was generally given to career soldiers of 45–50 years of age.
Praepositus of the Misenum fleet	Based at Misenum in Italy but with units posted at various locations.
Praefectus of Legion VI Victrix	Based at York in Britain from the early second century. A Praefectus Legionis was third in command and usually an experienced soldier of 50–60 years old.
Dux of the British legions	Dux was a temporary command of either a collection of troops or entire units or legions.
Procurator of Liburnia	Talented equestrian prefects sometimes obtained high civilian rank on retirement.

Table 11: The military career of Lucius Artorius Castus.

Owen and Keira Knightley. Various theories can be summarised as follows: Lucius Artorius Castus served in Britain alongside Sarmatian soldiers who carried with them tales which included concepts similar to some Arthurian themes. These tales, alongside battles fought by Artorius Castus, were remembered down the centuries and appeared much later.

The first problem with this is that we don't know how many Sarmatians, if any, arrived and what they did when they got to Britain. Even if Artorius was present at the same time we have no evidence that he met a single Sarmatian or fought a single battle in Britain. There is also no evidence of anything remotely Arthurian throughout the Roman period up to when Arthur is traditionally dated. Nor is there any hint from the later Arthurian tales which emerged in the middle ages of any concepts that are remotely Roman in nature.

Instead, every source that mentions Arthur places him in the same time frame c. 450–550. The *Annales Cambriae* and Geoffrey of Monmouth's *Historia Regum Britannia* place him in the early sixth century, dying at Camalnn in either 537 or 542. The earliest reference, the ninth-century *Historia Brittonum*,

KEY

1. Centurion of legion III Gallica, Syria
2. Centurion of legion VI Ferrata, Judea
3. Centurion of legion II Adiutrix, Pannonia
4. Centurion of legion V Macedonia, Dacia
5. Prima Pilus of legion V Macedonia, Dacia
6. Provost of the fleet of Misenum, Italy
7. Camp Prefect of legion VI Victrix, York, Britain
8. Dux of 'British legions'
9. Procurator of the Province of Liburnia, Dalmatia

Figure 34: Map of the career of Lucius Artorius Castus.

places him between the death of Saint Patrick and Hengest and the reign of Ida in Bernicia (c. 547), which could be as early as 450s or date from late 480s. None of the later French Romances or Welsh tales suggest anything other than this time frame.

It is also alleged Sarmatian traditions are similar to some Arthurian themes. However, a careful analysis of the nineteenth-century *Nart Sagas*, which themselves can't be linked to Sarmatians of the second century anyway, show no similarity with Arthurian tales. Let us not forget that those twelfth Arthurian tales were written 700 years after our hero is alleged to have lived. Even if one similarity presented itself, there's no way of knowing if the Arthurian legend travelled east and was copied into the nineteenth-century *Narts*. In summary, I found the so called 'Sarmatian connection' and Artorius-as-Arthur theory to be a modern myth, originating in the twentieth century.

We can, therefore, put this theory aside and concentrate on the real historical figure of Lucius Artorius Castus, a battle-hardened Roman soldier who served in the late second to early third century. Serving in the east and on the Danube, he achieved what for many would have been the pinnacle of a military career, that of praefectus castrorum of the Sixth Legion at York. However, he was chosen to take part in one last campaign, back to the east and the mountains of Armenia. Clearly, he survived and was able to retire as an equestrian procurator on the beautiful Dalmatian coast. We will finish this case study with figure 35 which shows the career path of Lucius Artorius Castus within the wider context of the tres militiae and cursus honorum. Pertinax, we recall, moved along the tres militiae before rising to senatorial rank and ultimately the highest office of all. The majority of the members of the Sixth lived and died as legionaries depicted at the bottom of the figure.

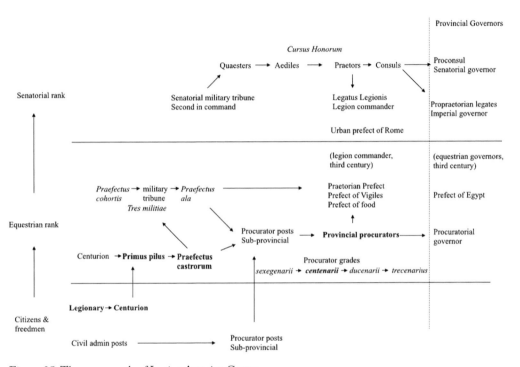

Figure 35: The career path of Lucius Artorius Castus.

Chapter 6

The Third Century, Crisis and Renewal

After the death of his father, Caracalla made peace with the barbarians, abandoned the forts north of the Antonine Wall and withdrew the troops. Treaties often entailed the provision of auxiliary troops for the Roman army. Evidence suggests that these may have been present on the German frontier as early as the following year. Inscriptions with the words 'Bittones dediticii' and 'Bittones gentiles' are found at Walldurn fort dated to c. 213.[1] Another inscription in Germania Superior dated to c. 232 suggests a Caledonian chieftain, Lossio Veda, may have been conscripted under Severus or Caracalla and was still serving twenty years later under Severus Alexander.[2]

We recall that Severus ordered the tribes to be exterminated. If this was only partially carried out and Caracalla conscripted large numbers of the survivors then the region may have been pacified for a generation or more. In fact evidence suggests the peace lasted for eight decades.[3] His greatest achievement was the *Consititutio Antoniniana*, or Edict of Caracalla, of 212 which declared that all free men in the Roman Empire would receive full Roman citizenship. Rather than a yearning for freedom or universal suffrage, in reality this was more of a tax-raising measure.[4] It did, however, promote a shared sense of *Romanitus*. As custom dictated, new citizens took their patrons' names, making Aurelian hugely common across the empire. Society was still heavily stratified between *honestiores* and *humiloiores*, high and low ranks respectively. The former, senators, equestrians and decurions for example, could not be tortured, beheaded or crucified. These reforms were to survive Caracalla.

Caracalla met his death on the side of the road from Edessa. In a scene reminiscent of the murder of Commodus, the praetorian prefect Macrinus, read correspondence that led him to believe he was next on the emperor's list to be executed. Accompanying the emperor, Macrinus had to act quickly before he arrived at the end of the road, both literally and metaphorically. As the emperor stopped to relieve himself, Macrinus instructed a centurion Martialis to do the deed and the murderous Caracalla met what many thought was a fitting end, stabbed to death with his pants down.

After Macrinus, who was killed the following year, the Severans were to last another eighteen years, but successive emperors died at the hands of their own troops. This led into a period known as the 'Crisis of the Third Century', generally dated c. 235–284. A time plagued by civil wars and political instability. Of the next eighteen emperors, not one was to die peacefully in bed, and only one had a cause of death other than murder or battle. One of the last was Valerian whose grisly end is worth noting. It indicates the weakening of Roman power and the rise of the Sassanid Empire. The emperor himself was taken prisoner by Shapur I of Persia at the end of a disastrous campaign into Mesopotamia. One story has him being kept in slavery for many years and used as a footstool for the Persian king to mount his horse. When he offered Shapur a huge ransom he was forced to swallow molten gold. In an even worse version he was flayed alive, his skin stuffed with straw and then kept on show, 'preserved for ages in the most celebrated temple in Persia'.[5]

Emperor	Date	Comments
Macrinus	217–18	Both executed after rebellion of Elagablus
Diadumenian	218	
Elagabalus	218–22	Assassinated by Praetorian Guard
Severus Alexander	222–35	Assassinated by troops
Maximinus Thrax	235– June 238	Assassinated by troops
Gordian I Gordian II	March-April 238	Committed suicide after loss of battle Died in battle against forces of Maximinus
Maximus and Balbinus	April-July 238	Killed by Praetorian Guard
Gordian III	238–44	Thought to have been assassinated on eastern campaign.
Philip	244–9	Died in battle of Verona against his successor
Decius	249–51	Killed at battle of Abritus against Goths
Aemilian	253	Assassinated by troops
Valerian	253–60	Defeated by Persians, died in captivity
Gallienus	253–68	Assassinated by troops. Son of Valerian.
Claudius Gothicus	268–70	Declared emperor by army of Gallienus. Died from plague.
Quintillus	270	Brother of Claudius Gothicus. Committed suicide when army supported Aurelian
Aurelian	270–5	Re-unified and stabilised empire. Murdered by Praetorian Guard.

Table 12: Emperors of the third century.

The Roman world descended into decades of instability which lasted, arguably, until Aurelian re-unified the empire. One notable change was that social position became less important. Instead military professionalism and performance on the field became the arbiters of who ruled. Equestrians began to emerge as more powerful than senators. Macrinus was the harbinger of things to come as the first equestrian emperor. The Praetorian Guard, instrumental in the death of Pertinax in 193, now made emperor killing a common occurrence. The Emperor Gallienus, 253–68, started to appoint equestrians as legionary commanders and provincial governors. These last were titled *praeses* with legion commanders called *praefectus legionis*.

Throughout this period we hear little from Britain and next to nothing about the Sixth. Up to the time of Caracalla only Roman citizens could join the legions. Only auxiliary units were open to Britons. With the Edict of Caracalla, citizenship was widespread and it is likely the legions of Britain began to recruit locally as well. York had grown into a bustling town and generations of soldiers had no doubt married and settled down, gaining citizenship for their sons. The families of retired auxiliary troops had also been eligible for citizenship. It is thus likely the Sixth Legion was already comprised of an ethnically diverse group from across the empire.

The Gallic Empire

One of the effects of all this upheaval was the fragmentation of the empire. In the east, following the death of Valerian in 260, the Palmyrene Empire consisted of Egypt, Syria and Arabia and Palestine. In the west, Postumus was chosen by the army on the Rhine. All of Gaul, Spain, Britain and two German provinces declared for this new western emperor. Gallienus was unable to wrest control back and we have little evidence from Britain. No doubt the civil and military administrations carried on as before. In 269 Postumus was able to put down a rebellion by a Laelianus. During a second rebellion, Postumus forbade his soldiers to sack Mainz and for this he was killed. The new Gallic emperor, Marius, lasted a few months, and was replaced by Victorinus in 269. By then Gallienus had been killed by his troops and the new emperor, Claudius Gothicus, sent an army against Victorinus. This failed but the Gallic emperor was assassinated, reportedly by one of his officers, a jealous husband, whose wife Victorinus had seduced. The last ruler of this breakaway empire was Esuvius Tetricus. Aurelian came to power in 270 and recovered the Palmyrene Empire in 272–3. A year later the Gallic Empire was similarly brought back under control after the battle of Châlons. Tetricus switched sides, either just before or during the battle. Aurelian allowed him not only to live but gave him a high-ranking position. He was awarded the title *Restitutor Orbis*, 'Restorer of the World', and so it may have seemed to many who had lived through such turbulent times. Given his lenient treatment of Tetricus, it is likely he left much of the governmental and military apparatus of Britain alone.

Emperor	Date	Comments
Postumus	260–8	Established after death of Valerian in response to barbarian invasions and instability in Rome. Initially included Britain, Spain and Gaul. Killed by own troops.
Marius	268	Reigned a couple of months. Killed by troops.
Victorinus	269–71	Killed by one of his officers
Tetricus	271–4	Defeated at battle of Châlons and surrendered to Aurelian.

Table 13: Emperors of the Gallic Empire.

We get little information concerning the Gallic Empire in Britain. A praeses Octavius Sabinus is recorded at Lancaster and may be dated to this period. A new *civitas Carvetiorum* is recorded at Carlisle from c. 260. It is thought some of the forts later attributed to the Saxon Shore command, such as Reculver and Brancaster, were constructed in the mid-third century.[6] British towns started to build defences, including stone walls in this period. This may be in response to Frankish and Saxon raids which appeared c. 250.

After the death of Aurelian, predictably killed by his own troops, two emperors, Tacitus and Florian, followed his demise within a year. Their successor, Probus, managed to last six years before he, too, was murdered. One relevant point during his reign is a report that he posted captured Burgundians and Vandals to Britain, 276–82: 'Living in the island they were useful to the Emperor when someone rebelled'.[7] Three emperors followed in quick succession: Carus, 282–3, Probus's praetorian prefect, and his two sons Carinus, 283–5 and Numerian, 283–4. All three met untimely deaths and another praetorian prefect, Aper, was linked to at least two of them. Carinus adopted the title *Britannicus Maximus* in 284, suggesting a successful campaign, although the details are lost. Together with the reference concerning Probus's Burgundians and Vandals, we can speculate that the long peace imposed by Severus and Caracalla decades before was under pressure towards the end of the third century.

Diocletian is the emperor often credited with ending 'The Crisis of the Third Century'. His reforms were certainly substantial and far-reaching. However, a witness at the beginning of his reign, 284, might be forgiven in thinking the future held more of the same. Once more a breakaway north-western empire emerged. Once more Britain was involved. Within two years of Diocletian claiming power a new usurper seized control in Britain and northern Gaul.

Carausius and Alectus

As Diocletian consolidated power he named Maximian Caesar. Maximian was soon declared Augustus and co-emperor. Events in Gaul required immediate action as rebels and deserters known as *Bagaudae* started to plague the countryside. Some were probably fleeing from raiders and invading barbarians. Others, however, were rebelling against punitive tax collectors. Maximian put down these rebellions and responded to raids by Alemanni and Burgundians in the Upper Rhine area. One of his decisions was to appoint a certain Carausius to command the channel fleet.

Carausius was born in Menapia, modern Belgium. He had humble origins and was a helmsman in his youth. The sources acknowledge his military skills, but refer to him as 'nothing but a barbarian'.[8] He was appointed to command the fleet based at Gesoriacum, Boulogne, and successfully cleared the area of Frankish pirates. However, he came under suspicion of corruption. The sources are instructive here:[9] not only was he keeping the booty for himself, but he was alleged to have allowed the barbarians passage to raid so that he could intercept them and keep the goods for himself.

Maximian prepared orders for his arrest and potential execution. Carausius, however, found out and proclaimed himself Augustus before moving the entire fleet to Britain in late 286. Maximian's initial attempts to end this new breakaway regime failed and an attempted invasion c. 289–90 was abandoned. Reluctantly, the two emperors had to accept the situation for a time.

In Britain Carausius tried to ingratiate himself with Diocletian and Maximian. He took their names, Aurelius and Valerius, and issued coins with the inscription 'Carausius and his brothers'. But this merely delayed the response. In 293 Diocletian founded the Tetrarchy. Each Augustus now had a Caesar with Maximian and Constantius I in the west and Galerius Caesar with Diocletian in the east. It was Constantius, Caesar of the west, who was tasked with destroying Carausius in Britain. He expanded the fleet and positioned small naval units around the coast to drive those of Carausius out to sea. He then blockaded Gesoriacum. Once this fell, Frankish allies were driven from the coastal area and shipping to and from Britain disrupted severely.

Carausius was now confined to the island of Britain and it is perhaps because of the loss of territory in Gaul that he was murdered by Allectus who assumed the title of Emperor in 293. He was to last just three years. Allectus was once thought to have been the treasurer of Carausius but more recent analysis suggests he was more likely his praetorian prefect or some other senior military figure.[10] Many of the Saxon Shore forts are thought to pre-date Carausius but there is clear evidence from coin deposits that they were extensively garrisoned during his rule. Whilst some date it to Probus, Pevensey seems to have been built under Allectus.[11]

Constantius prepared an invasion across the channel from Boulogne and Allectus positioned his army accordingly. However, another fleet led by the praetorian prefect Asclepiodotus from the mouth of the Seine landed near Southampton Water. A thick mist is recorded as having hidden their movements from the British fleet stationed ready to ambush off the Isle of Wight.[12] In, perhaps, a dramatic show of intent, when he landed he burned his boats and marched inland. Allectus withdrew from the coast where he was expecting Constantius and marched inland to head off Asclepiodotus. The sources claim he 'did not even form a battle-line or draw up all the forces he was leading, but, forgetting all his great preparations, charged headlong with the old ringleaders of that conspiracy and the units of barbarian mercenaries'.[13]

There is no mention of which British legions were present but we get a hint that Allectus relied heavily on 'barbarian mercenaries', most notably Franks. Allectus was defeated somewhere between the south-east coast and Hampshire, possibly near Silchester. Meanwhile, Constantius landed in the east and at some point met and destroyed Frankish mercenaries who had fled the battle against Asclepiodotus. Constantius marched into London, to be hailed as 'liberator' and the 'true light of the empire'.

By 301 all four tetrarchs had taken the title *Britannicus Maximus* and coins appear commemorating Constantius as 'restorer of the eternal light'. The western Caesar is seen mounted with a kneeling supplicant arms raised in welcome. Behind are the gates of a city with the letters LON below. Britain was now back in the empire and the Sixth were to play a significant role in its future.

Diocletian to Constantine

Diocletian now began various reforms, many of which were built on by Constantine. The first was to directly impact Constantine's rise to power. The establishment of the tetrarchy was intended to ensure the smooth transition of power and stabilise the empire. Diocletian, Augustus in the east, was assisted by his Caesar, Galerius. In the west, the Augustus Maximian was assisted by Constantius. All four men were Illyrians and they were bound together by marriage ties, with each Caesar marrying a daughter or step-daughter of their respective Augustus. However, in order to do so Constantius had to divorce his wife Helena, with whom he had a son, Constantine.

The numbers of legions were increased, almost doubled, but their size reduced drastically from over 5,000 to perhaps only 1,000. Central mobile forces, *comitatenses*, were formed away from border areas. The *comitatenses* were now the main field army units while the *limitanei* literally meant soldiers in the frontier districts. There was no particular difference in equipment or training.[14]

Civilian and military commands were separated. In general, the civilian governor was called praeses, and this would have been the case in Britannia Inferior. Military command was handed over to equestrian *duces*, who were generally placed on border areas and often commanded regions that crossed provincial borders.

The next major re-organisation was the increase in the number of provinces which approximately doubled. These new provinces were grouped together into a *Diocese* which, in Britain's case, was effectively the former single province before Caracalla's first division. Thus Britain was separated once more, from two to four provinces. All four came under the Diocese of the Britains administered by a *vicarus* in London. It is thought this occurred after the victory over Allectus in 296 but was certainly completed by 314 when the *Laterculus Veronensis*, Verona List, records all four provinces. Maxima Caesariensis was the only one with a consular governor, probably based in London. Britannia Secunda, capital at York, Flavia Caesariensis, Lincoln, and Britannia Prima at Cirencester or Gloucester, were each governed by a *praesides*.

The first of the *vicarii* of Britain is dated to 319 and he would have reported to the Praetorian Prefect of Gaul. Only one praeses is recorded for Britain before 305, Aurelius Arpagius, probably of Britannia Secunda, which would place him at York.

In 305 Diocletian abdicated and forced Maximian to do the same. Constantius and Galerius were both promoted to Augustus and each appointed a Caesar as their subordinate, Flavius Valerius Severus in the west and Maximinus II in the east. Constantine, the son of Constantius, was at the court of Galerius, possibly as an unofficial hostage. When Constantius prepared another campaign in Britain he requested his son, now about thirty-three-years-old, to accompany him.

Little is known of the campaign of 305–6 but it is thought it may have mirrored that of Severus nearly a hundred years earlier. Using York as a base, the army probably moved up the east coast and archaeological evidence, such as pottery from Carpow and Cramond, dates to this period. Literary sources suggest Constantius reached the 'furthest edge of the world'. The descriptions of forests and marshes are reminiscent of Cassius Dio the century before. Once again the emperor did not annex the territory he overran and returned south. In 306 Constantius, just like his predecessor, died at York.

In theory Flavius Valerius Severus should now have been Augustus but the army at York had other plans. There is nothing to suggest the Sixth were not still present and so we must conclude that, for the second time in a century, they were in the middle of pivotal events for the Roman Empire. One source tells us a king of the Alemanni called Crocus had accompanied Constantius to Britain and was key in elevating his son. The news would not have pleased Flavius or the eastern Augustus Galerius.

Civil war was averted when Constantine agreed to be Caesar to Flavius' Augustus in the west but matters were complicated when the Praetorian Guard in Rome declared another emperor, Maxentius, son of Maximinus I, the former Augustus. A complex series of shifting alliances, battles and the death of Galerius in 311 resulted in Constantine facing Maximinus in the east, Maxentius still in Rome and Licinius. This last-named new entrant had been appointed Augustus of the West by Galerius over the head of Constantine.

The first to fall was Maxentius in 312 when Constantine led a force of some 90,000 infantry and 8,000 cavalry to victory at the Battle of the Milvian Bridge outside Rome. The pretender died in the crush of retreating troops and was said to have fallen head-first in to the river when the bridge collapsed. The following year two important events occurred. The first was the Edict of Milan where Constantine and Licinius agreed to tolerate all religions, including, importantly, Christianity. Licinius eliminated Maximinus II that same year and ruled as Augustus of the east leaving, Constantine as Augustus of the west. A decade later Licinius was defeated at the Battle of Chrysopolis, leaving Constantine as the sole ruler.

After the Battle of the Milvian Bridge, the Praetorian Guard was disbanded. Praetorian prefects were kept and two new commands created: *magister militum* and *magister equitum*, master of the infantry and cavalry respectively. It is thought that he introduced the title of *Comes*, or Count. The *comitatenses* were posted back from the frontier areas and troops began to be billeted in towns. The frontier alae and cohortes units became *limitanei*, from the Latin limes, or frontier.

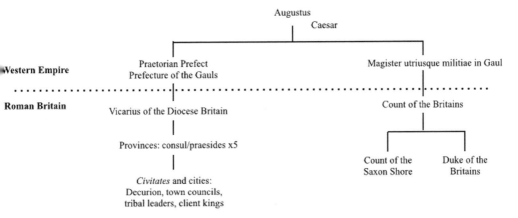

Figure 36: Administrative organisation of the late Western Roman Empire.

The second division of Britain

The first division of Britannia into Superior and inferior is dated to c. 213.[15] We know there were still at least two provinces in 297 as a panegyrist thanked Constantius for supplying craftsmen to Autun from Britanniae. Diocletian had re-organised other provinces early in his reign and it is likely he did the same in Britain after the reigns of Carausius and Allectus ended in 296. The governors of the provinces held the title praeses and were grouped under a vicarius, an over-governor. These vicarii of the western dioceses acted as deputies for the praetorian prefect sitting in Gaul. The *Laterculus Veronensis*, or Verona List, was compiled between 303 and 314 and listed the four provinces: Britannia

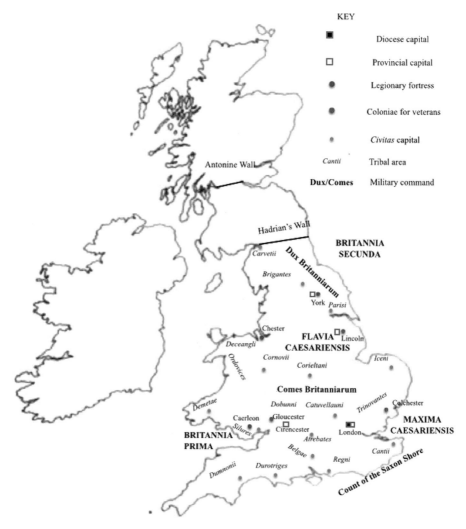

Figure 37: Map of Roman Britain in the fourth century.

Prima, Britannia Secunda , Maxima Caesariensis and Flavia Caesariensis. We can therefore date this drastic re-organisation fairly tightly to 296–313.

In 314 three Bishops from York, London and Lincoln travelled to the Council of Arles, and it is thought these represented the capitals of three of the provinces. The remaining province, Prima, is thought to have had its capital at Cirencester, due to an inscription (RIB 103) found there referring to a governor. The face reads: 'To Jupiter, Best and Greatest, His Perfection Lucius Septimius …, governor of Britannia Prima, restored (this monument),

Figure 38: Provinces of Roman Britain.

being a citizen of the Remi tribe'. The rear and side reads: 'This statue and column erected under the ancient religion Septimius restores, ruler of Britannia Prima'. However, this does not make it certain. As York and Lincoln were both *coloniae* it has been suggested that a third colonia, Gloucester, may have been capital of Britannia Prima.

Unfortunately, no document or source survives showing the provincial boundaries, let alone those of the *civitates*.[16] In addition, our understanding of political structures also remains poor.[17] A common version for the location of the provinces is as follows:[18]

- Britannia Prima covering the west country and modern-day Wales with the provincial capital at Cirencester
- Flavia Caesariensis covering the Midlands and Lincolnshire, the capital at Leicester and possibly later Lincoln.
- Britannia Secunda covering north of Hadrian's Wall up to Hadrian's Wall and at times beyond, the capital at York.
- Maxima Caesariensis covering the South East with London being both the capital of the Province and the Diocese.

Other options are possible and one example places Flavia Caesariensis and Britannia Secunda the other way round.[19] As Maxima Caesariensis was the only province at this point with a consular governor it is very likely that this was centred on the diocesan capital, and largest city, London. Birley suggests the re-organisation, starting under Diocletian, was completed under Constantine. This may have coincided with major changes in military structure. Above is a map of Roman Britain in the fourth century, followed by a simplified map of the possible boundaries of the four provinces.

The coastal defences of Roman Britain

During the third century the Romans constructed a series of forts in the south-east which formed part of a wider Gallic coastal system, including northern Gaul. A century or more later, the military commander on the coast of Britain was called *Comes Litoris Saxonici per Britanniam*, count of the Saxon shore in Britain. However, no such title existed when the first forts were constructed. It is possible they lay within the south-eastern province of *Maxima Caesariensis*.

Reculver and Brancaster are thought to have been built first, in the mid-third century, followed by the following forts dated to 270–90:[20] Burgh Castle, Bradwell, Walton Castle, Richborough, Dover and Lympne. Portchester in particular has been linked to the time of Carausius.

A few points are worth remembering later for our final two chapters. In the fourth century some sites show early abandonment: the forts at Lympne, Reculver, Caister and Burgh and many Yorkshire signal stations.[21] Richborough in Kent may have been one of the last Saxon Shore Forts garrisoned by troops in late Roman Britain. Not only is it recorded as the base for the Legio II Augusta in the early fifth century *Notitia Dignitatum*, but a huge number of bronze coins (20,000) have been found, suggesting it was an economic or financial centre.[22] Of the Saxon Shore forts, only Portchester in Hampshire shows occupations well into the fifth century, and a later Saxon presence.

How then did the south coastal command become known as 'The Saxon Shore'? It is notable that there are no examples of Roman defensive systems being named after an enemy.[23] Neither do we have evidence of the presence

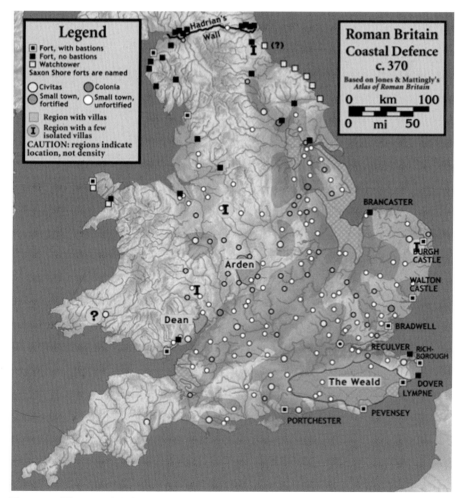

Figure 39: The coastal defences of Roman Britain. (*Wikimedia Commons*)

of Germanic warriors or settlers. However, on balance we can suggest it is likely that sometime in the fourth century Saxons began to settle, garrison or raid the south-eastern coast. The map above displays a number of interesting points aside from the Saxons Shore Forts and watch towers on the Yorkshire coast. We can see the extent of 'Romanisation' in the distribution of towns and villas. Interestingly, this will match the earliest evidence for the spread of Germanic material culture and burials in the fifth century.

Case study: Legionaries of the Sixth and others across the centuries

The social structure of citizens of the early empire had been based on three main classes: the aristocracy and senatorial class, the equestrian class and, finally, the plebs. All were citizens and ranked higher than freedmen. The changes of the third century, starting with the Constitution of Antoninus, or Edict of Caracalla, in 212, reduced these divisions to two: the *homestiores*, the aristocracy and richest equestrians, and the *humiliore*, which included much of the equestrian class and plebs. This squeezing of the middle classes produced huge inequalities between the very rich and very poor. The removal of the distinction between auxiliaries and legionaries was to have equally significant consequences.

In the mid-third century Emperor Gallienus introduced a number of reforms. Firstly, the senatorial class was excluded from military service. Secondly, mounted troops became more important. The legionary cavalry was increased six-fold to twenty-four turmae of thirty men, numbering 720 in total. More specialist mounted units were created. The legions were now commanded by an equestrian *praefectus legionis* rather than a senatorial legatus, a move begun under Septimius Severus when he raised three new legions in his Parthian campaign.

Another reform began under Severus and was built on by Gallienus, was the increase in importance, and number, of light troops. The *velites* of the republic era had given way to specialised auxiliary units. Now a new class of elite light skirmishers, the *antesignani*, made up the vanguard of each legion.[24] They were not a standing unit but drawn from the ranks of the existing cohorts to perform specific and temporary tasks: they were armed with oval shields and missile weapons such as javelins and light spears.

When Severus raised three new legions he created a new structure for them. Each cohort now had two centuries of light troops and four of heavy. These light troops became known as *lanciarii* after of their main weapon, the *lancea* spear. During the third century there was also an increase in the use of 'barbarian' units, infantry *numeri* and cavalry *cunei*. Initially, these had little structure, varied in size and fought in their own style under their own chieftains.

In the early fourth century the army was divided between *comitatenses*, the field army, and the *limitanei*, the frontier troops. Initially the latter had fewer privileges, such as tax exemptions, but they did receive land near their postings and, with their sons likely to join up as well, this created a hereditary class of military families. Senior units of the comitatenses became known as *palatini*. Constantine also disbanded the Praetorian Guard who were replaced by mounted guardsmen, the *Scholae Palatinae*.

The legions were reduced to 1,000–1,200 men and commanded by a *Tribunus*, a man of equestrian class and passed through the ranks of the *Protectores*. This was a type of imperial bodyguard and staff officer training created by Constantine. His second in command was a *Primicerius*, an experienced soldier with over twenty-five-years' service, similar to the rank of primus pilus. The legions now consisted of six *ordines* of 200 men, each commanded by a *Ducenarius*. Each *ordo* consisted of two *centuria*, the first led by the Ducenarius, with the second by a *Centenarius*. The century now consisted of ten contubernia, tent groups, commanded by a NCO, *semissalis*. The *auxilia palatina*, elite units of light infantry, consisted of three *ordines* of 200 each, totalling 600 men, half of the new legions. The *limitanei* were organised into former cohort-sized units. These were also commanded by a tribunus, with a primicerius as second in command. An *Ordinarius* commanded each century. In the mid-fifth century these units were again transformed into *numeri* but this was long after the Romans had left Britain.

The legionary cavalry evolved into a *vexillatio*, a unit of 600 consisting of three *ordines* of 200 with the same rank structure as the legions, led by a tribunus, with a *primicerius* as second in command. In 395 most infantry units were split in half.[25] The cavalry *vexillatio* was also halved and now numbered 300 men. They continued to be commanded by a *tribunus*. The frontier limitanei cavalry units retained alae of 600 whilst the irregular cunei units became more organised and consisted of ten turmae of thirty men each. Both the alae and cunei were led by a Tribunus. The question arises: was the Sixth split in half as well? If so, it would have now numbered just 600 and consisted of three ordines of 200 men each. It is likely that the Sixth Legion, during the reigns of Diocletian or Constantine, was reduced to 1,200 infantrymen, led initially by a tribunus.

In the mid-third century the *ballistae* started to be replaced by a heavier stone-throwing onager. Prior to this period, the Roman legions had ten heavy ballistae and fifty-nine light scorpiones. Now they began to create independent artillery units, perhaps the first in military history. The *Notitia Dignitatum* includes six of these *ballistarii* units.

Both legionaries and auxiliaries had generally been volunteers with conscription, *dilectus*, used rarely. After the reforms of Diocletian, service became hereditary, forcing the sons of serving soldiers or veterans to enlist. Thus, in the fourth century, many soldiers of the Sixth would have come from the settlements around the northern towns and forts, especially York. Citizens were also subject to an annual levy based on land tax, *indictio*. Rich landowners in rural areas had to provide a certain number of recruits, the standard of which inevitably declined. It also increased resentment and social friction, something we will come to in the final chapter.

From the time of Constantine the number of Germanic irregular troops increased: *bucellarii*, mercenaries; *laeti*, settler-soldiers; and *foederati*, allied troops. During the early empire cavalry units accounted for 20 per cent of the army. By the beginning of the fifth century this had risen to 35 per cent.[26] Mounted archers also became more important, as did archers and light troops. Battle tactics changed as well. The heavy infantry units were drawn up into a line several ranks deep. The light infantry, *auxilia palatina*, and mounted archers and light cavalry acted as skirmishers. To the rear archers and slingers were positioned. This formation was flanked by heavy cavalry. A large reserve of infantry and/or cavalry was to plug any gaps or respond to opportunities as they presented themselves.

Standardisation of uniform had deteriorated during The Crisis of the The Crisis of the Third Century. This was partially rectified under Diocletian and Constantine. Thirty-five state factories, *fabricae*, are recorded in the *Notitia Dignitatum*. Taxation in the eastern empire remained strong, often double that in the west. Consequently, soldiers of the late Western Empire were not as well equipped as in earlier centuries. The comitatensis had a higher degree of uniformity in clothing and equipment compared to the limitanei.[27]

Long-sleeved tunics, *tunica manicata*, became more common, adopted from Germanic custom. This was a T-shaped garment reaching to below the hips. Military tunics had narrow vertical bands coloured red and patterned roundels on shoulders and skirts. It was worn with a belt, *cingulum militiae*, and a *sagum*, a hip-length semi-circular-shaped cloak. In the late fourth century the cloak, along with specific types of broaches, became a sign of military service with officers wearing longer and richly-decorated cloaks. Common materials were wool for winter and linen for summer with red and white being the favoured colours. Helmets also changed, and we can see ornate ridge-type helmets replacing the Gallic-style helmet of the second century.

The lorica segmentata armour was phased out in the third century, being complex and difficult to produce. A legionary of the Sixth in the fourth century would likely be protected by lorica hamata. This armour took about two months to produce and was constructed with up to 30,000 5- to 7-mm rings.[28] This type was dominant in the west. Lorica squamata was more prevalent in the east. Scales measuring 0.5 to 0.8 mm thick were wired together and overlapped onto a cloth with leather backing. Lamellar armour was also more popular in the east and similar to squamata, although without the backing. It was made from plates of metal, leather or horn stitched together. This tended to be used by mercenary or federati troops. Officers often wore a 'muscle cuirass', consisting of two highly-ornamented pieces. This might have been worn by the tribunus of a reduced Sixth Legion in the fourth century or the 'praefectus legionis' recorded in the *Notitia Dignitatum*. The light infantry and light cavalry generally did not wear armour.[29]

Like the lorica segmentata plated armour, the scutum shield also fell out of use in the third century. It was replaced by oval or round shields. The gladius was also replaced by the longer spatha cavalry sword. This had been used by the cavalry for some time, having been copied from the Celts, just as the glades had been copied from the Spanish. The pilum was similarly abandoned in the mid-third century and replaced by two different types: a heavy javelin, *spiculum*, and the lighter *verutum*. Lead darts, *plumbatae* or *martiobabuli*, became more common and several could be attached to, and carried, on the rear of shields. The auxiliary units had long used spears or *lancea* and now, with the disappearance of the pilum, some legionnaires adopted the lancea. It is possible that soldiers of the Sixth in the fourth century were armed with spears and round or oval shields. They may well have carried two or three light spears in addition to five or six *plumbatae*.

Figure 40: Soldiers of the Sixth. (*Dave Grainger, Legio VI Victrix Eboracum re-enactment Group*)

Figure 41: Legionary infantryman from second century wearing lorica segmentata armed with pilum. (*Dave Grainger, Legio VI Victrix Eboracum re-enactment Group*)

Figure 42: Second-century officer wearing lorica squamata. (*Dave Grainger, Legio VI Victrix Eboracum re-enactment Group*)

Figure 43: An optio of the Sixth wearing lorica squamata. (*Dave Grainger, Legio VI Victrix Eboracum re-enactment Group*)

Figure 44: A signifier and centurion of the Sixth. (*Dave Grainger, Legio VI Victrix Eboracum re-enactment Group*)

A type of crossbow began to appear on the battlefield, *manuballista* or *cheiroballista*. Vegetius mentions an *arcuballista*. By the fourth century it was light and easy enough to operate to be used by mounted troops. Some cavalry units used the *contus*, a 13-feet long lance wielded two-handed. But other units would have used light javelins, lancea spears and the long spatha sword.

We can see the changing types of uniforms and armour in the pictures below.

Figure 45: Various uniforms from the fourth century. (*Ross Cronshaw, Magister Militum re-enactment Group*)

Figure 46: Fourth-century officer wearing lorica squamata with banner of *Ioviani Seniores*. (*Ross Cronshaw, Magister Militum re-enactment Group*)

Figure 47: Fourth-century Roman officer. (*Ross Cronshaw, Magister Militum re-enactment Group*)

Figure 48: Fourth-century Roman officer with light infantryman and archer. (*Ross Cronshaw, Magister Militum re-enactment Group*)

Figure 49: Late Roman officer and infantryman of the Sixth. (*Ross Cronshaw, Magister Militum re-enactment Group*)

Figure 50: Xanten ballista. (*Ross Cronshaw, Magister Militum re-enactment Group*)

Figure 51: Various examples of fourth-century late Roman soldiers. (*Ross Cronshaw, Magister Militum re-enactment Group*)

Figure 52: Auxiliary soldier second century. (*John Richardson, The Antonine Guard re-enactment group*)

Figure 53: Auxiliary archer second century. (*John Richardson, The Antonine Guard re-enactment group*)

Figure 54: Native warrior from a Numerus Exploratorum. (*John Richardson, The Antonine Guard re-enactment group*)

Figure 55: Native warrior from a Numerus Exploratorum. (*John Richardson, The Antonine Guard re-enactment group*)

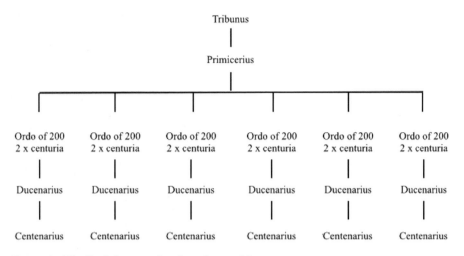

Figure 56: The Sixth Legion after the reforms of Constantine.

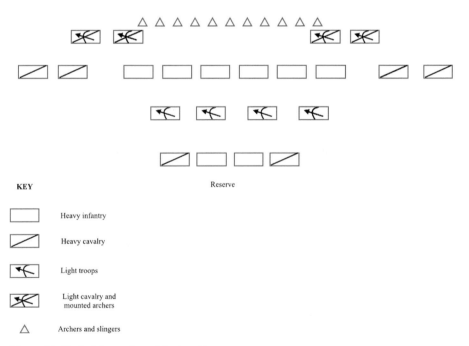

Figure 57: Typical formation of the late Roman army.

Chapter 7

Fourth Century Britannia,
a Province Fertile in Tyrants

After the death of Constantine in 337 the empire was split between his three sons: Constantine II, Constantius II and Constans. The relative stability of their father's reign did not last long. The three brothers began by killing a number of rivals, some of them close family and they soon fell out themselves. Constantine II, in the western provinces which included Britain, was aggrieved that, as the eldest son, he didn't receive the share he felt he deserved. When his younger brother Constans, in Italy, Africa and Illyricum, came of age Constantine marched across the Alps. He was ambushed and killed by Constans's troops outside Aquileia. Constans took over his brother's part of the empire and travelled to Britain in 343.[1] This came soon after he had defeated a Frankish incursion and the fact that he travelled in January or February, when the crossing is dangerous, suggests there was a pressing reason. Unfortunately, we have no further information but it is possibly an indication of northern raids which later were to prove more serious.

Constans's reign in the west was to end at the hands of another usurper. Having lost the support of the troops, he was forced to flee when the army on the Rhine frontier declared for Magnentius Augustus at Autun. Constans attempted to reach Hispania but was caught at a fortress on the Pyrenees and killed. As in the previous decades, the provinces of Britain sided with the western usurper. Civil war once again loomed but was delayed by conflict in the east with Persia. Overtures of peace broke down and Constantius, the remaining son of Constantine I, moved west to confront Magnentius. A major battle at Mursa Major in 351 left over 50,000 dead. Magnentius retreated west and his repeated offers of peace were rejected by Constantius who crossed the Alps. A final battle in 353 at Mons Seleucus in south-eastern France led to Magnentius fleeing to Lugdunum. In a scene reminiscent of Albinus Clodius, he was surrounded and committed suicide, falling on his sword. Constantius was now sole emperor.

Roman Britain in the mid-fourth century

The emperor sent an imperial notary, Paulus Catena, to Britain to stamp out supporters of Magnentius. Notorious for his cruelty, he began arresting people, sometimes with no evidence. An unsung hero of Roman Britain is perhaps Flavius Martinus, the vicarius of the diocese. His attempts to stop some of the injustices were met with an accusation of treason. Undeterred, he attacked Paulus with his sword. This failed and he was forced to commit suicide. Yet Britain continued to be a prosperous diocese, described by some as 'very wealthy'.[2] Most citizens of Britain, as across the empire, had a sense of Roman identity.[3] There was a 'substantial urban population',[4] plus evidence of maintenance and new construction within towns up to the mid-fourth century.[5] Many of the most luxurious and largest villas were built in this time.[6] In fact, it has been described as the 'heyday or Romano-British villas' within a 'wealth producing agricultural economy'.[7]

However, evidence points to a marked deterioration by the end of the fourth century. Towns became poorer and politically weaker.[8] There seems to have been a shift in political power from urban centres to country estates. The bulk of the population, around 90 per cent, had remained rural.[9] It is worth noting at this point the area which experienced the most 'romanisation' and urbanisation. This is approximately south and east of a line from Exeter to York,[10] a distinction that persisted after the end of Roman Britain.[11] This was the same area that later was to experience the earliest appearance of Germanic material culture and settlement in the fifth century.

In the mid-fourth century Britain was productive enough for Emperor Julian to order 600 grain ships from Britain to supply troops on the Rhine. Yet the diocese was shortly to suffer a number of significant raids from northern tribes. Picts and Scots attacked in 360 and again in 364, this time with Attacotti and Saxons. The most damaging incursion was in 367 when multiple tribes were alleged to have joined together in 'the barbarian conspiracy'. Irish, Picts, Scots and Germanic tribes, including Saxons, were involved. Some placed the blame on the *arcani*, Roman scouts posted in northern Britain, who sided with the barbarians.[12] The frontier was overrun and the *Dux Britanniarum*, Fullofaudes, was killed. So, too, was Necttaridus, the *comes maritime tractus*. It is suggested that this post is synonymous with the later *comes litoris Saxonici*; however, as the raiders are from the north, it is equally likely this is an unknown command.[13] The word *tractus* suggests a region rather than *litoris* which implies a coastline. Some have argued this alleged incursion was exaggerated or masked an internal insurrection. This idea has not gained wide support.[14]

Constantius had died in 361 and was replaced as sole emperor by Julian, 361–3, and then Jovian who ruled for less than a year. Remarkably, neither was murdered by their own troops nor were killed fighting a rival. Julian died from a wound sustained in battle against the Persians and Jovian reportedly from toxic fumes from a brazier. Valentinian ruled from 364 and made his brother Valens co-emperor in the east. It was Valentinian I who sent Theodosius to Britain to restore order after 367. Theodosius was named as *Comes Britannarium*. His son was to become Theodosius I, the last sole Emperor of both east and west. It would seem that, at this point, Britain was fully restored under Roman rule. A new province appears, although it is uncertain whether it was named after the recovery of a breakaway province or *civitas*.[15] It certainly appears in the *Notitia Dignitatum* as a separate province and so we must conclude that, for the last decades of the fourth century, Britain had five provinces.

Valentia, the fifth province

The fifth province of Britain has been an enigma with some historians claiming we can dismiss its existence. Our first piece of evidence comes from Ammianus Marcellinus c. 330–400[16] and comes after the 'barbarian conspiracy' of 367. He blames the incursion on the *arcani*, whose duty it was to scout and gather information. Instead, we read that these units had 'gradually become corrupted … led by the receipt, or the promise, of great booty … to betray to the savages what was going on among us.' Theodosius 'sallied forth' from Augusta, which Ammianus helpfully tells us was earlier called Londinium. He 'routed and put to flight' the attacking tribes and 'completely restored the cities and strongholds' and protected the frontiers by 'sentinels and outposts'.

But Ammianus hints at other reasons behind the unrest. A certain Valentinus, born in Pannonia, had been exiled to Britain because of a 'serious crime'. We read that he nursed a certain grudge against Theodosius and started to gather together exiles and soldiers, presumably to attack the emperor's general. But Theodosius found out and had Valentius executed along with his associates. This seems to have occurred after Theodosius had dealt with the barbarian tribes but, together with the reference to the arcani, indicates the Roman response was as much directed at internal forces as external ones. Whatever the cause of the events, we then come to the important passages about Valentia: 'after the danger had been wholly removed … so completely did he recover a province which had passed into the enemy's hands and restore it to its former condition, that, in the words of his report, it had a legitimate governor; and it was henceforth called Valentia'.

This has led some to speculate that, rather than creating a new province, he merely restored one that was lost. As the tribes came from the north and west, the most likely candidate is the northernmost province, whose capital was at York. However, there are two sources that confirm the presence of a fifth province. The first is the fifth century writer Polemius Silvius and the second the *Notitia Dignitatum*. The former adds a sixth province, Orcades, or Orkneys. The *Notitia* gives us the four from the second division, plus Valentia. One possibility is there was already a fifth province just prior to 367 and it was this that was recovered. As the Verona List of the early fourth century lists four provinces, it is possible a fifth was added by Constans in 343 when he visited Britain. Another argument is that a *dux* would normally command troops in more than one province. As the Dux Britanniarum was based at York and commanded troops over the entire former province of Britannia Secunda it is suggested this had been divided again at some point.[17]

On the balance of probabilities I would suggest our two latest sources, the *Notitia* and Polemius, confirm a fifth province by the end of the fourth century. The question arises: where was it? There seem to be a limited number of main contenders. The first would suggest perhaps the region directly south of and to the north of Hadrian's Wall, perhaps with its capital at Carlisle. The later sixth-century cleric Gildas writes that the Picts captured 'up to the wall', which would suggest Roman control north of the wall at the end of Roman authority and beyond into the early fifth century.

Another option comes from analysis of the *Notitia*. Only two provinces have governors of consular rank, Maxima Caesariensis and Valentia. All the other are provincial *praes*. It is tempting to conclude that the headquarters of

Figure 58: Valentia, the fifth province.

the two consular governors would have been at the two largest cities, London and York. If that is the case, then we are perhaps looking at an east-west divide of the northernmost province with the Pennines as the border. It's possible a new province carved out of North Wales and the Cumbrian coast was formed to combat the threat from western raiders. In truth we don't know and await archaeological evidence, such as from an inscribed stone. The maps above show just some possible scenarios.

Magnus Maximus to Constantine III

Another northern raid in 382 was subdued by Magnus Maximus who possibly held the post of *dux* or *comes Britanniarum*.[18] Maximus came from a poor Spanish family, possibly connected to the family of Theodosius, with whom he had served in Britain after the invasion of 367.[19] He gained more experience fighting in Africa in 373–5 against the rebellion of Firmus. Back in Britain the army grew dissatisfied with the rule of the western Augustus, Gratian, and declared Maximus emperor in 383. He moved to Gaul, taking much of the British garrison with him. This may have included elements of the Sixth.

Gratian's troops deserted him and he was forced to flee. En route to Lugdunum, fast becoming a graveyard for many a former emperor or usurper, he was overtaken and killed by Andragathius, the *magister equitum* of Maximus. The usurper soon had the support of the western provinces and the western Caesar, Valentinian II, and eastern Augustus, Theodosius I, were forced to accept the fait accompli and accept him as joint emperor. In 387, Maximus elevated his infant son, Flavius Victor, as Augustus and crossed the Alps. Valentinian fled to the east, seeking the protection of Theodosius.

By 388 Maximus had based himself at Aquileia and Andragathius led a force into Illyrium, only to suffer a reverse near Siscia. Theodosius advanced quickly and sent a substantial cavalry force towards Maximus's main forces near Poetovio on the River Save. A mainly Gothic and Alanic force was able to inflict heavy casualties and make a bridgehead on the northern bank as the main Theodosian army arrived. The usurper's forces regrouped and attacked the next day. They were beaten again and Maximus was forced to flee to Aquileia where he was besieged and eventually handed over to Theodosius. The emperor had sent his Frankish general, Arbogastes, on a northern route towards Trier where Victor, Maximus's son, was resident. Both Maximus and his son were executed. Theodosius and Valentinian were now emperors of the east and west respectively. However, with the latter still a teenager, Theodosius held the power. Four years later Valentinian was found hanged by the new western *magister militum*, Arbogastes.

Foul play was obviously suspected and, when Arbogast elevated a certain Eugenius as emperor, civil war ensued. The battle of the Frigidus in 394 left both dead and Theodosius as the sole ruler of an undivided empire. Theodosius died a year later and was succeeded by his two sons. The empire was once more divided, Arcadius in the east and Honorius in the west. They were aged seventeen and ten respectively and so Theodosius had sensibly given them experienced generals to advise them. In the east was the praetorian prefect Rufinus. In the west was Stilicho whose official title, *comes et magister utriusque militiae praesentalis*, made him the supreme military commander.

Victorious campaigns against Goths and Franks were followed by another serious raid in northern Britain in 398. A panegyric by the poet Claudian in c. 402 refers to 'the Saxon is conquered, the seas safe, the Picts defeated, and Britain secure'. Another specifically refers to Stilicho giving aid to Britain 'at the mercy of neighbouring tribes', mentioning Scots, Picts and Saxons. No more is known about this campaign. However, evidence suggests some repairing of Hadrian's Wall and after 402 Stilicho pulled out significant numbers of troops and, importantly, much of the coinage from Britain.

The last mint was closed in the reign of Maximus and no new coins seem to have reached Britain after 402.[20] The main purpose of these shipments was for the payment of soldiers and this may have contributed to the later rebellion under Constantine. Low-value coins fell out of circulation around 410–430, suggesting higher-value coins may have lasted a little later, c. 450–470.[21] This wouldn't, of course, mean that money ceased to be available, but the evidence does suggest the economic cycle and parts of Roman life were severely impacted.[22]

The third occasion troops were pulled out of Britain occurred just a few short years later. In the winter of 406 the Rhine froze over and several tribes took the opportunity to cross over into a weakened Roman Gaul, Vandals, Burgundians, Alemanni, Alans, Saxons and Gepids among them. This, coupled with Stilicho's recent actions in pulling troops and coins out of Britain, was perhaps the last straw. The Britons rebelled, appointing three different leaders in quick succession, Mark, Gratian and Constantine. Three contemporary sources, Orosius, Olympiodorus, and Sozomen, described the following events.

Mark and Gratian were both quickly killed before Constantine, 'a man of the lowest military rank, on account of the hope alone which came from his name and without any merit for courage, was elected'. Once elected Constantine crossed over to Gaul with his forces and became 'master of Gaul as far as the Alps'.[23] The question is: did these forces contain any of the Sixth legion? By 408 Stilicho was dead and the Gothic leader Alaric threatened Italy. Honorius had little choice but to accept Constantine as co-emperor. The *Gallic Chronicle* of 452 records a major raid on Britain for the following year, 409: Britain was 'devastated by an incursion of the Saxons'.[24] The Britons rebelled again, this time against Constantine.

Zozimus writing c. 500 records the events as follows:[25] The barbarian assaults caused 'Britain and some of the Celtic peoples to defect from the Roman rule ..... independent from the Roman laws'. The Britons freed their cities from the barbarian threat and interestingly, together with 'all Armorica and the other Gallic provinces', expelled Roman officials and set up a constitution 'as they pleased'. Zozimus blames the assaults squarely on Constantine and his 'carelessness in administration'. The Britons appealed directly to Honorius in Ravenna.

The reply, *The Rescript of Honorius,* was to the *civitates* and directed them to look to their own defences. It is interesting that the reply is not to the diocese or provinces. Perhaps these structures had broken down or possibly some were still loyal to Constantine and could not be trusted. There is some debate concerning whether this order really was to Britain rather than Bruttium in Italy.[26] However, subsequent events make this rather academic. Sozomen c. 439 makes no mention of Britain when he states the province, most likely Gaul, returned its 'allegiance to Honorius'. Procopius c. 540 states: 'However the Romans never succeeded in recovering Britain, but it remained from that time on under tyrants.'[27]

What may have seemed a good idea to Constantine in 408 quickly turned sour in 409. His general Gerontius was unable to secure Spain from barbarian incursions and he sent his son Constans to take over. Gerontius rebelled and declared another Maximus as emperor. Constans was killed and Gerontius moved into Gaul and besieged Constantine and his surviving son, Julian, in Arelate, Arles in southern France. The future Constantius III advanced from Italy on behalf of Honorius, forcing Gerontius back into Spain where he was killed. Constantine merely changed besiegers and eventually was forced to surrender. Both he and his son were killed en route to Ravenna despite assurances of safe passage.

Events had now been set in motion. In the east Theodosius II succeeded his father Arcadius in 408 and was to rule for forty-two years. In the west, Rome had been sacked by the Gothic king Alaric in 410. The western empire was to suffer continued barbaric raids and a slow fragmentation of power and authority. Only Aetius was able to hold back the tide for a generation, culminating in his great victory over Attila the Hun at the Battle of the Catalaunian Plains in 451. His murder in 454 was followed by a succession of weak emperors and strong Germanic generals which ended when Odoacer deposed the last Roman emperor in the west, Romulus Augustulus, in 476.

What little we know of Britain from these last decades of Roman authority in the west will be covered in the last chapter. We have seen how Britain may have been denuded of troops by Maximus, Stilicho and, finally, Constantine III. However, we have one contemporary document that may shine a light on the military situation in Britain around c. 400 and on the fate of the Sixth.

Notitia Dignitatum

The *Notitia omnium Dignitatum et administrationum tam civilium quam militarum*, more commonly known as the *Notitia Dignitatum*, is the earliest written evidence for the military and civil organisation of fifth-century Britain. It can be split into two halves: a *Notitia Dignitatum Occidentis*, *Register of Offices in the West*, and N*otitia Dignitatum Orientis*, *Register of Offices in the West*. The earliest copy is from the now lost, eleventh-century, *Codex Spirensis*. It is generally dated to 390–425. It thus gives a snapshot of the structure of the late Roman Empire. It may be an early-fifth-century copy of an earlier document that itself was depicting an ideal rather than reality on the ground.[28] It is possible it was out of date when completed.

The civilian and military authorities of Britain reported to the *Prefectis Praetorians per Gallias*, the Praetorian Prefect of the Gauls. The civilian authority was led by the *Vicarius Britanniae*, one of six vicars in the west. In Britain a governor from each of the five provinces reported to him. These included two consular provincial governors, *Consularis per Maxima Caesariensis* and *Consularis per Valentia*, and three provincial praeses, *Praesidis per Britannia prima*, *Praesidis per Britannia secunda* and *Praesidis per Flavia Caesariensis.*

The military authority was controlled by six military counts in the west who also reported to the praetorian prefect in Gaul. In Britain there were two such men, the *Comes Britanniarum* and *Comes Litoris Soxonicum per Britannias*. In the north the *Dux Britanniarum* was one of thirteen dukes in the west and reported to the *Comes Britanniarum*. The staff of the *vicarus* included the following: a chief of staff, chief deputy, two receivers of taxes, chief clerk, custodian, chief assistant, keeper of the records, assistants, secretaries, notaries and 'the rest of the staff'. The tables below list the units under each command.

Name of unit	Location
Praepositus numeri Fortensium, Othonae	Bradwell
Praepositus militum Tungrecanorum, Dubris	Dover
Praepositus numeri Turnacensium, Lemannis	Lympne
Praepositus equitum Dalmatarum Branodunensium, Branoduno	Brancaster
Praepositus equitum stablesianorum Gariannonensium, Gariannonor	Burgh Castle
Tribunus cohortis primae Baetasiorum, Regulbio	Reculver
Praefectus legionis secundae Augustae, Rutupis	Richborough
Praepositus numeri Abulcorum, Anderidos	Pevensey
Praepositus numeri exploratorum, Portum Adurni	Portchester

Table 14: Troops and Offices of the Count of the Saxon Shore.

Table 15: Troops and Offices of the Dux Britanniarum.

Name of unit, with location	Location
Praefectus legionis sextae	York
Praefectus equitum Dalmatarum, Praesidio	Newton Kyme
Praefectus equitum Crispianorum, Dano	Doncaster
Praefectus equitum catafractariorum, Morbio	Piercebridge
Praefectus numeri barcariorum Tigrisiensium, Arbeia	South Shields
Praefectus numeri Nerviorum Dictensium, Dicti	Wearmouth
Praefectus numeri uigilum, Concangios	Chester-le-Street
Praefectus numeri exploratorum, Lauatres	Bowes
Praefectus numeri directorum, Uerteris	Brough
Praefectus numeri defensorum, Braboniaco	Kirkby Thore
Praefectus numeri Solensium, Maglone	Old Carlisle
Praefectus numeri Pacensium, Magis	Burrow Walls
Praefectus numeri Longovicanorum, Longouico	Lanchester
Praefectus numeri superuenientium Petueriensium, Deruentione	Malton
Tribunus cohortis quartae Lingonum, SeConduno	Wallsend
Tribunus cohortis primae Cornouiorum, Ponte Aeli	Newcastle
Praefectus alae primae Asturum, Conderco	Benwell
Tribunus cohortis primae Frixagorum, Uindobala	Rudchester
Praefectus alae Sabinianae, Hunno	Halton Chesters
Praefectus alae secundae Asturum, Cilurno	Chesters
Tribunus cohortis primae Batauorum, Procolitia	Carrawburgh
Tribunus cohortis primae Tungrorum, Borcouicio	Housesteads
Tribunus cohortis quartae Gallorum, Uindolana	Chesterholm

Name of unit, with location	Location
Tribunus cohortis primae Asturum, Aesica	Great Chesters
Tribunus cohortis secundae Dalmatarum, Magnis	Carvoran
Tribunus cohortis primae Aeliae Dacorum, Amboglanna	Castlesteads
Praefectus alae Petrianae, Uxelodunum or Petrianis	Stanwix
Luguuallii	Carlisle
Praefectus numeri Maurorum Aurelianorum, Aballaba	Burgh-by-Sands
Tribunus cohortis secundae Lingonum, Congauata	Drumburgh
Tribunus cohortis primae Hispaniorum, Axeloduno	Bowness
Tribunus cohortis secundae Thracum, Gabrosenti	Moresby
Tribunus cohortus primae Aeliae classicae, Tunnocelo	Ravenglass
Tribunus cohortis primae Morinorum, Glannibanta	Ambleside
Tribunus cohortis tertiae Neruiorum, Alione	Lancaster
Cuneus Sarmatarum, Bremetenraco	Ribchester
Praefectus alae primae Herculeae, Olenaco	Ilkley
Tribunus cohortis sextae Neruiorum, Uirosido	Bainbridge

The *Comes Britanniarum* appears to have controlled the whole of the diocese and thus would have authority over the Dux Britanniarum and, possibly, the *Comes Litoris Soxonicum per Britannias*.

Infantry units	Cavalry units
Secunda Britannica, legio comitatenses	Equites Catafractarii Iuniores, vexillatio comitatenses
Victores Iuniores Britanniciani auxilia palatinae	Equites Scutarii Aureliaci, vexillatio comitatenses
Primani Iuniores, legio comitatenses	Equites Honoriani Seniores, vexillatio comitatenses
Secundani Iuniores, legio comitatenses	Equites Stablesiani, vexillatio comitatenses
	Equites Syri, vexillatio comitatenses
	Equites Taifali, vexillatio comitatenses

Table 16: Units under the Comes Britanniarum.

The three commands at the end of the Roman period could be summarised as follows.[29]

	Cavalry units (alae)	Infantry cohorts
Count of the Britains	6	4 (comitatenses)
Count of Saxon Shore	2	7 (limitanei)
Duke of the Britains (York)		
Along Hadrian's wall	5	18 (limitanei)
Reserves	3	11 (limitanei)
Overall total	16	40

Table 17: Military commands of Roman Britain.

It is estimated that, by the end of the fourth century, the army had dropped to between 12,000 and 20,000 men compared to a force of perhaps 50,000 in the second century.[30] One estimate places the army size as low as 6,000 by the year 400.[31] We must remember that this is before Constantine crossed over to Gaul with a sizeable force.

The occupation of the VI Legion at York can be attested up to the middle of the third century. After this date it is a little difficult to confirm. In theory, it could have been disbanded, destroyed or moved. We do see elements of the Second Augusta throughout the *Notitia* such as the Secunda Britannica, legio comitatenses and the *Secundani Iuniores, legio comitatenses*, both under the command of the Comes Britanniarum, plus the Praefectus legionis secundae Augustae based at Rutupis, Richborough. This might suggest that the second was broken up when the legions were reduced in size and re-organised under Diocletian and Constantine. Unit names on the continent such as Secunda Britannica and *Secundani Britones* might also hint at a redistribution. The Twentieth Legion from Chester disappears from the record completely. However, there are some clues that point to the Sixth's survival.

The fourteen prefects not stationed on Hadrian's Wall are as follows: Sextae, Praesidio, Dano, Morbio, Arbeia, Dicti, Concangios, Lauatres, Uerteris, Braboniaco, Maglone, Magis, Longouicio and Deruentione. This suggests that being the unit was at a place known as Sextae rather than a reference to the unit's number. Thus the command could mean either 'the Prefect of the Sixth Legion' or 'the Prefect of the legion stationed at Sextae'. The second entry is for the unit Equitum Dalmatarum, located at Praesidio. This might be equated with Praetorio, which is used in the British section of the Antonine itinerary. If so we can read this as 'headquarters'. This has led some to speculate that the location has been entered on the wrong line or that both the legionis sextae and the Equitum Dalmatarum were based at the headquarters of the Sixth Legion. This, of course, would suggest York. Alternatively, some have suggested the copyist simply left this out as its base was so well known. The

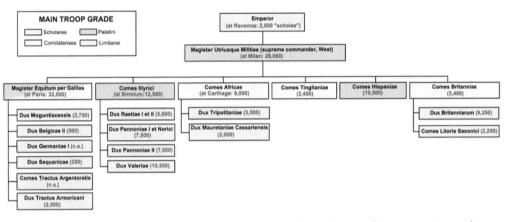

Figure 59: Late Roman army command structure of the Western Empire. (*Wikimedia Commons*)

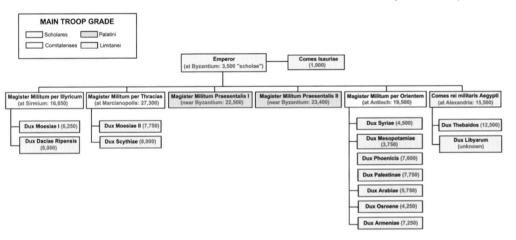

Figure 60: Late Roman army command structure of the Eastern Empire. (*Wikimedia Commons*)

Notitia appears to follow recognised routes, most likely roads and this fact all points to our acceptance of York. The surviving manuscript does have illustrations which show Sextae and Praesidio as two separate places, although in the illustration it is Praesidium. However, this might simply be a medieval addition. Leaving the location to one side what can we say about the fate of the Sixth?

The main options are as follows: it was broken up or disbanded sometime after Carausius, possibly during the re-organisation of Diocletian or Constantine; it survived intact at York; the reference in the *Notitia* can be interpreted as the evolution of the Sixth Legion into a smaller unit of limitanei or comitatenses under the command of the Dux Britanniarum. There can be very little certainty, but on balance the last option appears most likely. A legion-sized unit in the fourth century might have numbered approximately 1,200 troops. By the end of the fourth century many units were again divided but, if it was led by a Praefectus legionis, perhaps it survived as a larger unit. To support this proposal we need to take a closer look at York in the fourth century.

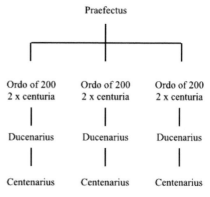

Figure 61: The Sixth Legion c. 395.

Late Roman York

John Wacher, in *The Towns of Roman Britain*, describes the last two centuries of Roman York as follows:[32] he dates its elevation to colonial status probably in the reign of Caracalla around the same time it became a provincial capital. An altar found at Bordeaux demonstrates it was certainly a colonia by 237. During the third century the governor of Britannia Inferior would also have been the legate of the Sixth Legion; the legionary praetorium in the fortress would have served as his headquarters. Towards the end of the third century the civil and military authority was separated and York became the military headquarters for the Dux Britanniarum who controlled all the units in the north. York was also the seat of the provincial administration. In addition, by 314 it was also a bishopric and a certain Eborius attended the Council of Arles in 314.

York maintained its status in the first half of the fourth century. By 350 the important naval base at Brough-on-Humber, twenty-six miles to the south-east, had been abandoned. The town at Brough, like Aldborough north-west of York, shows a decline in maintenance along with reduced occupation. In York Wacher finds a 'tenuous suggestion of fifth-century civilian occupation in the legionary fortress'.[33] Hypocausts and baths become disused and there is a general deterioration in building techniques.

However, there is still evidence of refurbishment in the fortress in the second half of the fourth century.[34] Nearby forts at Bainbridge and Ilkley also show signs of reconstruction and five signal stations appear on the Yorkshire coast, 'probably later than 367'.[35] These consisted of towers, possibly 65 feet high, in a wall courtyard, over 160 feet across, protected by a bank and ditch.

A distinct change has been detected and dated to c. 380. The headquarters basilica and first cohort barracks were largely demolished whilst the kitchen buildings remained. The colonia settlement to the south-west of the Ouse appears to have remained occupied and defended. Other areas of the former vicus give limited evidence for continued occupation. The road to the south-west seems to have been narrowed to half its width.

There is some evidence for the presence of Alemmanic troops and the legionary fortress shows signs of continued occupation, although similar signs for survival of the town is lacking.[36]

A defensive ditch was built inside the eastern wall indicating that parts of the fortifications were still being used.[37] It would thus appear that York did indeed survive, albeit in a much reduced and contracted state. A century or more later there are few signs that the Roman infrastructure was exploited by Anglo-Saxons.[38] Excavations under York Minster show no activity from the fourth to the seventh centuries. Germanic material culture, burial sites and settlements, associated with Angles, appear from the mid-sixth century, such as Heslington. However, there is no evidence of structural continuation from the early-fifth century.[39]

Patrick Ottaway, in *Roman York*, declares that, by the end of Roman Britain, 'there can have been few soldiers at Eboracum worthy to be considered heirs to the proud tradition of Petilius Cerialis and his men of 71'.[40] Nevertheless, the evidence of continuation within the fortress and colonia suggests some did remain. By the late-fifth century York was possibly at the borders of two emerging petty kingdoms. To the west was the British kingdom Elmet and to the east the Anglian Deira. Bede, writing in c.730, records the presence of the Northumbrian king, Edwin, at York in the early-seventh century. We thus have evidence of occupation of York into the early-fifth century and occupation by Anglo-Saxon Kings a century later, albeit no new building work has been detected. How long the remaining Romano-Britons at York may have held authority into the fifth century and what form that may have taken will be discussed in the final chapter. If we accept the presence of a *praefectus legionis* of the Sixth at York when the *Notitia Dignitatum* was written, then there is no reason to believe the Sixth was not still present in the early-fifth century.

Chapter 8

A Whimper Rather Than a Bang

Roman Britain suffered an extreme economic shock in the early-fifth century. The end of the coin supply and Roman governance disrupted the economic cycle and parts of Roman life failed suddenly and irrevocably.[1] This seems to have been more sudden and complete than elsewhere in the western empire.[2] Many villas were abandoned in the early-fifth century and urban life effectively ended.[3] However, some towns clearly continued, even if what is often called 'town life' did not.[4] Britain, free from Roman rule, beset by raiding and economic decline, limped into the fifth century. Yet it was able to defeat these initial incursions and was able to hire and post mercenaries across the diocese a generation after Roman authority ended. Indeed parts of the former diocese, for example modern Wales and Cornwall, retained their independence and a distinctive Roman-Brittonic culture for many centuries. The important question for the Sixth Legion is what does the evidence tell us about northern Britain in the fifth century?

Hadrian's Wall and the northern military frontier

Importantly the archaeology or contemporary literary sources do not suggest Hadrian's Wall was abandoned at the end of the fourth century.[5] Several forts all show occupation and activity continued well into the fifth century: South Shields, Vindolanda, Birdoswald, Carlisle and south of the wall at Binchester, Piercebridge and York.[6] In fact, Piercebridge on the River Tees shows the defences were used until the late-sixth century.[7] There is evidence for a change in material culture in East Yorkshire in the mid-fifth century and of this spreading through the eastern half of the wall in the sixth century.[8] Despite the lack of Anglo-Saxon burials in the region for this period, we do see the presence of Germanic material culture. However, there is little support for the literary sources which place Germanic mercenaries 'near the wall'.

It is useful at this point to describe what the region evolved into a century or more later. The Anglo-Saxon kingdom of Northumbria initially consisted of two kingdoms, Deira and Bernicia, both with Brittonic etymologies, *Bernech* and *Deura*. The latter covered the *civitas* of the Parisii, north of the Humber. The boundary between the two is traditionally thought to have been the

River Tees.[9] The *Historia Brittonum* names the first king of Bernicia as Ida c. 547. The first attested king of Deira was Aelle, c. 568–598.[10] The *Historia Brittonum* names Soemil as being the first king to separate Deira from Bernicia five generations before Aelle. Interestingly, the archaeological evidence does show evidence of material culture from the second half of the fifth century around York and Catterick.[11] These are often associated with Romano-British military centres.[12] Outside these isolated pockets there is little evidence of any Anglo-Saxon materials in the fifth or sixth centuries.[13]

The Brittonic kingdom of Elmet, perhaps bordering York, was not overrun until 616. Additionally the *Historia Brittonum* describes four powerful British kings nearly pushing the Angles of Bernicia into to the sea at Lindisfarne in the late-sixth century. Other Welsh poems describe Urien of Rheged as the '*Ruler of Catraeth*'.[14] The famous, possibly seventh-century poem, *Y Gododdin* tells of a heroic battle of 300 men attacking the Angles of Deira at Catraeth. All this points to heirs of the former Roman province as still being the power in the north with the early Anglo-Saxon kingdoms struggling to hold on. If Urien really was 'Lord of Catraeth' it implies a far more complex political situation with the Angles aiding the Briton Urien against the Gododdin from the Lothian region and their allies. It would thus appear that Anglo-Saxon settlement in the north was confined to just north of the Humber, possibly up to York, and potentially isolated pockets at former military sites.

In *Hadrian's Wall and the End of Empire*, Collins lays out four scenarios for the fate of the troops of northern Britain.[15]

- There remained an effective imperial garrison into the fifth century
- Major changes and decline in the fourth century left a skeleton force and the frontier became a military backwater
- Major changes in the fourth century left a more regional or localised force that remained effective.
- Changes in the fourth century caused the frontier to evolve into local command/polities served by militia or barbarian *foederati*

Of these four choices, Collins finds the first two options unlikely and states the evidence points to a fragmentation of the northern command into local polities. The question arises when did this fragmentation occur?

St Germanus and St Patrick

There is one contemporary account of life in post-Roman Britain that gives us a brief glimpse at life a generation after Roman rule. Constantius of Lyon, writing c. 480, described the visit of St Germanus of Auxerre in 429. He was sent by Pope Celestine to combat the Pelagian heresy which is confirmed by an earlier record from Prosper c. 455:[16] 'at the persuasion of the deacon Palladius, Pope Celestine sent Germanus, bishop of Auxerre, as his representative, and having rejected the heretics, directed the British to the catholic faith'. Pelagius is described as a British monk who favoured the concept of freewill over that of original sin resulting in Anti-Pelagian legislation appearing in 418. Subsequently Agricola, a Pelagian supporter, fled to Britain suggesting the island was a safe haven for his followers. Prosper also records another deputation, this time to Ireland, in 431: 'Palladius was sent by Pope Celestine to the Scots [Irish] who believed in Christ, and was ordained as their first bishop.'

Germanus is able to travel to Britain where he is welcomed by crowds and wins a theological debate against the Pelagians. The large crowds might suggest London as the most likely venue as he then travels to St Albans to visit the saint's shrine. Our hero cures the blind daughter of a 'tribune' and then has to deal with an incursion of Picts and Saxons. Whilst we should be sceptical of these accounts, the last is interesting since it indicates a functioning military force a generation after the Romans had left. It is worth describing the events in more detail.[17]

The army of the Britons had already marched out, located the enemy and were in camp when they sent for Germanus. The reason for the request for help was 'their apprehension of the numbers' rather than any inability or unwillingness to fight. The Picts and Saxons learn of the Britons' location and advance but the defenders show a 'decisive superiority in reconnaissance' and lay an ambush. Germanus led 'lightly armed men' across country and, when the enemy appears, they cry 'Alleluia' three times and the terrified enemy flee without a blow being struck, many drowning in a nearby river.

All this tells us of a very Christian and Roman-sounding society. One with tribunes, wealthy 'richly dressed' Pelagian-supporting aristocrats and a functioning military force. A second visit occurs a decade or more later. Three dates are possible given that we know the length of Germanus' tenure as bishop: 437, 442 and 448. The first date of 437 is considered most likely.[18] After this visit the heretics are arrested and exiled rather than just 'confounded' and beaten in a debate. This suggests a growth in the power and influence of the Roman church.

Constantius, writing perhaps fifty years later, describes Britain as an 'opulent island', secure and peaceful.[19] Prosper, writing earlier, states that Pope Celestine, 'while he labours to keep the Roman island Catholic he has also made the barbarian island Christian'.[20] So here we have two writers concerned with events twenty years after Roman rule and just before what some call *adventus saxonum*, the coming of the Saxons. The picture is one of a Romanised province, if not a Roman one.

St Patrick is perhaps a little later than Germanus, although his date is insecure. He wrote two works, the *Confessio* and *Epistola*. From the former, we learn he was born in a small country estate, *Bannavem Taburniae*, an unknown location in the west of Britain. His father, Calpornius, was a decurio, a member of town council and a deacon in the church whilst his grandfather, Potitus, was a priest.[21] The dates for his death range from c. 457 to 493. However, it is thought some records conflate him with the earlier Palladius sent by Celestine in 431 and thus his death is accurately recorded in the *Annals of Ulster* as 493.[22] The letter to a King Coroticus, complains of the killing or enslaving of the 'newly baptised' to be sold to the 'apostate Scots and Picts'. Coroticus has been identified as a king of Alt Clud in Strathclyde c. 450, although this is not certain.[23] The words Patrick uses are of interest as he accuses Coroticus of not behaving as a Christian or Roman citizen. The fact these are considered insults suggests that in one part of Britain at least some people still considered themselves to be both.

These two contemporary sources, from possibly either side of the mid-fifth century, give a picture of a Romanised and Christian society. However, it is one where the danger from raiding is very real. Ammianus Marcellinus states that raids by Franks and Saxon were common in the late fourth century.[24] Sidonius Apollinaris in the fifth century makes similar comments concerning Saxon attacks on Gaul. The letter to Coroticus suggests British rulers were resorting to similar tactics and perhaps indicates the breakdown of central control.

The adventus saxonum

By c.440 an entire generation of Britons had lived outside Roman rule. However, older and wiser heads might have lived through similar upheavals during the reigns of Magnus Maximus and Constantine III. They may well have recalled their parents and grandparents telling them about the usurper Maxnentius or the barbarian conspiracy of 367. One might be forgiven in thinking the situation was a temporary suspension of the natural order of things as occurred many times before, such as the Gallic Empire and under Carausius and Allectus. However, this time really was different and events unfolded, both in Britain and the western empire, that were to have far-reaching consequences.

It is likely Germanus witnessed a still functioning diocese and provincial structure. By the end of the sixth century that had all been swept away and in its place several competing petty kingdoms vied for control. Many of these were based on the old *civitates* which themselves were often based on pre-Roman tribal areas. Those in the north and west retained a distinctive Romano-British culture; the south and east did not. The interesting point here is that it is the most Romanised and urbanised areas that evolved into the earliest Anglo-Saxon kingdoms. How then did this happen?

The first question to address is when? Two versions of the *Gallic Chronicles* give us the date c. 440–1: *GC* in 452 states: 'The Britains, which to this time had suffered from various disasters and misfortunes, are reduced to the power of the Saxons.' The *GC* in 511 writes: 'The Britains, lost to the Romans, yield to the power of the Saxons.' Here then we have a firm date from a usually reliable source. Although we must keep an open mind what 'reduced to' and 'yield to' mean. It clearly does not mean the entire island since we know significant areas retained independence for many centuries.

Bede, writing in c. 731, gives us more details. He gets much of his narrative from the sixth-century writer Gildas, and is in turn followed by the later *Anglo-Saxon Chronicles*. Bede suggests these events started with the arrival of Germanic foederati troops in 449, posted in 'the east of the island', later by the wall to fight the Picts and later still given land 'in their [the Britons] midst'. They subsequently rebel, which, assuming a few years have passed since their initial arrival, puts Bede's dates at odds with the *Gallic Chronicle*. One, admittedly very unreliable, source gives a reasonable explanation. The ninth century *Historia Brittonum* was written in northern Wales and is likely more about the politics of that time and place than an accurate historical account. However, it tells the story of an initial group of mercenaries followed by a marriage between the British king Vortigern and Hengest's daughter, named by the even more unreliable Geoffrey of Monmouth in the twelfth century, as Renwein. Vortigern cedes Kent, allows further arrivals and eventually Hengest becomes a kind of *magister militum*. Vortigern's son Vortimer drives the Saxons out but they return and a new treaty is agreed. But the Saxons treacherously murdered 300 British nobles at a peace conference, captured Vortigern and demand control over Essex, Middlesex, Sussex and 'other regions'.

Here is a tale that might explain the discrepancy between the *Gallic Chronicle* and Bede. The first refers to the rise of influence of Germanic mercenaries over the British central authority. The second refers to the later war and massacre. Whatever the case, the mid-fifth century appears to be the turning point. In western Europe, too, Roman authority was shrinking. The defeat of Attila in 451 was perhaps the last high point. The murder of the last great Roman general, Aetius, in 455 was followed by a succession of weak, short-lived emperors and the growing power of Germanic tribes. By 476 the last emperor was deposed by the Germanic general Odoacer.

But the Britons were not finished. In fact we have examples from several different sources referring to military victories by the Romano-Britons. We have already heard of St Germanus leading a force against raiders. Gildas refers to repeated raids, the third of which allowed the Picts to seize the 'whole northern part of the land as far as the wall'. Gildas is scathing of the army: 'slow to fight, unwieldy for flight, incompetent by reason of its cowardice of heart.' An appeal to Aetius, 'thrice consul', is dismissed and they are forced to fight back alone. However, eventually, 'for the first time, they inflicted upon the enemy ... a severe slaughter.' As in Bede, we get the arrival of the Saxon *foederati* troops. Only the *Historia Brittonum* gives us the great victories of Vortimer. Both Bede and Gildas then tell of the rebellion and the subsequent revival. The Britons once more fight back under the command of Ambrosius Aurelianus, 'a man of unassuming character, who, alone of the Roman race chanced to survive in the shock of such a storm.' This culminates in the siege of Mons Badonicus. Gildas states that forty-four years has passed and 'external wars' have ended, but he is unable to access certain shrines, among them St Alban's. Bede dates Ambrosius Aurelianus to 'the time of Zeno', 474–91 and the battle to the 490s.

What does all this mean for the Sixth? Were elements involved in the 'Alleluia victory' of St Germanus in 429? Were these the troops Gildas referred to as being 'dragged from the walls and dashed to the ground' by 'the barbed weapons of their naked enemies' when they 'abandoned their cities and lofty wall'? Or did they survive to win the great victory against the Irish and Pictish raiders, presumably after 445 when Aetius was consul for the third time? The sources all seem to agree that there was no invasion as such and the events were the result of hiring mercenaries. This might suggest that the northern units were so depleted they were unable to function. If the Sixth limped into the fifth century as a skeleton force at York, then it is possible it did not survive beyond the events leading up to the *adventus saxonum*. However, there is one scenario that might make that plausible.

The end of the Sixth?

It is very tempting to suggest a dramatic end to the Sixth, fighting a heroic battle against waves of Picts, Irish or Anglo-Saxon invaders. Perhaps being part of Vortimer's army or even that of Ambrosius Aurelianus. Evolving into the armies of the Romano-Britons, perhaps even fighting at Badon. A more speculative, though perhaps entertaining thought, might be to include them as a core unit fighting alongside Arthur in the twelve battles in the *Historia Brittonum*. However, it is a very real possibility that the *Notitia Dignitatum* does indeed reflect the presence of the remnants of the Sixth at York. It is equally possible that Constantine III left behind some units in the north. It is therefore worth considering what a 'rump' Sixth Legion might have evolved into.

To do this we must first look at the nature of the Germanic settlement. The sources are remarkably consistent; instead of an invasion there was a revolt of federate forces, followed by a steady increase of peoples. Archaeological evidence points to an increase in Germanic material culture after 425. This increases steadily after the mid-fifth when the *Gallic Chronicle*, Gildas and Bede all point to a shift in power. There is a very rough correlation between archaeology and the likely provincial boundaries. Cremations and other evidence associated with Angles are found predominantly between the Humber and north of the Thames Valley roughly in the former province of Flavia Caesariensis. Evidence of Saxon inhumations and material culture are confined to the south and Thames Valley. DNA studies are mixed with estimates of the immigrant population ranging from around 15 to 25 per cent.[25]

In specific areas some estimates of 'continental influences' rise to 38 per cent,[26] whilst in Wessex and East Anglia it is as low as 10 per cent and 20 per cent respectively.[27] An interesting study found a warrior elite of only 10 per cent, spread over many decades, could account for up to 50 per cent towards the gene pool within five generations due to reproductive advantages.[28] A summary of the evidence suggests 'a significant level of immigration into south-eastern England during the fifth century in the order of between 10 and 20 per cent'.[29] This leads to an estimate for a total Germanic immigrant population in the mid-fifth century of between 100,000 to 250,000 in to a population of roughly two million.[30] This would have occurred over several decades which equates to low thousands of people per year.

Bede, writing 200 years later, describes 'three Germanic tribes', Saxons in Wessex, Sussex and Essex, Jutes in Kent and Hampshire, and Angles in East Anglia, Mercia and Northumbria.[31] However, it is often forgotten that he also later lists many other settlers: Frisians, Rugians, Danes, Huns, Old Saxons and Bructeri.[32] We must also remember that the Roman army had significant Germanic elements, many of whom would have settled in Britain after their service. Emperor Probus sent Burgundians and Vandals to Britain around 276–82.[33] Carausius had a significant Germanic presence in his army. Allectus used Frankish mercenaries and it was a king of the Alemanni, Crocus, who declared Constantine Emperor at York in 306. Plus the Saxon Shore Command suggests the coast was either manned by Saxon foederati or settled by their families. This is in addition to the Germanic troops in the legions and the many auxiliary units.

We can thus make a number of statements. The Roman army of the early-fifth century had significant numbers of Germanic troops: the Sixth Legion would have been no different. The earliest evidence of Germanic material culture and settlement is confined to the most romanised and urbanised areas of the south and east. The area around York did not experience settlement until later in the fifth century and that was confined to the civitas of the Parisii. When mercenaries were hired by Vortigern it is likely some were posted to the north to fight the Picts. The subsequent rebellion, spreading from east to west, may well have involved other elements of the army sympathetic to their comrades, especially if they also had not been paid. The later emergence of petty kingdoms suggests a distinction between Anglo-Saxons on one side and Romano-Britons on the other. However, terms such as 'Anglo-Saxon' and 'Welsh' did not evolve for many centuries and we should not assume that the political and social context was that simple.

Cultural change

Gaul in the fifth century could be described as a game of two halves. In the first half-century the Romans battled to control waves of immigrant tribes. For a time Aetius was successful in playing one group off against another. But his death in 455 was perhaps the turning point. Tellingly, we also get evidence that the people themselves were becoming disillusioned with Roman authority. Salvian of Marseilles, writing in the mid-fifth century, claimed that the Romans under barbarian rule desired to never again 'pass under Roman authority'.[34] He writes, 'even those of not obscure birth' choose to live among the barbarians to avoid Roman 'iniquity and cruelty'. This was a view widespread among the 'Roman plebs' or free Roman citizens. He declares, 'the *Romana respublica* is now dead … strangled, as if by thugs, with the bonds of taxes.'[35] He places the blame on local elites, such as town councillors, *principales* or *curiales*, who 'glory in this name of *tyrannus*'. Freeborn Roman citizens found themselves branded as *bacaudae*, outlaws, and subject to 'vicious campaigns of repression'.[36]

If the bulk of the population in the most romanised parts of Britain felt this way we can see why they may have rejected Roman rule in c. 410. No doubt the political and social situation was as fractious as at any other time in human history. If we add to the mix economic collapse, de-urbanisation, the removal of coinage, repeated raids and an unpaid army, we can see how the situation may have been even more fraught than usual. One possible timeline of events has the diocesan structure lasting up to the rebellion of the mercenaries c. 450. The subsequent war left the provincial structures fragmenting with the romanised south and east developing a Germanic material culture. Emerging petty kingdoms start to appear from the collapsing provinces and civitates.

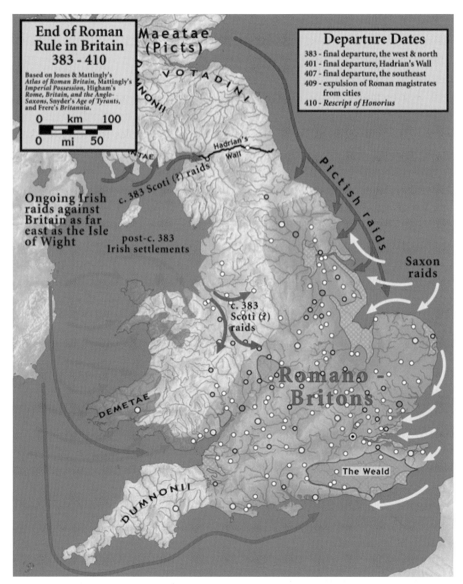

Figure 62: Map of the end of Roman Britain. (*Wikimedia Commons*)

The emergence of the warband

The Britons and Germanic peoples came to share a common institution; the *comitatus* or warband includes the Anglo-Saxon hearth-companions and Welsh *teulu*, or family.[37] At first, this was centred on close kinship groups but evolved into something much wider where warriors were bound to their lord who, in return for their loyalty, gave them shelter and food. By the time of Bede events had turned full circle as social structures coalesced around kingdoms based on a territorial area rather than a 'people'. However, in the late-fifth or early-sixth century, the warband had become the dominant social force. This 'warband' culture, centred on a 'lord' evolved out of the wreckage of the diocesan and provincial structures.

The principle function of the *comitatus* was raiding and warfare and we see many references in the poems and sagas of the early middle ages. The warbands of the Britons, Irish, Picts and Germanic peoples would have likely numbered less than 100.[38] Gildas hints at this cultural change when he talks of the five tyrant kings and their 'military companions'. How then might these cultural changes affect the remnants of the Sixth at York or elsewhere?

As central control broke down the economy, and perhaps more importantly the coin supply, suffered a catastrophic contraction. Ironically, the average peasant, living in rural Britain, may have felt little change or even an increased prosperity with the end of high taxes and the need to supply resources such as grain to the Roman regime. As power became 'localised' those in charge of town councils or important villa estates became more autonomous. There is strong evidence linking *decurions*, the leaders of town councils, to the word 'tyrant' in the fifth century.[39] Salvian, writing at the time, complains that there are as many *tyranni* as *curiales* in municipalities but interestingly they 'glory in this name of *tyrannus*'. Vortigern is thought to stem from 'overlord' being a compound of ver/wor/wer meaning 'over' and -tigern meaning 'lord'. Whilst, in this case, it seems to be a personal name similar versions stemming from *tigernos* are found in aristocratic names in Britain and Gaul. In Brittany the title *machtiern* meant 'fine' or 'great' lord and in Old Irish *macthigern* also meant 'overlord'. It is argued that these Celtic words for 'lord' reflect how provincial people would refer to the local *decurion* or *curiale*.[40]

After Roman rule broke down it may be useful to view the following events as consisting of two stages:[41] The first was a late Roman material culture where villas and urban centres were still important. The local elites shared a social identity, heavily influenced by Roman culture and laws. They thus continued to govern through 'economic relationships' such as tax collectors or landlords.[42] This is the likely situation that St Germanus witnessed when he visited in 429 and again in c. 437. At this point there was still a functioning army of sorts a generation after Roman rule. This suggests political, social and military structures survived. Recruitment, pay and training continued. There's no reason to think York was abandoned or the Sixth disbanded at this point.

The second stage begins roughly just before the mid-fifth century and lasts to the late-sixth. Hill-forts are re-occupied and urban centres contracted or abandoned. The western areas see an increase in Mediterranean material culture, whilst the south and east turn to a more Germanic material culture.

There seems to have been a rejection of aspects of Roman culture in the very areas that had experienced the greatest influence under the empire. At the same time there was a shift to a more martial material culture and symbols reflected a more individual and paramilitary world view.

Conclusion

In summary we can say it is very likely the Sixth Legion is indeed represented in the *Notitia Dignitatum* and thus survived into the fifth century. Even after Maximus, Stilicho and Constantine III, detachments at least were left behind, most likely at York and possibly various other forts across the north. The ending of coinage, economic collapse and de-urbanisation contributed to a fragmentation of political and military organisation in the diocese.

All these forces suggest that whatever was left of the Sixth Legion probably shared the same fate as many other units in Britain. They may have hung on to their cohesion up to the mid-fifth century. The foederati rebellion and subsequent fragmentation of the provincial structure resulted in localised seats of power emerging. Many of these would later evolve into the petty kingdoms of the seventh century, often based on the former civitates of Roman Britain. With no coin supply and no central authority to resource, equip, train or maintain a regular army, units simply faded away or evolved into local warbands. If there was still a praefectus of the unit or a decurion of the town council at York, he may well have become the local *tigernos* or 'tyrant'.

One last point to bear in mind is this. Some might assume that any surviving force might have fought against Saxons and Picts in the first half of the fifth century, or fought with Vortimer, Vortigern or even Ambrosius Aurelianus against the invading Anglo-Saxons. However, the actual political and cultural situation was far more complex. We have no way of knowing the ethnic make-up of surviving units any more than their political views. It is just as likely that they supported the foederati who rebelled against Vortigern as they fought against them.

For nearly 300 years the Sixth were the dominant military force in northern Britain. They helped to build, and defend, two of the most famous defensive walls in history. Like so many other military units in Roman Britain, they seem to have ended with a whimper rather than a bang, slowly fading into a slow death as Roman Britain disintegrated. The importance of York, however, continued. What replaced the former Roman provincial and military structures was a warband culture that eventually evolved into the kingdoms of Anglo-Saxon England. It is interesting that the borders of the powerful kingdom of Northumberia often resembled the northern province of Roman Britain. The last soldiers of the Sixth may well have witnessed the arrival of Hengest and Horsa. They may have fought alongside these mercenaries against the Picts and Irish raiders from the north and west. Who their sons and grandsons fought for is open to debate. Many may have found themselves on different sides of a widening divide in emerging cultural identities.

I will finish with a timeline of the Sixth Legion and the major events affecting Roman Britain.

Table 18: Timeline of the Sixth Legion in Roman Britain.

Year (AD unless stated)	
41 BC	Fought at Perugia, Italy for Augustus
	Sixth posted to Spain.
29–19 BC	*Bellum Cantabricum et Asturicum* in Spain
43	Roman invasion of Britain
54–68	The name *Victrix*, or 'Victorious' first attested during the reign of Nero
68	Fought for Glba in 'Year of the Four Emperors'
70	Sixth sent to Rhine border during Batavian rebellion. Victory at Vetera. Based at Novaesium in Germania Inferior.
89	Sixth sent to quell a rebellion in Germany Superior. Awarded the title *Pia Fidelis Domitiana*, Dutiful and Loyal of Domitian.
96	Domitian assassinated, title *Pia Fidelis Domitiana* dropped.
c. 110	Posted to Vetera on the Rhine
119	Unrest in Britain, coins issued with BRITTANIA signifying a campaign
121	Construction of limes in Germania
c. 122	Coins issued c. 122 allude to *expeditio Augusti*, suggesting possible campaign by Hadrian
122	Legion posted to Britain. Construction of Hadrian's Wall begins
c. 130	The Sixth by now based at York
138	Hadrian dies. Antoninus Pius emperor.
138–42	Unrest in northern Britain. Urbricus 'overcame the Britons' and emperor awarded title of *imperator*.
c. 142–154	Construction of Antonine Wall
155–60	Unrest in northern Britain, Antonine Wall abandoned, Hadrian's Wall re-occupied.
161	Antoninus dies. Marcus Aurelius Emperor. Parthian war 161–6.
180	Marcus Aurelius dies, Commodus emperor

Year (AD unless stated)	
182–4	War in Britain. Tribes cross the wall and kill a 'general' and his troops. Evidence of damage to northern forts. Put down by Marcellus.
185	Legions rebel and attempt to declare Junius Priscus emperor. 1,500 'javelin men' sent to Rome from Britain.
185–7	Pertinax sent as governor. Legions attempt to declare Pertinax emperor, mutiny and nearly kill him.
193	Year of the Five Emperors after Commodus killed. Ends with Clodius Albinus Caesar in Britain and Septimius Severus Emperor in Rome.
196	Albinus declares himself Emperor and crosses to Gaul with army.
197	Battle of Lugdunum, likely presence of Sixth. Albinus defeated and killed. Severus 'settles affairs' in Britain and rebuilds and repairs the Wall and northern forts.
208–11	Attacks by Caledonians and Maeatae results in Roman invasion of Scotland. Evidence of the Sixth at Capow.
211	Severus dies, Caracalla fails to get support of legions in Britain and returns to Rome.
212	First division of Britain forms two provinces, Britannia Inferior and Britannia Superior. Edict of Caracalla grants citizenship to all freemen across empire.
235–84	Crisis of the Third Century
253–68	Emperor Gallienus reforms military. Equestrians now legion commanders.
260–74	Gallic Empire includes Britain
284	Diocletian emperor.
286–93	Carausius declares himself emperor and takes fleet to Britain
293	Allectus assassinates Carausius and takes control of Britain. Diocletian introduces tetrachy and other reforms
296	Allectus defeated in southern Britain.
c. 300	Second division of Britain into four provinces within one diocese. Legions reduced from c. 5,000 to c. 1,000 troops.
305	Constantius made Western Augustus and campaigns in northern Britain
306	Constantius dies at York. Constantine declared emperor.
313	Edict of Milan allowed freedom of religion for Christians
324	Christianity becomes official state religion
337	Constantine dies, succeeded by his three sons.
343	Constans travels to Britain, possible campaign.
350	Magnentius emperor of western provinces including Britain.
353	Magnentius killed at Lugdunum, Constantius II sole emperor.

Year (AD unless stated)	
367	Barbarian conspiracy in Britain put down by Theodosius. Fifth province of Valentia created.
383–88	Magnus Maximus declared emperor in Britain, takes troops to Gaul and kills Gratian. Killed at Aquileia.
402	Stilicho campaigns in north before removing troops and coinage from Britain
406	In Britain three emperors declared in succession. Constantine III takes troops from Britain to Gaul
408	*Gallic Chronicle* records major Saxon raid
409	Britons rebel from Constantine and appeal to Honorius. They are told to look to own defences.
410	Rome sacked by Goths
411	Constantine killed and Britain is 'forever lost to the Romans'
Early fifth century	Gildas records Britain raided by Picts and Irish in three major incursions.
429	St Germanus visits Britain. Last contemporary record of functioning 'Romanised' civilian and military structure.
Mid-fifth century	Gallic Chronicle records Britain 'falls to the power of the Saxons' c. 440 Gildas: Appeal to Aetius, 'thrice consul' (c.446) rejected. Britons defeat Irish and Picts. Gildas records Saxon mercenaries hired and then rebel. Bede dates this to c. 449–56
476	End of Western Roman Empire
c. 500	Fightback by Ambrosius Aurelianus and battle of Badon Emergence of warband culture and petty kingdoms.

Appendix

Table 19: Sixth Legion inscriptions.

Inscription (building inscription unless stated)	Location	RIB number	Date 43–410 unless stated
The Sixth Legion Victrix (built this)	Near Milecastle 42, Hadrian's Wall	1680	
The Sixth Legion Victrix (built this)	Piercebridge	1025	
The Sixth Legion Victrix (built this)	Birrens	2113	
The Sixth Legion Victrix (built this)	Birrens	2112	140–165
The Sixth Legion Victrix (built this)	Corbridge	1159	
The Sixth Legion Victrix Pia Fidelis (built this)	Corbridge	1160	
Dedication: To the Concord of the Sixth Legion Pia Fidelis and of the Twentieth Legion Valeria Victrix	Corbridge	1125	
Dedication: To Jupiter, Best and Greatest, for the welfare of the detachments of the Twentieth Legion Valeria Victrix and of the Sixth Legion Victrix the soldiers on garrison-duty	Corbridge	1130	
Dedication: To the Invincible Sun-god a detachment of the Sixth Legion Victrix Pia Fidelis set this up under the charge of Sextus Calpurnius Agricola, emperor's propraetorian legate	Corbridge	1137	162–8
A detachment of the Sixth Legion Pia Fidelis under the charge of Virius Lupus, of senatorial rank and consular governor, (built this)	Corbridge	1163	197–202
A detachment of the Sixth Legion Pia Fidelis rebuilt this	Corbridge	1162	
Fragment: the Sixth Legion Victrix	Corbridge	1190	
The Sixth Legion Victrix (built this)	Birdoswald	1916	
The Sixth Legion Victrix (built this)	Birdoswald to Castlesteads sector	1966	

Inscription (building inscription unless stated)	Location	RIB number	Date 43–410 unless stated
The Sixth Legion Victrix (built this)	Birdoswald to Castlesteads sector	1967	
The Sixth Legion Victrix (built this)	Birdoswald to Castlesteads sector	1968	
The Sixth Legion Victrix (built this)	Birdoswald to Castlesteads sector	1934	
The Sixth Legion Victrix (built this)	Birdoswald to Castlesteads sector	1938	
Fragment: The Sixth Legion Victrix …	Birdoswald to Castlesteads sector	1939	
Quarry: The Sixth Legion Victrix Pia Fidelis (made this)	Birdoswald to Castlesteads sector	1953	
Altar: To the god Cocidius a detachment of the Sixth Legion Victrix willingly and deservedly fulfilled its vow	Birdoswald to Castlesteads sector	1961	
The Sixth Legion Victrix (built this)	Castlesteads	2000	
Altar: To the god Cocidius the soldiers of the Sixth Legion Victrix Pia Fidelis (set this up)	Castlesteads to Stanwix sector	2020	
The Sixth Legion Victrix and the Twentieth Legion Valeria Victrix built this	Halton Chesters	1430	
The Sixth Legion Victrix Pia Fidelis built this	Halton Chesters	1429	
Dedication: For the Emperor Caesar Trajan Hadrian Augustus the Sixth Legion Victrix Pia Fidelis (built this) under Aulus Platorius Nepos	Halton Chesters	1427	122–6
[For the Emperor Antoninus Pius … a detachment] of the Sixth Legion Victrix…	Halton Chesters	3291	
The Sixth Legion Victrix built this	Binchester	1038	
The Sixth Legion Victrix built this	Halton Chesters to Chesters sector	1438	
The Sixth Legion Victrix built this	Housesteads to Great Chesters sector	1635	
The Sixth Legion Victrix (built this)	Chesters	1471	
Dedication: For the Emperor Titus Aelius Hadrianus Antoninus Augustus Pius, father of his country, in his second consulship, the Sixth Legion Victrix (built this)	Chesters	1460	139

Inscription (building inscription unless stated)	Location	RIB number	Date 43–410 unless stated
Dedication: For the Emperor Titus Aelius Hadrianus Antoninus Augustus Pius, father of his country, in his second consulship, the detachment of the Sixth Legion Victrix Pia Fidelis (built this)	Chesters	1461	139
The Sixth Legion Victrix (built this)	Papcastle	884	
The Sixth Legion Victrix Pia Fidelis (built this)	Croy Hill	2161	
The Sixth Legion Victrix Pia Fidelis (built this)	Croy Hill	2163	140–154
Altar: To the Nymphs a detachment of the Sixth Legion Pia Fidelis under Fabius Liberalis (set this up)	Croy Hill	2160	140–65
The Sixth Legion (built this)	Croy Hill	2162	140–65
The Sixth Legion Victrix Pia Fidelis (built this)	Risingham	1239	
The Sixth Legion Victrix Pia Fidelis (built this)	Bowness-on-Solway	2061	
Altar: To Neptune the Sixth Legion Victrix Pia Fidelis (set this up)	Newcastle upon Tyne	1319	Possibly 122
Altar: To Ocianus the Sixth Legion Victrix Pia Fidelis (set this up)	Newcastle upon Tyne	1320	
For the Emperor Antoninus Augustus Pius, father of his country, the detachment (of men) contributed from the two Germanies for the Second Legion Augusta and the Sixth Legion Victrix and the Twentieth Legion Valeria Victrix, under Julius Verus, emperor's pro-praetorian legate, (set this up).	Newcastle upon Tyne	1322	155–9
A detachment of the Sixth Legion Victrix Pia Fidelis (built this): of the Sixth Legion Pia Fidelis	Netherby	981	
The Sixth Legion Victrix Pia Fidelis Gordiana rebuilt this	Hadrian's Wall near Carlisle	2027	
Dedicateon: To the Nymphs the detachment of the Sixth Legion Victrix (set this up)	Carrawburgh	1547	
The Sixth Legion Victrix Pia Fidelis (built this)	Carrawburgh to Housesteads sector	3320	158
A detachment of the Sixth Legion Victrix (set this up)	Near Carlisle	1019	

Inscription (building inscription unless stated)	Location	RIB number	Date 43–410 unless stated
The Sixth Legion (built this)	Cartlise	3464	
Fragment: Sixth Legion Victrix	York	669	
Altar: To the African, Italian, and Gallic Mother Goddesses Marcus Minucius Audens, soldier of the Sixth Legion Victrix and a pilot	York	653	
To the holy god Serapis Claudius Hieronymianus, legate of the Sixth Legion Victrix, built this temple from the ground	York	658	190–212
A detachment of the Sixth Legion Victrix Pia Fidelis (built this)	High Rochester	1283	
Altar: To the Mother Goddesses of the household a detachment of the Sixth Legion Victrix Pia Fidelis (set this up)	Burgh-by-Sands to Drumburgh sector	2050	
Second Legion Augusta (and) ... Sixth Legion Victrix Pia Fidelis (built this)	Hadrian's Wall, unknown location	2075	
From the Sixth Legion Victrix Pia Fidelis, and from the seventh cohort the century [...] ...	Hadrian's Wall, unknown location	2076	
The Sixth Legion Victrix Pia Fidelis rebuilt this in the consulship of Tertullus and Sacerdos; S(...) F(...).	Benwell to Rudchester section	1389	158
Of the Sixth Legion Victrix the tenth cohort completed this	Benwell to Rudchester section	1388	158
Dedication: To Fortune detachments of the Second Legion Augusta and Sixth Legion Victrix Pia Fidelis gladly and willingly set this up	Castlecary	2146	142–180
Altar: To the god Mercury soldiers of the Sixth Legion Victrix Pia Fidelis, being citizens of Italy and Noricum, set up this shrine	Castlecary	2148	140–90
Distance slab: Victrix Pia Fidelis (built this) for a distance of 3,666½ paces	Balmuildy	2194	139–61
Fragment: ... with the equipment ... he had vowed ... of the Sixth Legion Victrix ... consuls	Brougham	783	
Distance slab: Victrix Pia Fidelis (built) for a distance of one mile	Kirkintilloch	2185	142=61
The Sixth Legion Victrix(built this)	Vindolanda	3353	
Of the Sixth Legion Victrix Pia Fidelis, a detachment built (this)	Bewcastle	3480	163

Inscription (building inscription unless stated)	Location	RIB number	Date 43–410 unless stated
Distance slab: To the Emperor Caesar Titus Aelius Hadrianus Antoninus Augustus Pius, father of his country, a detachment of the Sixth Legion Victrix Pia Fidelis (built this) for a distance of 3,666½ paces.	Castlehill	2196	142–61
Distance slab: For the Emperor Caesar Titus Aelius Hadrianus Antoninus Augustus, father of his country, a detachment of the Sixth Legion Victrix Pia Fidelis did the construction of the rampart for 3240 feet.	Duntocher	2200	142–61
Distance slab: For the Emperor Caesar Titus Aelius Hadrianus Antoninus Augustus, father of his country, a detachment of the Sixth Legion Victrix Pia Fidelis (did) the construction of the rampart for 4,141 feet.	Old Kirkpatrick	2205	142–80
The Sixth Legion (built this)	South Shields	1061	

Table 20: Soldiers of the Sixth inscriptions.

Inscription	Location	RIB number	Date 43–410 unless stated
Dedication: To … Gaius Julius Maximinus, centurion of the Sixth Legion Victrix, in accordance with his vow, set up this statue with its	Wallsend	1305	
Centurial stone: Under the direction of Flavius Hyginus, centurion of the Sixth Legion Victrix	Corbridge	1161	
Altar: To the god Maponus Apollo, Publius Aelius …, centurion of the Sixth Legion Victrix, willingly and deservedly fulfilled his vow	Corbridge	1122	
a detachment of the Sixth Legion Victrix Pia Fidelis (set this up) under Gnaeus Julius Verus, emperor's legate, through the agency of Lucius …, military tribune.	Corbridge	1132	155–9
Altar: To Apollo Maponus, Quintus Terentius Firmus, son of Quintus, of the Oufentine voting-tribe, from Saena, prefect of the camp of the Sixth Legion Victrix Pia Fidelis, gave and dedicated this	Corbridge	1120	

Inscription	Location	RIB number	Date 43–410 unless stated
Funerary: To Lucius Valerius Justus, soldier of the Sixth Legion, Egnatius Dyonisius and Surius Justus, his heirs, had this set up.	Corbridge	1175	
Dedication: To the goddess Fortune Sosia Juncina, (wife) of Quintus Antonius Isauricus, imperial (legionary) legate, (set this up)	York	644	mid-130s
Building stone: The century of Calpurnius Victorinus	York	669	
Altar: To the African, Italian, and Gallic Mother Goddesses Marcus Minucius Audens, soldier of the Sixth Legion Victrix and a pilot	York	653	
Funerary: To the spirits of the departed (and) to Aurelius Super, centurion of the Sixth Legion, who lived 38 years, 4 months, 13 days; his wife, Aurelia Censorina, set up this memorial.	York	670	
Funerary inscription: To the spirits of the departed: Lucius Bebius Crescens, of Augusta Vindelicum, soldier of the Sixth Legion Pia Fidelis, aged 43, of 23 years' service; his heir had this set up to his friend	York	671	
Funerary inscription: To the spirits of the departed (and) of Titus Flavius Flavinus, centurion of the Sixth Legion Victrix; his heir, Classicius	York	675	
Funerary inscription: To the spirits of the departed; [...]lius Cresces, son of ..., of the ... voting-tribe, from ..., veteran of the Sixth Legion Victrix, ...	York	679	
Funerary inscription: Simplex, made this: centurion of the Sixth Legion Victrix	York	690	
Funerary inscription: To the spirits of the departed (and) of Flavia Augustina; she lived 39 years, 7 months, 11 days; her son, Saenius Augustinus, lived 1 year, 3 days, and [...]a, (her daughter), lived 1 year 9 months, 5 days; Gaius Aeresius Saenus, veteran of the Sixth Legion Victrix, had this set up for his beloved wife and himself	York	685	

Inscription	Location	RIB number	Date 43–410 unless stated
Funerary inscription: To the shades of the dead. Antonius Gargilianus, of equestrian rank, sometime prefect of the Sixth Legion Victrix, aged 56 years, 6 months. Claudius Florentinus, decurion, his son-in-law (set this up).	York	3201	early 3rd century
Altar: To Cocidius and to the Genius of the garrison Valerius, soldier of the Sixth Legion Victrix Pia Fidelis, set this up as his vow	Housesteads	1577	
Fragmentary dedication: centurion of the Sixth Legion Victrix Pia Fidelis, gladly, willingly, and deservedly fulfilled his vow	Housesteads	1609	
Altar: To the Fortune of the Roman People Gaius Julius Raeticus, centurion of the Sixth Legion Victrix, (set this up)	Vindolanda	1684	
Altar: To Fortuna Conservatrix Lucius Senecianius Martius, centurion of the Sixth Legion Victrix (set this up)	Manchester	575	
Dedication: To the god Hercules Gaius Vitellius Atticianus, centurion of the Sixth Legion Victrix Pia Fidelis, (set this up)	Whitley Castle	1199	
To the Victory of the Sixth Legion Victrix Valerius Rufus willingly and deservedly fulfilled his vow	North-East of Manchester	582	
Dedication: Gaius Julius Speratus, by tribe a Mattiacan, ... of the Sixth Legion Victrix Pia Fidelis, gladly, willingly, and deservedly	Castlecary	2151	
Altar: Sacred to Fortune: Gaius Antonius Modestus, centurion of the Sixth Legion Victrix Pia Fidelis, willingly and deservedly	Slack	624	
Funerary inscription: Sacred to the spirits of the departed (and) to Nigrina, (who) lived 40 years: Aurelius Casitto, centurion of the Sixth Legion Victrix Pia Fidelis, had this set up.	Great Chesters	1746	
Funerary inscription: To the spirits of the departed (and) of Gaius Julius Ingenuus, son of Gaius, of (colonia) Flavia [...], soldier of the Sixth Legion Victrix Pia Fidelis	High Rochester	1292	

Inscription	Location	RIB number	Date 43–410 unless stated
Altar: To the goddess Sulis for the welfare and safety of Aufidius Maximus, centurion of the Sixth Legion Victrix, Marcus Aufidius	Bath	144	
Altar: To the Genius of this place … of the Sixth Legion Victrix, Forianus gladly, willingly, and deservedly fulfilled his vow xx	Bath	139	
Altar: To the goddess Sulis for the welfare and safety of Marcus Aufidius Maximus, centurion of the Sixth Legion Victrix, Aufidius	Bath	143	after 122
Funerary inscription: To the spirits of the departed (and) of Gaius Julius Calenus, of the Galerian voting-tribe, from Lyons, veteran from the Sixth Legion Victrix Pia Fidelis; his heir made this to the memory of him	Lincoln	252	
Fragment: … fallen down through age, under the charge of … centurion of the Sixth Legion Victrix … Postumius Urbanus … of Upper Britain … .	Greta Bridge	747	3rd-4th century
Funerary inscription: To the spirits of the departed: Flavius Agricola, soldier of the Sixth Legion Victrix, lived 42 years, 10 days; Albia Faustina	London	11	after 197
Fragmentary dedication: To … Lucius Junius Victorinus Flavius Caelianus, imperial legate of the Sixth Legion Victrix Pia Fidelis, (set this up) because…	Stanwix to Burgh-by-Sands sector	2034	mid-2nd century
Centurial stone: Of the Sixth Legion Victrix, the century of Paternus (built this)	South Shields	3273	138–92
Centurial stone: Of the Sixth Legion Victrix [Pia Fidelis], the century of […] Severus (built) 102 feet	South Shields	3274	138–92
Fragmentary centurial stone: Of the Sixth Legion Victrix Pia Fidelis, of the Third Cohort, [the century of … (built this)]	South Shields	3275	
Fragmentary dedication: Julius Verax, centurion of the Sixth Legion …	South Shields	1057	

Inscription	Location	RIB number	Date 43–410 unless stated
Funerary inscription: [Sacred to the spirits of the departed;] Publius Aelius Bassus, son of Publius, of the Sergian voting-tribe, [from Mursa], once centurion of the Twentieth Legion Valeria Victrix, lived ... years .[...] and Privatus, his freedmen and heirs, through Aelius Surinus, centurion of the Sixth Legion Victrix, had this erected. If anyone brings another corpse into this tomb, let him pay to the treasury of our Lords [...]; set up under the direction of Aelius Surinus, [...	Watercrook, Lancashire	754	
Funerary inscription: Sacred to the shades of the dead. Gaius Cossutius Saturninus of Hippo Regius, soldier [of the Sixth Legion Victrix] Pia Fidelis ...	Birdoswald	3445	
Dedication: ... Lucius Vereius Fortunatus, centurion of the Sixth Legion	Birdoswald	1907	
The century of Florianus of the eighth (?) cohort of the Sixth Legion (built this)	Birdoswald to Castlesteads	1937	
Funerary inscription: To [deity] and the Divinity of the Emperor, Sammius Victor, centurion of the Sixth Legion Victrix [Pia Fidelis].	Ebchester	3265	
Dedication: To the holy god Apollo Maponus for the welfare of our Lord (the Emperor) and of Gordian's Own Unit of Sarmatian cavalry of Bremetennacum Aelius Antoninus, centurion of the Sixth Legion Victrix, from Melitene, acting-commander and prefect, fulfilled his vow willingly, deservedly. Dedicated 31 August in the consulship of the Emperor Our Lord Gordian for the second time and of Ponpeianus.	Ribchester	583	238–44
Altar: Sacred to the celestial Silvanae and Quadriviae. Vibia Pacata, (wife) of Flavius Verecundus centurion of the Sixth Legion Victrix, with her family paid her vow willingly, deservedly.	Westerwood	3504	
Altar: To Fortune Audacilius Romanus, centurion of the Sixth, Twentieth, and (Second) Augusta Legions, (set this up).	Carvoran	1179	

Inscription	Location	RIB number	Date 43–410 unless stated
Dedication: To Jupiter Dolichenus Best and Greatest, for the welfare of the detachments of the Sixth Legion Victrix and of the army of each Germany under the charge of Marcus Lollius Venator, centurion of the Second Legion Augusta. They paid their vow willingly, deservedly	Piercebridge	3253	217
Dedication: To the God, Lucius Sentius Castus, (centurion) of the Sixth Legion, set this up as a gift	Rudchester	1398	

Below is a list of other officers of the Sixth Legion known from other sources.

Legates of the Sixth

Marcus Pompeius Macrinus Neos Theophanes, c. 100–10, Germania Inferior (CIL XIV, 3599)

Marcus Valerius Propinquus c. 122 (CIL II, 6084)
Probably the son of the equestrian officer, Marcus Valerius Propinquus Grattius Cerealis of Liria.

He was likely elected to the senate as a tribune or aedile after serving as an equestrian officer.

He is thought to have served as legate of the Sixth in Germania Inferior for a year or two before traveling with the Sixth to Britain where he handed command to Tullius Varro. A year later he was governor of a province beginning with A, very likely Aquitania, in c. 123–6.

Publius Tullius Varro c. 122 (CIL X, 3364)
From Tarquinii in Etruria, Italy, his father was proconsul of Macedonia. After a praetorship he commanded the XII Fulminata in Cappadocia. It was rare to command more than one legion but the transfer of the Sixth may have been a good enough reason. He subsequently served as proconsul of Baetica and prefect of the Treasury before a consulship in 127. Later he served as Tiber curator, legate of Moesia Superior and proconsul of Africa in 142.

Lucius Minicius Verus c. 130 (CIL XIV, 3599)
From Barcelona, he was tribune in three successive legions, the last being XIV Gemina in Pannonia Superior whist his father was governor c. 112–7.

He entered the senate as a quaestor before serving as legate, again under his father who was by this time proconsul of Africa. He served as Tribune of the Plebs and was Hadrian's candidate for the praetorship. He won the four-horse chariot race in the Olympic Games of 129 as an 'ex-praetor' and likely came to Britain soon after to lead the Sixth. Birley states he was described as 'extremely wealthy, somewhat vain, and a devotee of various religious cults'. Lucius was a consul in 139 and added the governorship of Moesia Inferior and proconsulship of Africa to his list of achievements.

Quintus Antonius Isauricus c. mid-130s (CIL VII, 233)

A stone dated to just after Verus was found at York. It reads: 'To the goddess Fortune Sosia Juncina, (wife) of Quintus Antonius Isauricus, imperial (legionary) legate, (set this up)'.

Birley dates him to 'late in Hadrian's reign, c. 135' but nothing else is known of his career.

Publius Mummius Sisenna Rutilianus c. 135–8 (CIL XIV, 3601)

From Baetica in Spain he was described as 'a man of good family and tested in many Roman offices, but utterly sick as far as the gods were concerned'. He was a tribune in V Macedonia before three urban magistrate posts, the last in c. 134. His father was governor of Britain in 135 and it is likely he was legate during this period. Born in c. 105 he died aged 70 in c. 175 having served as governor in Moesia Superior c.150 and proconsul of Asia c. 160–1.

Quintus Camurius Numisius Junior c. 155–8 (CIL XI, 5670)

From Attidium in Umbria, his wife was Stertinia Luci and they had a son, Quintus Cornelius.

Tribune of IX Hispana c. 138–40, followed by posts as questor, aedile and praetor in Rome by 150.

A legionary command (unreadable on stone inscription) pre-dated his command of the Sixth. He achieved consul in 161. He was thought to have been born prior to 120 and was legate of the Sixth in the mid-150s.

Junius Priscus Gargilius Quintilianus c. 184

An attempted mutiny in Britain around 184 involved a certain Priscus which Birley argues is the very same man the legions in Britain tried to make emperor in 184 under Commodus. A stone inscription (CIL vi.41127) records him later as a propraetorian legate of the Emperor of the Second Legion Italica. Interestingly, as he is not recorded as governor, this suggests the legion was operating outside its normal base of operations. A command of vexillations of three British legions may be the 1,500 javelin men recorded by Dio who marched on Rome. Another posting was as legate of V Macedonia followed by further distinguished posts: Iuridicus, praetor, Tribune of the Plebs and quaestor. If Birley is correct then we can piece together events in this career. A second legate post is unusual, but the failed mutiny in Britain may have prompted his removal to the Danube with the Fifth Macedonia. Perhaps the delegation of 1,500 javelin men was led by Priscus. A German expedition under Commodus is dated to c. 188 and if he sent the Second Italica out of their normal base in Noricum, he left the governor in situ. If so a new legate was required to lead them and his previous loyalty may have raised the profile of Priscus.

Lucius Junius Victorinus Flavius Caelianus, mid-second century
Fragmentary dedication found between Stanwix and Burgh-by-Sands: 'To … Lucius Junius Victorinus Flavius Caelianus, imperial legate of the Sixth Legion Victrix Pia Fidelis, (set this up) because of successful achievements beyond the Wall.'

A legate of the sixth, Lucius Junius Victorinus Flavius Caelianus has a dedication for 'successes beyond the wall' which could be dated to Antonine or early Severan period.[43]

Lucius Claudius Hieronymianus, c. 190s (CIL VII, 240): An early-third century source, Papinian killed by Caracalla, allows us to date him before 212. Another source, Tertullian, refers to the fate of Roman officials who persecuted Christians. We read that Hieronymianus in Cappadicia who was angry at his wife's conversion and treated the Christians cruelly. He subsequently fell ill with plague and 'festering with worms'. Reportedly, he was the only one in the praetorium to suffer and asked for it to be kept secret, 'lest the Christians rejoice'. We are told he repented and died 'nearly a Christian'. Birley dates this governorship to 202–12 and his legionary command to the 190s. As it's likely to be after the defeat of Albinus in 197 suggesting he may have been appointed by Septimius Severus.

Tribunus laticlavius
Second in command and of senatorial rank, this was usually a young man in his twenties.

Lucius Funisulanus Vettonianus c. 58 in Hispania Tarraconensis (CIL III, 4013 and XI, 571)

Gaius Calpetanus Rantius Quirinalis Valerius Festus c. 60 in Hispania Tarraconensis (CIL V, 531)

Marcus Pontius Laelianus, 122 (CIL VI, 1497): He served as propraetorian legate in three provinces Syria, Pannonia Inferior and Pannonia Superior. His later career was exceptional:

> 'comes of the deified Verus Augustus, decorated with military decorations in the Armenian and Parthian war by the Emperors Antoninus and the deified Verus, the Augusti, with crowns, a wall one, a rampart one, a naval one, a gold one, four pure spears, four vexilla, comes of the Emperors ... in the German war, likewise comes of the Emperor Antoninus Augustus Germanicus Sarmaticus,

Legate of the first Legion Minervia'. Importantly, the same inscription states he was 'military tribune of the Sixth Legion Victrix, with which he crossed from Germany to Britain'. If he was 20 years of age at this point he would have been 60 when he fought in the Parthian War of Lucius Verus, 161–6. It is during the reign of Marcus Aurelius that Fronto praises his 'old fashioned discipline' which ties in with Hadrian's reign and the emperor's reputation with the army.

Quintus Licinius Silvanus Granianus Quadronius Proculus, c. 120s (CIL II, 4609)
Possibly the son of Q. Licinius Silvanus Granianus from Spain.

Tribunus angusticlavius
One of five equestrian military tribunes advising the legate
Gaius Minicius Italus c. 80 in Hispania Tarraconensis (CIL VIII, 875 and III, 12053)
Lucius ? (RIB 1132): 'a detachment of the Sixth Legion Victrix Pia Fidelis (set this up) under Gnaeus Julius Verus, emperor's legate, through the agency of Lucius ..., military tribune'
Marcus Macrinius Avitus Catonius Vindex c. 160s (CIL VI, 1449)
Publius Helvius Pertinax c. 170s

Sources for Images and Maps

Author's own unless listed below:

Figure 4: Map of Imperial and Senatorial provinces AD 117. Image from Wikimedia Commons. https://commons.wikimedia.org/w/index.php?curid=23100228

Figure 11: Map of Roman Britain c. 68. Image from Wikimedia Commons. CC BY-SA 3.0, https://commons.wikimedia.org/w/index.php?curid=11357177

Figure 12: Map of Agricola's campaigns 78-84. Image from Wikimedia Commons. CC BY-SA 3.0, https://commons.wikimedia.org/w/index.php?curid=8494910

Figure 13: Map of Northern Britain c. 84. Image from Wikimedia Commons. Primarily Frere's Britannia, CC BY-SA 3.0, https://commons.wikimedia.org/w/index.php?curid=8496882

Figure 17: Model of Fort Horsesteads on Hadrian's Wall. Image from Wikimedia Commons. CC BY 2.0, https://commons.wikimedia.org/w/index.php?curid=62988972

Figure 20: Bust of Hadrian. Image from Wikimedia Commons. Author: Carole Raddato. From Hadrian's Mausoleum, possibly created following the emperor's death in 138 AD Vatican Museums, CC BY-SA 2.0, https://commons.wikimedia.org/w/index.php?curid=74822013

Figure 22: Map showing Roman military organisation in the north. Image from Wikimedia Commons. CC BY-SA 3.0, https://commons.wikimedia.org/w/index.php?curid=8496901

Figure 26: Section of a Roman street of Pompeii. Image from Wikimedia Commons. CC BY-SA 3.0, https://commons.wikimedia.org/w/index.php?curid=20085736

Figure 27: Map of Roman roads of Britain. Image from Wikimedia Commons. CC BY-SA 3.0, https://commons.wikimedia.org/w/index.php?curid=11465812

Figure 32: Map of northern campaign of Septimius Severus c. 208-11. Image from Wikimedia Commons. BY-SA 3.0, https://commons.wikimedia.org/w/index.php?curid=8496914

Figure 39: The coastal defences of Roman Britain. Map from Wikimedia Commons. CC BY-SA 3.0, https://commons.wikimedia.org/w/index.php?curid=11734746

Figure 40: Soldiers of the Sixth. A variety of uniforms and armour from the second century. Photograph by kind permission of Dave Grainger of Legio VI Victrix, Eboracum.

Figure 41: Legionary infantryman from 2nd century wearing lorica segmentata armed with pilum. Photograph by kind permission of Dave Grainger of Legio VI Victrix, Eboracum.

Figure 42: Second century officer wearing lorica squamata. Photograph by kind permission of Dave Grainger of Legio VI Victrix, Eboracum.

Figure 43: An optio of VI Victrix wearing lorica squamata. Photograph by kind permission of Dave Grainger of Legio VI Victrix, Eboracum.

Figure 44: On the left a signifier of VI Victrix wearing lorica hamata with legion banner. On the right a centurion of the Sixth with his medals on his cuirass. Photograph by kind permission of Dave Grainger of Legio VI Victrix, Eboracum.

Figure 45: Various uniforms from the fourth century. Lorica segmentata replaced by hamata and squamata armour. Photograph by kind permission of Ross Cronshaw of Magister Militum. Uniforms and armour of the fourth century.

Figure 46: Fourth century officer wearing lorica squamata with banner of *Ioviani Seniores*. Photograph by kind permission of Ross Cronshaw of Magister Militum.

Figure 47: Fourth century Roman officer wearing lorica squamata armour and ornate late Roman ridge helmet. Photograph by kind permission of Ross Cronshaw of Magister Militum.

Figure 48: Fourth century Roman officer with light infantryman and archer. Photograph by kind permission of Ross Cronshaw of Magister Militum.

Figure 49: Late Roman officer and infantryman of the Sixth. Photograph by kind permission of Ross Cronshaw of Magister Militum.

Figure 50: Xanten ballista recently acquired by the VIII Legio Augusta. Photograph by kind permission of Ross Cronshaw of Magister Militum.

Figure 51: Various examples of fourth century late Roman soldiers. Photograph by kind permission of Ross Cronshaw of Magister Militum. The general and cavalry commander at the front are equipped with full fighting kit, as are the sagittarius and marine behind them. The infantryman follows in a lavish decorated tunic but still armoured with a helm, manica and greaves - equipped as a middle-rank soldier in an infantry block.

Figure 52: Auxiliary soldier 2nd century. Photograph by kind permission of John Richardson of The Antonine Guard re-enactment group. An auxiliary soldier of the Sixth Cohort of Nervians.

Figure 53: Auxiliary archer 2nd century. Photograph by kind permission of John Richardson of The Antonine Guard re-enactment group. An auxiliary soldier in the first Cohort of Hamian Archers.

Figure 54: Native warrior from a Numerus Exploratorum. Photograph by kind permission of John Richardson of The Antonine Guard re-enactment group. A native Celtic warrior from a Numerus Exploratorum, raised from the local Dumnonii tribe and employed by the Romans as an irregular scout.

Figure 55: Native warrior from a Numerus Exploratorum. Photograph by kind permission of John Richardson of The Antonine Guard re-enactment group. A native Celtic warrior from a Numerus Exploratorum, raised from the local Dumnonii tribe and employed by the Romans as an irregular scout.

Figure 59: Late Roman army command structure of the Western Empire. Image from Wikimedia Commons. https://commons.wikimedia.org/w/index. php?curid=12237367

Figure 60: Late Roman army command structure of the Eastern Empire. Image from Wikimedia Commons. https://commons.wikimedia.org/w/index. php?curid=12237360

Figure 62: Map of the end of Roman Britain. Image from Wikimedia Commons. CC BY-SA 3.0, https://commons.wikimedia.org/w/index. php?curid=11817590

Notes

Introduction
1. Pollard and Berry, 2015: 93
2. Birley, 205: 227
3. Pollard and Berry, 2015: 94
4. Pollard and Berry, 2015: 83
5. Dando-Collins, 2010: 142

Chapter 1
1. Beard, 2016: 59
2. Beard, 2016: 60
3. Beard, 2016: 373
4. McLynn, 2009: 10
5. Levick, 2000: xix
6. McLynn, 2009: 13
7. Webster, 1981: 113
8. Webster, 1981: 109
9. Milner, 2011: 72
10. Milner, 2011: 44
11. McLynn, 2009: 325
12. Webster, 1981: 146
13. Webster, 1981: 150
14. Pollard and Berry, 2015: 82–105
15. Breeze and Dobson, 2000: 163
16. Polybius, book 6.23
17. Milner, 2011: 13
18. Livy, book 31.34
19. Caesar, Gallic wars book 1.25
20. https://www.youtube.com/
    watch?v=EfgMfSZiQSU
21. Underwood, 1999: 25
22. Goldsworthy, 2003: 180
23. Underwood, 1999: 32–34
24. Esposito, 2018: 111
25. Marren, 2006: 10
26. Travis, 2012: 116
27. Webster, 1981: 151
28. Mortimer, 2011: 169
29. Esposito, 2018: 93
30. Hughes, 2020: 45
31. Esposito, 2018: 93
32. Webster, 1985: 151

33. Milner, 2011: 104
34. Tacitus, The Histories 5.16
35. https://www.livius.org/articles/place/
    xanten/xanten-victory-monument/
36. Tacitus Annals, book 14, chapters 34–37
37. Tacitus, *Life of Agricola*, chapter 30
38. Clarkson, 2019: 17
39. Tacitus, Agricola chapter 21
40. Tacitus, Agricola chapter 14

Chapter 2
1. Breeze and Dobson, 2000: 17
2. Milner, 2011: 10
3. Milner, 2011: 89
4. Milner, 2011: 24 & 80–81
5. Milner, 2011: 10
6. Breeze, 208: 39
7. Webster, 1985: 119
8. Southern, 2013: 257
9. Goldsworthy, 2003: 192
10. Ammianus Book 23.4
11. Goldsworthy, 2003: 244
12. Cassius Dio book 60.20
13. Birley, 2002: 44–5
14. Birley, 2002: 43
15. Birley, 2002: 76
16. Birley, 2002: 95
17. Birley, 2002: 96
18. Birley, 2002: 80
19. Birley, 2002: 99
20. Birley, 2002: 15
21. Grant, 1997: 77
22. Grant, 1997: 77
23. Grant, 1997: 79
24. Grant, 1997: 79
25. McLynn, 2009: 27
26. McLynn, 2009: 32
27. Breeze and Dobson, 2000: 25
28. Breeze and Dobson, 2000: 25
29. Birley, 2002: 74–5
30. Symonds, 2021: 56

31. Historia Augusta, Hadrian, 10.2
32. Birley, 2005: 123
33. Historia Augusta, Hadrian 11.4–7
34. Birley, 2005: 122
35. Birley, 2005: 244
36. Tomlin, 2018: 92–3
37. Tomlin, 2018: 94–6
38. Birley, 2005: 284
39. Birley, 2005: 122
40. Tomlin, 2018: 92
41. Birley, 2005: 228–30
42. Breeze and Dobson, 2000: 23
43. Breeze and Dobson, 2000: 12
44. Breeze and Dobson, 2000: 13
45. Breeze and Dobson, 2000: 15
46. Historia Augusta, Hadrian, 11.2
47. Breeze and Dobson, 2000: 47
48. Breeze and Dobson, 2000: 40
49. Breeze and Dobson, 2000: 42
50. Breeze and Dobson, 2000: 53
51. Breeze and Dobson, 2000: 54
52. Tomlin, 2018: 107
53. Tomlin, 2018: 114
54. Tomlin, 2018: 128
55. Tomlin, 2018: 311
56. Birley, 2005: 250
57. Birley, 2005: 250–1
58. Ottaway, 2004: 24
59. Ottaway, 2004: 26
60. Ottaway, 2004: 31
61. Bishop, 2020: 3
62. Bishop, 2020: 17
63. Bishop, 2020: 104
64. Bishop, 2020: 70–71
65. Bishop, 2020: 66
66. Bishop, 2020: 85
67. Bishop, 2020: 76
68. Bishop, 2020: 20–21
69. Bishop, 2020: 20
70. Bishop, 2020: 99
71. Bishop, 2020: 80
72. Bishop, 2020: 20
73.
74. Elliott, 2019: 16
75. Elliott, 2019: 15
76. Collins, 2020: 26
77. Collins, 2020: 28
78. Collins, 2020: 23
79. Southern, 2016: 224
80. Southern, 2016: 225
81. Webster, 1985: 120
82. Webster, 1985: 120
83. Southern, 2016: 247
84. Webster, 1985: 14
85. Webster, 1985: 264–8
86. McLynn, 2009: 10
87. McLynn, 2009: 13
88. Davenport, 2019: 316
89. Speidal et al, 2009: 350

Chapter 3
1. Historia Augustus, Antoninus Pius 5.3
2. Breeze, 208: 36
3. Tomlin, 2018: 197–8
4. Birley, 2005: 139
5. Breeze, 208: 13
6. Breeze, 208: 22
7. Breeze, 208: 21
8. Southern, 2016: 377–81
9. Arrianus, Ektaxis kata Alanon
10. Breeze, 208: 35
11. Breeze, 208: 18
12. Breeze, 208: 40
13. Breeze, 208: 48
14. Tomlin, 2018: 129
15. Tomlin, 2018: 169
16. Tomlin, 2018: 209
17. Birley, 2005: 147
18. Birley, 205: 148
19. Tomlin, 2018: 143
20. Tomlin, 2018: 149
21. Birley, 2005: 155
22. Travis, 2012: 125
23. https://www.youtube.com/
    watch?v=uDRBw1Hl_Qg&t=261s
24. https://www.youtube.com/watch?v=jr9-
    uT58Z08&t=1497s
25. https://www.youtube.com/
    watch?v=65n3PpjPK04
26. https://www.youtube.com/
    watch?v=Xu8QGkqLjno
27. Travis, 2015: 113
28. https://www.youtube.com/watch?v=ni-
    h8SH1yUw
29. Lindybiege: https://www.youtube.com/
    watch?v=afqhBODc_8U
30. Legio V Macedonia: https://www.
    youtube.com/watch?v=jnoiTX0xZ0Y
31. https://www.warhistoryonline.com/
    ancient-history/archers-roman-army.
    html

32. https://www.youtube.com/
    watch?v=eYsr81y0Aeo
33. Travis, 2012: 125
34. Plutarch, The life of Crassus, 24
35. Milner, 2001: 3

Chapter 4
1. McLynn, 2009: 123
2. Birely, 2005: 156–7
3. Tomlin, 2018: 162
4. Tomlin, 2018: 359
5. McLynn, 2009: 185
6. Birley, 2005: 173
7. Taylor, 2016: 110
8. McLynn, 2009: 353
9. Cassius Dio, book 72.17
10. Cassius Dio, book 72.16
11. Tomlin, 208: 160
12. Breeze and Dobson, 2000: 163
13. Cunliffe, 2019: 322
14. McLynn, 2009: 87
15. McLynn, 2009: 418
16. McHugh, 2015: 57
17. Birley, 2005: 166–7
18. Moffatt, 2017: 206–7
19. McHugh, 2015: 97–8
20. Moffatt, 2017: 206–7
21. Cassius Dio book 73.9
22. Birley, 2005: 260–1
23. Herodian 1.9
24. Historia Augusta, Commodus, 6.1
25. Birley, 2005: 261
26. Herodian 1.10.1–3
27. Birley, 2005: 262
28. Birley, 2005: 261
29. Herodian 1.10.4
30. Herodian 1.12.4–5
31. Cassius Dio book 73.13.6
32. Herodian 1.13.8
33. Epplett, 2020: 67
34. Hopkins and Beard, 2011: 115
35. McHugh, 2015: 192
36. Herodian 1.17.1
37. Herodian 1.17.3–4
38. Taylor, 2016: 176

Chapter 5
1. Herodian 3.5–8
2. Cassius Dio Book 76.6
3. Birley, 2005: 184
4. Breeze and Dobson, 2000: 216

5. Breeze and Dobson, 2000: 219
6. Tomlin, 2018: 211
7. Tomlin, 2018: 212–3
8. Birley, 2005: 265
9. Tomlin, 2018: 216
10. Tomlin, 2018: 216
11. Cassius Dio, book 72.11
12. Herodian 3.14–15
13. Birley, 2005: 202
14. Birley, 2005: 263
15. Tomlin, 2018: 372
16. Tomlin, 2018: 370–1
17. Herodian 3.15–4.6
18. Cassius Dio book 78.2
19. Birley, 205: 333
20. Tomlin, 2018: 231
21. McLynn, 2009: 87
22. McLynn, 2009: 88
23. McLynn, 2009: 90
24. Tomlin, 2018: 257
25. Birley, 2005: 342–3
26. Tomlin, 2018: 277
27. Tomlin, 2018: 256
28. Birley, 2005: 333
29. http://christophergwinn.com/arthuriana/
    lac-sourcebook/#etymology
30. Birley, 2005: 355
31. Tomlin, 2018: 156
32. Higham, 2018: 35–38
33. Davenport 2019: 493
34. Xavier Loriot. 1997: 85–86
35. Birley, 2005: 355

Chapter 6
1. Southern, 2013: 251
2. Breeze and Dobson, 2000: 220
3. Southern, 2013: 251
4. Southern, 2013: 261
5. Grant, 1996: 165
6. Southern, 2013: 270
7. Zosimus 1.68.3
8. Birley, 205: 371
9. Birley, 205: 373–4
10. Birely, 205: 386
11. Birley, 205: 383
12. Birley, 205: 389
13. Birely, 205: 390
14. Goldsworthy, 2000: 168
15. Birley, 205: 397–8
16. Gerrard, 2016: 215
17. Rippon, 2018: 327

18. Bedoyere, 2006: 89
19. Salway, 2001: 230
20. Southern, 213: 288
21. Pearson, 2010: 168
22. Pearson, 2010: 169
23. Goldsworthy, 2010: 341
24. Esposito, 2018: 37
25. Esposito, 2018: 57
26. Esposito, 2018: 71
27. Esposito, 2018: 80
28. Esposito, 2018: 93
29. Esposito, 2018: 96

Chapter 7
1. Southern, 213: 313
2. Dark, 1994: 10
3. Halsall, 2014: 457
4. Dark, 1994: 16
5. Dark, 1994: 15
6. Goldsworthy, 2010: 344
7. Dark, 2000: 17
8. Salway, 2001: 277
9. Gerrard, 2016: 55
10. Bedoyere, 2006: 183
11. Halsall, 2014: 363
12. Higham, 2014 :21
13. Salway, 2001: 280–281
14. Gerrard, 2016: 23–25
15. Salway, 2001: 293
16. Ammianus, book 28.3–8
17. Birley, 205: 399–400
18. Salway, 2001: 297
19. Grant, 1997: 274
20. Salway, 2001: 316
21. Gerrard, 2016: 168
22. Higham and Ryan, 2015: 42
23. http://www.vortigernstudies.org.uk/
    artsou/orosius.htm
24. http://www.vortigernstudies.org.uk/
    artsou/chron452.htm
25. http://www.vortigernstudies.org.uk/
    artsou/zosim.htm
26. Oosthuizen, 2019: 27
27. http://www.vortigernstudies.org.uk/
    artsou/procop.htm
28. Hughes, 2020: 34–35
29. Storr, 2016: 56
30. Goldsworthy, 2010: 337
31. Evans, 2000: 26
32. Wacher, 1995: 167
33. Wacher, 1995: 188

34. Ottaway, 2004: 140
35. Ottaway, 2004: 143
36. Wacher, 1995: 188
37. Wacher, 1995: 401, 406–407
38. Carver, 2019: 37
39. Carver, 2019: 169
40. Ottaway, 2004: 144

Chapter 8
1. Higham and Ryan, 2015: 42
2. Hills, 2011: 9
3. Halsall, 2014: 358
4. Gerrard, 2016: 163
5. Collins, 2012: 1
6. Collins, 2012: 110
7. Collins, 2012: 103
8. Collins, 2012: 138
9. Yorke, 2013 :74
10. Dumville, 1993: III.9
11. Dumville in Bassett, 1989: 215
12. Dumville, 1993: III.5
13. Loveluck and Laing, 2011: 541
14. Bartrum, 1993: 634
15. Collins, 2012: 106–110
16. Wood in Dumville and Lapwood, 1984: 8
17. Thompson, 1968: 39–46
18. Hughes, 2020: 93
19. Oosthuizen, 2019: 29
20. Charles-Edwards, 2014: 227
21. O Croinin, 2017: 46
22. Dumville, 1999
23. Bury, 1998: 192
24. Mortimer, 2011: 173
25. Cunliffe, 2013: 242
26. Higham and Ryan, 2015: 91
27. Eagles, 2018: xxx
28. Moffatt, 2013: 182
29. Cunliffe, 2013: 424
30. Cunliffe, 2013: 242
31. Hills 2011: 10
32. Bede volume 5 chapter 9
33. Zosimus 1.68.3
34. Mathisen, 1993: 68–69
35. Brown, 2012: 448
36. Brown, 2012: 446
37. Evans, 2000: 1
38. Evans, 2000: 28
39. Snyder, 1998: 107
40. Snyder, 1998: 107
41. Gerrard, 2016: 179
42. Gerrard, 2016: 155–156
43. Birley, 2005: 263

Bibliography

Beard, Mary, *SPQR A History of Ancient Rome*, (Profile Books, London, 2016).

Birley, Anthony, *Garrison Life at Vindolanda, A Band of Brothers*, (Tempus, Stroud, 2002).

Birley, Anthony, *The Roman Government of Britain*, (Oxford University Press, Oxford, 2005).

Bishop, M.C., *The Secret History of the Roman Roads of Britain*, (Pen and Sword, Barnsley, 2020).

Bishop, M.C., *Lucius Verus and the Roman Defence of the East*, (Pen and Sword, Barnsley, 2018).

Breeze, David, J. and Dobson, Brian, *Hadrian's Wall*, (Penguin Books, London, 2000).

Breeze, David, *Edge of Empire, Rome's Scottish Frontier, The Antonine Wall*, (Birlinn, Edinburgh, 2008).

Bruun, Christer and Edmondson, Jonathan, The Oxford Handbook of Roman Epigraphy, (Oxford University Press, Oxford, 2015).

Carver, Martin, *Formative Britain, An Archaeology of Britain Fifth to Eleventh Century* AD, (Routledge, Abingdon, 2019).

Casey, P.J., *Carausius and Allectus*, (Yale University Press, New Haven, 1994).

Charles-Edwards, T.M., *Wales and the Britons 350–1064*, (Oxford University Press, Oxford, 2014).

Chrystal, Paul, *A Historical Guide to Roman York*, (Pen and Sword, Barnsley, 2021).

Clarkson, Tim, *The Men of the North*, (Berlinn Ltd, Edinburgh, 2016).

Clarkson, Tim, *The Picts: A History*, (Berlinn Ltd, Edinburgh, 2019).

Clearly, S., *The Ending(s) of Roman Britain* in Hamerow, H, Hinton, D, and Crawford, S, *The Oxford Handbook of Anglo-Saxon Archaeology*, (Oxford University Press, Oxford, 2011).

Collins, Rob, *Hadrian's Wall and the End of Empire*, Routledge, New York, 2012).

Collins, Rob, *Living on the Edge of Empire*, (Pen and Sword, Barnsley, 2020).

Crook, J.A., *Law and Life of Rome, 90 B.C. – A.D. 212*, (Cornell University Press, New York, 1967).

Cruse, Audrey, *Roman Medicine*, (Tempus, Stroud, 2004).

Cunliffe, Barry, *Britain Begins*, (Oxford University Press, Oxford, 2013).

Czajkowski, Kimberley, Eckhardt, Benedikt, *Law in the Roman Provinces*, (Oxford University Press, Oxford, 2020).

Dando-Collins, Stephen, *Legions of Rome, The Definitive History of Every Imperial Roman Legion*, (Thomas Dunne Books, St Martin's Press, New York, 2010).

D'Amato, R. and Negin, A., *Decorated Roman Armour, from the Age of the Kings to the Death of Justinian the great*, (Frontline Books, Barnsley, 2017).

D'Amato, Raffaele and Sumner, Graham, *Arms and Armour of the Imperial Roman Soldier, from Marius to Commodus, 112* BC- AD *192*, (Frontline Books, London, 2009).

Dark, K.R., *Civitas to Kingdom; British Political Continuity 300–800*, (Leicester University Press, London, 1994).

Dark, Ken, *Britain and the End of the Roman Empire*, (Tempus Publishing Ltd, Stroud, 2000).

Davenport, Caillan, *A History of the Roman Equestrian Order*, (Cambridge University Press, Cambridge, 2019).

Davies, Hugh, *Roman Roads in Britain*, (Shire Archaeology, Oxford, 2008).

De La Bédoyère, Guy, *Domina*, (Yale University Press, New Haven, 2018).

De La Bédoyère, Guy, *Eagles over Britannia*, (Tempus Publishing, Stroud, 2001).

De La Bédoyère, Guy, *Gladius, Living Fighting and Dying in the Roman Army*, (Little Brown, London, 2020).

De La Bédoyère, Guy, *Roman Britain, A New History*, (Thames and Hudson, London, 2006).

De La Bédoyère, Guy, *The Real Lives of Roman Britain*, (Yale University Press, New Haven, 2015).

Elliott, Paul, *Everyday Life of a Soldier on Hadrian's Wall*, (Fonthill, 2015).

Elliott, Paul, *The Life of a Roman Soldier in Britain* AD *400*, (Spellmount, Stroud, 2007).

Elliott, Simon, *Pertinax*, (Greenhill Books, Barnsley, 2020).

Elliott, Simon, *Roman Britain's Missing Legion*, (Pen and Sword, Barnsley, 2021).

Elliott, Simon, *Roman Legionaries, Soldiers of Empire*, (Casemate, Oxford, 2018).

Elliott, Simon, *Romans at War*, (Casemate, Oxford, 2020).

Elliott, Simon, *Sea Eagles of Empire, The Classis Britannica and the Battles for Britain*, (History Press, Stroud, 2016).

Elliott, Simon, *Septimus Severus in Scotland*, (Greenhill Books, Barnsley, 2018).

Esposito, Gabriele, *Armies of the Late Roman Empire* AD *284–476, History Organisation and Equipment*, (Pen and Sword Books, Barnsley, 2018).

Gerrard, James, *The Ruin of Roman Britain an Archaeological Perspective*, (Cambridge University Press, Cambridge, 2016).

Goldsworthy, Adrian, *Pax Romana*, (Weidenfeld and Nicolson, London, 2016).

Goldsworthy, Adrian, *The Fall of the West*, (Phoenix, London, 2010).

Goldsworthy, Adrian, *The Complete Roman Army*, (Thames and Hudson, London, 2003).

Goldsworthy, Adrian, *Roman Warfare* (Phoenix, London, 2000).

Grant, Michael, *The Antonines*, (Routledge, London, 1994).

Grant, Michael, *The Roman Emperors*, (Phoenix, London, 1997).

Halsall, Guy, *Barbarian Migrations and the Roman West 376–568*, (Cambridge University Press, Cambridge, 2014).

Hamilton, Walter, *Ammianus Marcellinus, The Later Roman Empire* AD *354–378* (Penguin Books, London, 1986).

Hobbs, R. & Jackson, R., *Roman Britain*, (The British Museum Press, London, 2015).

Hughes, Ian, Patricians and Emperors, (Pen and Sword, Barnsley, 2015).

Istvanovits, Eszter, and Kulcsar, Valeria, *Sarmatians, History and Archaeology of a Forgotten People*, (Romisch-Germanisches Zentralmuseum, Germany, 2017).

Kershaw, Stephen, *Barbarians, Rebellion and Resistance to Ancient Rome*, (Robinson, London, 2019).

Laycock, Stuart, *Britannia The Failed State*, (The History Press, Stroud, 2011).

Levick, Barbara, *The Government of the Roman Empire*, (Routledge, London, 2000).

Low, D.M, *Gibbon's The Decline and Fall of the Roman Empire*, (Chatto and Windus, London, 1981).

MacDowell, Simon, *Twilight of Empire, The Roman Infantryman 3rd to 6th Century* AD, (Osprey, Oxford, 1994).

Marren, Peter, *Battles of the Dark Ages*, (Pen and Sword, Barnsley 2006).

Mathisen, Ralph, *Roman Aristocrats in Barbarian Gaul, Strategies for Survival in the Age of Transition*, (University of Texas Press, Texas, 1989).

McHugh, John, *Emperor Alexander Severus*, (Pen and Sword, Barnsley, 2017).

McHugh, John, *The Emperor Commodus, God and Gladiator*, (Pen and Sword, Barnsley, 2015).

McLynn, Frank, *Marcus Aurelius, Warrior, Philosopher, Emperor*, (Vintage, London, 2010).

Milner, N, P, *Vegetius: Epitome of Military Science 2nd Ed* (Liverpool Universety Press, Liverpool, 2011).

Mitchell, Stephen, and Greater, Geoffrey, *Ethnicity and Culture in Late Antiquity*, (Duckworth and The Classical Press of Wales, London, 2000).

Moffatt, Alistair, *The Wall, Rome's Greatest Frontier*, (Birlinn, Edinburgh, 2017).

Moorhead, Sam, and Stuttard, David, *The Romans who Shaped Britain*, (Thames and Hudson, London, 2016).

Morris, J., *Arthurian Period Sources Volume 7 Gildas*, (Phillimore, Chichester, 1978).

Morris, J., *Arthurian Period Sources Volume 8 Nennius*, (Phillimore, Chichester, 1980).

Moscsy, Andras, *Pannonia and Upper Moesia, A History of the Middle Danube Provinces of the Roman Empire*, (Routledge, Abingdon, 2014).

Ottaway, Peter, *Roman York*, (Tempus Books, Stroud, 2004).

Pearson, Andrew, *The Roman Shore Forts*, (The History Press, Stroud, 2010).

Penrose, Jane, *Rome and Her Enemies*, (Osprey Publishing, Oxford, 2005)

Pitassi, Michael, *The Roman Navy, Ships, Men and Warfare 350 BC – AD 475*, (Seaforth Publishing, Barnsley, 2012).

Pollard, Nigel and Berry, Joanne, *The Complete Roman Legions*, (Thames and Hudson, London, 2015).

Richards, Mark, *Walking Hadrian's Wall Path*, (Cicerone, Cumbria, 2015).

Richardson, John, *The Romans and the Antonine Wall of Scotland*, (Lulu.com, 2019)

Rivet, A.L.F., and Smith, Colin, *The Place-Names of Roman Britain*, (Batsford, London, 1982).

Rogan, John, *Roman Provincial Administration*, (Amberley Publishing, Stroud, 2011).

Sage, Michael, *Septimius Severus and the Roman Army*, (Pen and Sword, Barnsley, 2020).

Salway, Peter, *A History of Roman Britain*, (Oxford University Press, Oxford, 2001).

Scarre, Chris, *Chronicle of the Roman Emperors*, (Thames and Hudson, London, 2007).

Sheldon, Rose Mary, *Rome's Wars in Parthia*, (Vallentine Mitchell, London, 2010).

Shotter, David, *The Roman Frontier in Britain*, (Carnegie Publishing, Preston, 1996).

Southern, Patricia, *Roman Britain, A New History 55 BC- AD 450*, (Amberley Publishing, Stroud, 2013).

Southern, Patricia, *The Roman Army, A History 753 BC- AD 476*, (Amberley Publishing, Stroud, 2016).

Summerton, Nick, *Greco-Roman Medicine*, (Pen and Sword, Barnsley, 2021).

Symonds, Matthew, *Hadrian's Wall, Creating Division*, (Bloomsbury, London, 2021).

Syvanne, Ilkka, *Caracalla, A Military Biography*, (Pen and Sword, Barnsley, 2017).

Syvanne, Ilkka, *Military History of Late Rome 425–457*, (Pen and Sword, Yorkshire, 2020).

Tacitus, *Agricola and Germanis*, (Penguin Classics, London, 2009).

Taylor, Don, *Roman Empire at War*, (Pen and Sword, Barnsley, 2016).

Todd, Malcolm, *A Companion to Roman Britain*, (Blackwell Publishing, Malden, USA, 2007).

Tomlin, R.S.O., *Britannia Romana, Roman Inscriptions and Roman Britain*, (Oxbow Books, Oxford, 2018).

Travis, Hiliary and Travis, John, *Roman Body Armour*, (Amberley, Stroud, 2012).

Travis, Hiliary and Travis, John, *Roman Helmets*, (Amberley, Stroud, 2016).

Travis, Hiliary and Travis, John, *Roman Shields*, (Amberley, Stroud, 2016).

Underwood, Richard, *Anglo-Saxon Weapons and Warfare*, (Tempus Publishing Ltd, Stroud, 1999).

Wacher, John, *The Towns of Roman Britain*, (BCA, London, 1995).

Wallace-Hadrill, J.M, *The Barbarian West 400–1000*, (Blackwell, Oxford, 1999).

Wallace-Hadrill, J.M, *The Long-Haired Kings*, (Methuen & Co, London, 1962).

Webster, L & Brown, M, *The Transformation of the Roman World AD 400–900*, (British Museum Press, London, 1997).

Webb, Simon, *Life in Roman London*, (The History Press, Stroud, 2011).

Webster, Graham, *The Roman Imperial Army*, (A & C Black, London, 1981).

White, Roger, *Britannia Prima, Britain's Last Roman Province*, (Tempus, Stroud, 2007).

Wilson, Roger J.A, *A Guide to the Roman Remains in Britain*, (Constable & Company, London, 1980).

Wilkes, J.J., *Dalmatia*, (Routledge and Kegan Paul, London, 1969).

Xavier Loriot, *Un mythe historiographique : l'expédition d'Artorius Castus contre les Armoricains* (Bulletin de la Société nationale des antiquaires de France, 1997), Pg. 85–86.

Index